cha

Raag
dream

2/24 £6

chasing
the
Raag
dream

A LOOK INTO THE WORLD OF
HINDUSTANI MUSIC

ANEESH PRADHAN

HarperCollins *Publishers* India

First published in India by
HarperCollins *Publishers* in 2019
A-75, Sector 57, Noida, Uttar Pradesh 201301, India
www.harpercollins.co.in

2 4 6 8 10 9 7 5 3 1

Copyright © Aneesh Pradhan 2019

P-ISBN: 978-93-5357-017-0
E-ISBN: 978-93-5357-018-7

Typeset in 12/14.7 Arno Pro at
Manipal Digital Systems, Manipal

Printed and bound at
Thomson Press (India) Ltd

MIX
Paper
FSC FSC® C010615

This book is produced from independently certified FSC® paper to ensure
responsible forest management.

To my parents, Kisan and Vasant Pradhan, whose commitment to justice, equality and free speech has always been an inspiration

Contents

Preface

Hindustani music, the art music system of northern India, transports music lovers to an abstract world of sublime experience far removed from the maddening reality that surrounds us every day. Only a few would be aware that this oasis of solace and beauty is actually created in an ecosystem ridden with contradictions, which have frequently led to conflicting opinions about its very future. Undoubtedly, this music is only a small part of India's musical landscape, and every system and form of music faces its share of challenges. In this book, I have focused on the challenges that this music and its practitioners face today; a subject I am familiar with as a student, performer, teacher and researcher.

Conditions in the past were also difficult, as would be evident from a brief overview of those times. Until the last quarter of the nineteenth century, Hindustani music was pursued professionally only by members of musician and courtesan families. Royal courts were the primary source of patronage and musicians had to travel to princely states across the country in the hope of procuring professional positions as court musicians. They often tried to obtain letters of recommendation from previous benefactors with a view of approaching prospective patrons. Family and professional networks helped them secure work. Some also received patronage by default, when they inherited professional positions occupied by senior members of their family. In other words, musical merit played an important role in procuring patronage, but it was not the sole criteria. In order for the dream and desire to perform successfully in princely courts to become a reality, great hardship, uncertainty and risk were involved.

After the decline of royal patronage in the second half of the nineteenth century, musicians migrated to colonial cities like Calcutta (Kolkata) and Bombay (Mumbai) in search of patronage from the commercial, industrial and intellectual elite. They taught and performed, evolving adaptive strategies, reinventing themselves to survive in the new environment and to establish their credentials to a largely uninitiated audience. Gharana, a modern incarnation of bani and gayaki (both referring to vocal styles) and baaj (referring to instrumental style), did not merely assert stylistic distinctiveness, but also defined identity through familial and guru–shishya or master–disciple linkages. Perhaps this would be similar to terms like 'brand name' and 'brand equity' in today's consumerist world.

During this period, Hindustani music found support from the intellectual elite. Driven by nationalistic fervour, the intellectuals sought to construct a pan-Indian cultural identity by promoting certain aspects of indigenous culture to counter the colonial claim of racial superiority. Endeavours to classicize Indian music and to propagate it as a symbol of an ancient culture dating back to a supposed glorious Hindu-Sanskritic past were part of this nationalist scheme. Prompted by the colonial perspective of Indian history that was decidedly communal, these intellectuals blamed Muslim rulers and 'illiterate' performers for the disconnect, which was apparent between contemporary Hindustani music and the music theory enshrined in Sanskrit treatises. These 'reformists' spoke in favour of systematizing Hindustani music and cleansing it of its relationship with professional women performers and their male associates.[1] Music educationists in different parts of the country agreed with this view and gradually music clubs, music circles and music schools were set up to accord Hindustani music and its practitioners with what was considered much-needed respectability in the eyes of society and to give an institutional credibility to the idea of a classical, pure and ancient music.

Hereditary musicians were forced to negotiate these new reformist ideas, in addition to bearing the burden of surviving on an irregular income obtained from teaching and performing. They often sought alternative or supplementary means of livelihood by taking up employment as composers, actor-singers and accompanists with itinerant theatre companies. Later, musicians also joined film studios as composers and members of orchestras.

There was virtually no state patronage for Hindustani music under colonial rule.[2] If at all there was any, it was only when Indians enjoying a close association with the administrators convinced them to extend financial support.[3] Other than such infrequent cases of pecuniary support, there were few occasions when British officials presided over musical programmes.[4] But neither the sporadic monetary support nor the rare presence of British dignitaries at Hindustani music concerts were indicative of any overarching state policy related to indigenous music. The only official policy in this regard came much later in the form of broadcasts of Hindustani music on All India Radio (AIR), a policy that had little to do with the consideration of promoting Hindustani music.

On the Indian side, efforts by the middle-class intelligentsia at classicizing this music and establishing it as a symbol of national culture found support among some important leaders of the national movement for independence. For instance, prominent

nationalist and educationist Dadabhai Naoroji (1825–1917) was
the president of the Parsi Gayan Uttejak Mandali, perhaps the
first formal music club in Bombay, from 1885 to 1890. Prior to
this, he frequently advised the mandali between 1870–1883 and
was made its honorary member on 11 October 1884.[5] Vocalist
and music educationist Vishnu Digambar Paluskar (1872–1931)
also received encouragement and support for his educational
activities from prominent leaders like Lala Lajpat Rai (1865–
1928), Madan Mohan Malaviya (1861–1946), Sarojini Naidu
(1879–1949), Lokmanya Tilak (1856–1920) and Mahatma
Gandhi (1869–1948).[6] These leaders were too involved in
the hurly-burly of the independence movement to concern
themselves with Hindustani music at a deeper level. Even the
Government of India Act, 1935, that led to the formation of
ministries led by the Indian National Congress in seven out of
eleven provinces, did not expressly include culture as a part of
the subjects that were allocated to these provincial ministries.
Instead, culture appeared in an indirect manner through sections
concerning performances and cinema, institutions such as
libraries and museums, and education.[7]

The possibility of a well-planned and sustained patronage from
the state emerged only in the post-Independence era, although
that too had to wait for a few years as the new nation grappled with
more immediate problems concerning the economy and society.[8]
The observations by India's first prime minister, Jawaharlal Nehru
(1889–1964), during his speech at the inauguration of the Indian
Council of Cultural Relations in 1950, are pertinent in this context:

> ... [I]t is just folly to talk of culture or even to talk of God, when
> human beings starve and die. The first thing that one has to do is
> to provide the normal essentials of life to human beings before
> you can talk about anything else and there economics comes in
> [sic], and human beings today are not in a mood to put up with
> this suffering and starvation and inequality when they see that the

burden is not equally shared. Others profit while they only have to bear the burden.[9]

The authors of the Constitution of India, in their wisdom, did not deem it fit for the state to engage overtly in formulating a cultural policy pertaining to the arts, and instead prescribed to it the role of a facilitator. It is possibly for this reason that only subjects related to tangible heritage were included in the Union and State Lists to be dealt with by the Union and state governments respectively.[10]

In keeping with the idea of facilitating activities related to the arts, the Union government established autonomous arts institutions. A separate ministry of culture did not exist until much later, as since 1961, culture had been grouped in different forms with ministries dealing with subjects as varied as scientific research, education, tourism, youth affairs and sports. A separate Department of Culture at the Centre was set up as late as in May 1971 and an independent Ministry of Culture at the Centre was formed even later, in September 2001.[11]

While connections between culture and education, tourism and youth affairs are obvious, those with others like scientific research appear tenuous and seem to reflect a lack of serious intent in facilitating its progress. An alternative interpretation may be found in scholar Kapila Vatsyayan's observation that the linkages had to be made with other subjects which were being taught at the school or university levels. She says:

> Institutions of science and culture had to be linked, institutions of culture and education had to be interlinked, institutions of anthropology and tribal arts and crafts had to be interlinked with tribal and rural development.[12]

Over the years, political parties across the board have seldom paid attention to Indian culture, even in its broadest context. A quick look at some of their websites will reveal that there is no mention of culture in most cases.[13] The Bharatiya Janata Party (BJP), the single-largest party heading the coalition, the National Democratic Alliance (NDA) government at the Centre, makes a departure by listing culture as a key area in the 'Vision of Modi', a section that is declared to be at the heart of Prime Minister Narendra Modi's development model. It states:

> The comprehensive vision laid out by Shri Modi builds on the heritage of India's rich social and cultural diversity, its tradition, the talent of our human resource and the aspirations of the youth and women.[14]

This section includes 'Tradition' as one of the five sectors which have 'the potential to make India a global power' and will be the focus of 'Brand India'. 'India's Culture' heads the seven-point 'Rainbow of India', which 'envisions seven key focus areas that will be the overarching theme of all initiatives to make India a developed nation'.[15] Sadly, there is little else that the website has to offer in terms of strategy beyond these broad statements.

In contrast to other political parties that do not comment on cultural policy, the website of the Shiv Sena, a member of the NDA, used to have a tangible plan of developing a Kala Academy, an institution devoted to all the arts, though it does not contain this information any longer.[16] An institution of this nature was inaugurated in Mumbai in 2002 and called the P.L. Deshpande Maharashtra Kala Academy, as a tribute to P.L. Deshpande (1919–2000), the well-known author, playwright, composer and multi-faceted creative genius.[17] The academy lists, among its objectives, the preservation and promotion of Maharashtra's cultural heritage and 'the Classical, Traditional and Contemporary Performing Arts including Music, Dance and Drama and Visual Arts in the form of Painting, Sculpture, Photography and Graphics'.[18] Its objectives also include 'promotion, growth and revival of Music, Dance and

Drama and for preservation, documentation and dissemination of materials relating to diverse forms of Music, Dance and Drama and for the recognition of contributions to the performing arts by outstanding artists'.[19] Until recently, the Maharashtra Navnirman Sena, a breakaway party from the Shiv Sena, had featured a separate section on its website devoted entirely to the arts in Maharashtra, which included information about Hindustani music and musicians in the state.[20]

But moving away from the limited cultural vision of political parties, there is no doubt that the ministries like the Ministry of Information and Broadcasting, Ministry of Education, Ministry of Human Resource Development, Ministry of Culture at the national level, and others at the state level, have initiated fragmented policies related to culture in general and to Hindustani music in particular, in the past seven decades. Government, quasi-government and autonomous institutions, including the Prasar Bharati and its constituent media units, that is, All India Radio or Akashvani, and Doordarshan (DD), as well as the Sangeet Natak Akademi (SNA), the Indian Council for Cultural Relations (ICCR), National Culture Fund (NCF) and the Cultural Zonal Centres (CZC) are of particular relevance here. The objectives of many of these agencies are based on a nationalist and pan-Indian cultural perspective, as is evident from the repeated assertion that their activities preserve and promote the unity of the nation while respecting its diversity. A detailed analysis of the manner in which this perspective has influenced the programmes and working of these institutions and those at the regional level would require a separate study.[21]

Meanwhile, over the past several decades, the number of professional and semi-professional musicians increased exponentially, as music performance and teaching were no longer pursued solely by hereditary musician families. Scores of first-generation musicians took to Hindustani music as a career option after changed social conditions gave the profession respectability, which it was denied earlier. In this situation, other than the support received from institutions established by the government, patronage of Hindustani music and musicians has also come from individual patrons and organizations music circles and clubs set up by civil society groups and corporate houses. In addition, record labels and social media platforms have played an important role in propagating this music among wider audiences. Institutionalized music education has increased the number of music students at all levels. Hindustani music has also been performed overseas over the past several decades, drawing listeners from expatriate Indian communities and from the locals. In fact, many non-Indians have become professional performers now. Documentation, research and archiving have also seen a rise during this period.

With patronage offered from sources mentioned here and the increased interest in Hindustani music nationally and globally, one would imagine that the ecosystem is in a healthy position and will progress in the future. However, there have been voices of discontent among some sections. Several musicians, particularly those from the younger generation, believe that there is a dearth of performance opportunities and financial assistance. Organizations established by civil society groups complain of rising costs, depleting resources and a lack of younger listeners. Corporate houses consider sponsorship to Hindustani music concerts as an unprofitable venture, as they feel these concerts do not attract many listeners. Social media platforms have challenged conventional modes of distributing music and have rendered them commercially unviable. Most established record labels are not producing and distributing new recordings. The situation in the field of music education is equally alarming due to the rise in the number of certified teachers, many of whom are not inspired enough to teach, but have to do so as they do not find other suitable employment opportunities. Audience opinions are divided on the quality of performances taking place and the future of the music tradition.

It is imperative to discuss each of these problems in detail. In particular, the aims and objectives of all the agencies need to be examined to assess how they have impacted the patronage that is being offered to performers. I have attempted to do so in this book and, in the process, have sought to raise questions to find possible solutions and ensure a healthier future for this music tradition. I must admit that I have not tried to analyse specific trends in performance or teaching, as they would require an entire book by themselves.

Some of the issues discussed here have been deliberated upon elsewhere too.[22] This study is based on the firm belief that musicians play a central role in the ecology of Hindustani music, and that their opinions need to be appropriately deliberated upon and represented on all forums. While doing so, I am acutely aware that the experiences of the members of hereditary musicians and courtesan families would be vastly different from those of other musicians, since the former have lost their position as sole interpreters of the tradition. But it is also true that hereditary and non-hereditary performers are not monolithic entities marked merely by a Hindu–Muslim communal divide, as is often simplistically projected. Each category is stratified into groups like soloists and accompanists, vocalists and instrumentalists, and gurus and shishyas. I have tried to address the problems that some of these groups face today, but in most cases I have used the term 'musicians' for those who are performing or teaching Hindustani music as a profession, irrespective of whether they are hereditary or non-hereditary musicians or whether they belong to any particular group.

This book is based on primary and secondary source material published in four languages, namely, English, Hindi, Marathi and Gujarati, and from my personal interactions with musicians, concert organizers, sponsors and listeners. The appendices provided at the end of the book include questionnaires that were earlier circulated as a part of surveys conducted among students and practitioners of Hindustani music. Information gathered through these surveys has been referred to in the appropriate sections of the book. I have also drawn upon the experience that I have gained in well over four decades.

A historical background to many of the institutions or trends discussed here has been included, as I feel this has greatly impacted the present and can provide vital clues to forging the path ahead. I have tried to provide empirical evidence to back my arguments, but in cases where such evidence is hard to come by in the public domain, I have described the situations based on my experience. The internet has been a boon in providing ready access to empirical evidence, but I must hasten to add that a few websites that I have referred to in the course of my research may not be available anymore, may have deleted previous information, or may have re-located. I crave the indulgence of readers for any changes that may have occurred since the time the book went into press. I have made it a point to indicate the fact that official websites of some public organizations have not been updated or do not provide adequate information as would be expected of agencies run on public funds. Official websites are primary sources for research, and should be regularly updated. In fact, public organizations must make all relevant information available to citizens, particularly when the ruling dispensation takes pride in going digital. This would go a long way in demonstrating transparency and accountability on their part.

I have chosen to include diverse viewpoints throughout the book, because I believe that many of the issues are often the result of a lack of much-desired transparency in policy-making and working relations. I hope and trust that a fruitful and sustained dialogue between all individuals and agencies connected to Hindustani music will begin, sooner rather than later.

Introduction

Before discussing the specifics related to different stakeholders in the Hindustani music ecosystem, it would be relevant to take stock of the major problems concerning this music tradition which have become talking points in private conversations as well as public discourse.

The first to head the list of stumbling blocks for performers is that the limited concert opportunities are unable to accommodate the increasing number of performers. Amarendra Dhaneshwar, music critic, organizer and vocalist, argues that the number of concerts has risen today and that there is no dearth of talent, but there is a serious lack of equality of opportunity for the talented. He goes further to suggest that an almost insidious pattern exists in the manner that performers are chosen for concerts. He states, 'Almost the same musicians are chosen to perform in all the festivals. So when we look at the performance scene we also need to look at the – I would use a little strong word, but politics of concert organizing [sic].'[1]

Concerts that enjoy corporate sponsorship often do not feature a large number of lesser-known musicians, as organizers prefer to present celebrated musicians to ensure a good turnout that will satisfy sponsors. The average turnout at concerts does not seem encouraging, although mega festivals and concerts featuring specific performers draw large audiences from diverse social strata.

In most cases, performers are paid poorly, thus further aggravating the problem. Age, experience and the public stature of performers determines the fee they usually command or that the organizer would offer, keeping in mind the total budget for the programme. Relatively unknown musicians, therefore, can neither command nor demand a fee and have to, perforce, accept a token honorarium in the hope of reaching out to a large audience. Often, this honorarium barely covers the travel costs incurred by performers. Those who have not been able to establish successful careers maintain that petty politics and commerce in the field control performance opportunities. For them, decisions related to the choice of performers and their fees for prime concerts are carefully orchestrated moves by some musicians and concert presenters. They believe that this unholy nexus has given rise to favouritism, nepotism and corruption, all of which adversely affect the music. Journalist Sumana Ramanan asks '. . . why those with the most knowledge and dedication remain on the sidelines while those peddling meretricious fare hog the limelight and much more?'[2]

Some musicians have taken to arranging sponsorship and then organizing concerts that feature themselves. Often, they include other performers too, who may return the favour by inviting them to perform in concerts that they organize. Dhaneshwar mentions, 'Musicians are either connected with some music institutions or musicians float their own institutions and then a kind of barter system develops among musicians.'[3] Words like 'marketing', 'public relations' and 'networking' have been added to the contemporary musician's vocabulary, reflecting the consumerist world that we operate in. Having found easy acceptance even among musicians otherwise unfamiliar with the English language, these activities are regarded by contemporary Indian musicians as necessary to further their career prospects.

With the increase in the number of performers, it is only natural that they are all keen to share their work with wider audiences, not only through live concerts but also by utilizing all available formats of distributing music. Airplay time for Hindustani music has declined on public broadcasting networks, with the result that hundreds of young musicians can no longer look forward to these channels to relay their music on a regular basis. These networks, apart from some private and public institutions, are large repositories of archival recordings which need to be made easily accessible to listeners. But a lot needs to be done in this direction for concrete results to be discernible.

Propagation of Hindustani music through commercial recordings has also been adversely impacted in recent years, as established record labels have stopped producing new recordings. New independent labels have introduced younger musicians to listeners, but they lack resources to reach wider audiences. Added to this, the urge even among diehard fans of Hindustani music to acquire free music recordings through illicit copying and transferring of music files does not help the situation.

Digital technology has made available many online platforms, which have been used successfully by musicians and music lovers alike. But there are often inadequacies in the quality of musical content and its production.

In the context of music education, there has been an exponential increase in the number of music schools and departments of music at universities, but the quality of performers, teachers and academics trained solely at these institutions, often appears wanting.

Many musicians participate in concerts that do not necessarily fall within the purview of conventional Hindustani music recitals.

Some of these are intercultural collaborations with non-Indian musicians or are concerts involving Indian musicians experienced in diverse systems of music, such as Carnatic or south Indian art music, folk music, jazz, rock and others. Justifying their participation in such musical collaborations, more popularly categorized as 'fusion music', musicians often claim that such projects not only offer performance opportunities but they also popularize Hindustani music and make it more accessible to the uninitiated and young audiences.[4]

But there are others who are more circumspect about such projects. They believe that they have been true to the traditional form and that most intercultural fusion work is merely a means to introduce novelty. Ravi Shankar(1920–2012), the world-renowned sitar player and India's pre-eminent cultural ambassador stated:

> I have never tried to do anything like fusion. The basis of all my
> music is in the raga and tala format. If I have done anything else, it
> has been mostly with the folk music of India, the many folk tunes
> that have inspired me. So whatever I have tried is a new texture or
> sound for experimentation, but not fusion. Many people are trying
> some interesting things, but I find that most of it is very gimmicky
> in order to sell the record, something new that catches [people's
> fancy]. And it does catch [on], but unfortunately within a year or
> two, something else comes along that takes its place.[5]

Many critics of such collaborations use the word 'confusion' while evaluating their musical worth. Sarangi maestro Ram Narayan says, 'Fusion? I call it confusion! If there's no integrity and natural flow, there's nothing to be gained. . . . I am happy only with my pure music.'[6]

Those involved in such collaborative work strongly feel that they need to devise new ways of connecting with the listeners of today, particularly the youth. They consider it old-fashioned and conservative when others criticize them for resorting to gimmicks in performance and vehemently reject all talk about the supposed consequential dilution of music. Some even point out that Hindustani music has been the result of fusion experiments that took place centuries ago. For instance, tabla maestro Zakir Hussain says:

> The north Indian classical music that anybody performs, be it Ravi Shankar, Vilayat Khan or Bhimsen Joshi, is actually a fusion . . . [Amir Khusro] took the forms from temples and the kaul and kalbana and meshed them together and came up with the form of music now known as khayal, which all north Indian classical musicians perform. So, the fusion began then.[7]

Given this complex picture of a tradition that is regarded as one of the best examples of India's cultural heritage, there are concerns among some senior connoisseurs, musicians and scholars, many of them with several years of listening experience, about the quality of performances today. They are apprehensive that the 'purity' and 'authenticity' of the tradition are being lost as a result of the impatience and the lack of restraint, which they believe are being exhibited by the young musicians of today. They feel that these musicians, in an attempt to gain performance opportunities and ensure professional success, allow themselves to be carried away by the breakneck speed that present society embodies. This impacts the manner in which they create music. Their music is found wanting in depth, gravitas and breadth of vision. The shallow and superficial quality of the music is due to the excessive emphasis given by young performers to the flashy and the spectacular. They also alter the dynamic and tonal range of voice and instruments with the help of digital systems. This is further exacerbated by what the seniors consider is an unleashing of gimmicks, like performing at great speeds, indulging in savaal–javaab (musical call and response) sequences with percussion accompanists and such drama. The seniors firmly state that the absence of sustained taaleem and scholarship, the keenness to self-gratify and to captivate audiences through the sensual, rather than the abstract and intangible, leads to music that is made with a view to appeal to the lowest common denominator. They castigate musicians for introducing changes in their performance practice and concert repertoire, ostensibly to please a varied listenership. They view this as a 'commercial approach' to music-making.

Some of these sentiments are expressed in the statement made by Ram Narayan:

[T]oday, depth and dedication are rarely to be seen. Everyone is trying to impress. The fastest and the loudest are the ones who are popular! A raga is often replaced by the mere presentation of the scale! The aaroha-avaroha, gale ki taiyari, haath ki taiyari, gimmicky exchanges with the tabla player, sawal jawab . . . over emphasis on looks and attire . . . I see these as symptoms of deterioration.[8]

Similarly, in the words of dhrupad maestro Zia Fariduddin Dagar (1932–2013):

[T]oday's performer is quick to wind up, collect his payment and disappear! Earlier, the best of artistes used to sit in the front rows, before the general public. The performer had to give his best to measure up to the challenge of impressing the knowledgeable. And even ordinary listeners got the benefit of it! Today, everything is mercenary there's no heart. Each one if busy trying to promote and project himself! Trying to get the media to acknowledge his dubious 'innovations'.[9]

Comparing the past with the present, Dagar added:

About thirty years ago, there were some musicians who were really great. Today, there's hardly a vocalist who satisfies [the listener]. Some good instrumentalists are still there, but they too are deviating from their path. There are no sadhaks today, there's no sadhana. Our classical character itself is in jeopardy.[10]

Company director, musician, organizer and critic Kumar Prasad Mukherji even criticized celebrated musicians for declining artistic standards. He complained that their frequent performances qualitatively hamper the musical output. Putting it plainly, he wrote:

[B]ig artistes sometimes create conditions themselves that are not conducive to good recitals, especially if they accept too many successive bookings in different parts of the country. Singing or playing at midnight with a plane ticket for an early-morning flight in the pocket does not always contribute to quality performance.[11]

In contrast to these opinions, celebrated musicians of our times maintain that change is inevitable, that it has always occurred throughout history, and that it is necessary and beneficial in order to prevent the tradition from stagnating. In this context, Ravi Shankar stated:

People talk about tradition and Nada Brahma, and that's fine. But we're not singing Vedic hymns now, and we're not playing what was played even two hundred years ago. People don't realize that. The link is there, definitely, but it spread into so many different channels that we call gharanas. So many names have been invented by individuals to stamp something as their trademark, like 'Made in the USA'.[12]

Going a step further, Shankar maintained that a professional musician could not but compromise his music to satisfy audiences. He said:

Ultimately, we try to please people. You cannot charge a fee and sell tickets to an audience, and then just sit there and do whatever you want, or play alap for the entire concert. Some people may get bored. Or if you show your virtuosity right from the very beginning, playing for the gallery, people get tired of that also. So now it is a beautiful compromise that everybody is trying to do. In the beginning we always start with the alap, which is supposed to be more spiritual, and then we gradually accelerate into a faster tempo. That is the usual format.[13]

Some eminent musicians believe that every generation blames the successive one for diluting the music, both in terms of scholarship and performance. They feel young musicians are a talented lot and see a bright future for Hindustani music. They suggest that musicians need to be open to other musical influences, collaborate in intercultural music projects, as they believe this is a new and welcome way of projecting this tradition of music to the world and have musical conversations with musicians from other parts of the world.[14]

Setting aside for a moment the opposing views I have described, it may be apt to note that concerns about the purity of Hindustani music were voiced even in earlier times. Even trends in the late nineteenth and early twentieth centuries demonstrate that musicians employed adaptive strategies with regard to performance practice, concert repertoire and so on, displaying remarkable artistic zeal to push the accepted boundaries of tradition. There is enough evidence to show that they also altered their musical trajectory during trying times in a bid to reach a wider audience.[15]

Some censured such changes, while others welcomed them. Writing in the first quarter of the twentieth century, music educationist Vishnu Narayan Bhatkhande (1860–1936) criticized contemporary young khayal singers for indulging in vocal acrobatics without caring whether their voices were melodious or if this was in consonance with the import of the song-text.[16] Although he accepted that the musical tradition in India had transformed since ancient and medieval times and that further change was inevitable, even extending to the incorporation of Western influences, he obviously did not view the transformation as a favourable occurrence. This explains his statement that the situation was unavoidable since the purpose of music was to entertain people. He felt these changes occurred primarily due to the lack of notation and the absence of detailed theoretical explanation of the subject. His project of preparing modern normative texts that would explicitly lay down the rules and grammar for current musical practice to guide contemporary musicians and help plot the future course of Hindustani music was in answer to the concerns raised by him.[17] But there were others who believed that the very period that Bhatkhande was commenting on was a high point of this music. Commentator Vamanrao Deshpande (1907–1990) averred:

> The period from the middle of the nineteenth century to 1947 when India became free might well be regarded as the Golden Age of Hindustani music. The various gharanas of music, i.e., Gwalior, Rampur, Agra, Kirana, Patiala, Jaipur, etc., and the various aesthetic traditions of music developed and were invested with dignified status during this period.[18]

Deshpande strongly believed that the quality of music was at its best during this phase because of the accomplishments and discipline of the performers and teachers during those times, as well as due to the patronage they received from royal families and initiated listeners at music circles and conferences.[19]

Thus, diametrically opposite opinions about the quality of music-making have been expressed in the past too. Germane to this discussion is that most critiques of Hindustani music and musicians, whether in the past or now, often ignore the fact that this music has always been in a state of flux. Tradition is expected to remain in the state that it existed in several centuries ago. This perspective does not seem to take cognizance of the fact that a tradition from a distant past cannot remain static, even though it is based on information, knowledge and wisdom handed down through generations. Every generation has absorbed elements from the past, reinterpreted them and passed them on to the next, thus colouring what was considered 'traditional' until then. With the passage of time, innovations have ceased to be regarded as such, and have been subsumed into the vast repository of tradition itself. As in the case of other existing traditions, Hindustani music has also encountered challenges and responded to new stimuli. This movement of ideas over a considerably long period and across geographical spaces has made it a living tradition.

The comprehension and construction of the past is often clouded by a sense of nostalgia and by prejudices or personal choices, giving rise to dogmatic positions about what should constitute 'pure and authentic' music. This underestimates artistic impulses and ignores social, political and economic processes, which shape the trajectory of music-making. A careful perusal of the recordings made through the twentieth century shows that there is no single, monolithic and absolute Hindustani music aesthetic. Instead, it changed over the period, almost unnoticeably. The problem is further compounded by the reality that this music has essentially been an oral tradition, thus giving rise to multiple interpretations. Misguidedly, a celebration of this diversity is sometimes overtaken by a dogmatic approach. This is similar to the approach to Indian culture. As stated by historian Romila Thapar:

> The historical process is decisive to the definition of culture, yet the understanding of Indian culture is poorly served in this respect, for it is assumed that the historical process has a static interpretation and has remained broadly unchanged over the last century, or, that culture is a one-time event which has survived untampered with from the past to the present.[20]

The root of the present yearning for the hallowed past lies in the nineteenth-century discourse on Hindustani music, led by members of the educated middle class. Fired by nascent nationalism, they sought to project a pan-Indian cultural identity which would prove India's 'glorious' legacy and 'golden' past. To this effect, they strove to establish the antiquity of this musical tradition and to promote this music as a symbol of ancient Indian heritage. This endeavour was in keeping with the orientalist approach that sought to link different aspects of Indian society with an ancient exotic Hindu-Sanskritic civilization. These claims of antiquity ignored the contribution of Muslim royal patrons, musicians; or the contribution of Muslim musicians was acknowledged grudgingly. Instead, they were regarded as an illiterate lot who had been incapable of comprehending theoretical information enshrined in Sanskrit treatises and had therefore caused a disjunct between age-old theoretical norms and current musical practice.[21]

The forcefulness with which this interpretation of the past was reiterated has deeply influenced successive generations. It is not surprising, therefore, that most people and well-known institutions hold fast on to the impression that Hindustani music is a tradition that has deeply Hindu religious or spiritual connections with an ancient past dating back several thousand years. Raised to the level of an absolute truth, any interpretation to the contrary invites scorn and disdain, as it would shake the belief that we have been living with for many years and would also challenge those who matter in the world of Hindustani music now.

This brief description of the current environment of Hindustani music provides only a glimpse of the incredible maze of contradictions that lie behind the music that so many appreciate. No doubt, concerns about the present and future of this music have grown in the past few decades. The ring of urgency sounded in certain quarters today is probably due to the speed with which radical changes have been brought about in the last decade of the twentieth century and the early part of the twenty-first century, and their widespread repercussions. While accepting that change is inescapable, Ravi Shankar observed:

Our music has always gone through changes, becoming more and more developed and sophisticated through centuries. We today feel the onslaught of disturbing elements because the changes are very rapid for us to adjust [sic]. Those days the media of communication was limited to live concerts.

Then came the gramophone, the radio and then the television. But now with the age of computers and instant access it is really overwhelming. I am not saying that this is good or bad but it is a fact. Every kind of music has and in fact is going through changes more rapidly now than ever before, and who am I to say if it's for better or worse.[22]

Indeed, technological changes have made access to Hindustani music much easier today than was the case several decades ago. Technology has equipped music lovers with information about the music that performers, teachers, and government and non-government institutions should not underestimate. As stated by Ashok Da. Ranade (1937–2011):

[R]epeated and massive exposure to music has changed the type and quality of Patronage. Though our audiences cannot be considered knowledgeable they are no more ignorant! One cannot fool this audience. These audiences now are able to know the artist's repertoire, and the depth of his knowledge.[23]

One would imagine that easy access to information has made it possible for other stakeholders to also apprise themselves of one another's activities and work towards a healthy interaction. Regrettably, however, various groups act in isolation and often take unilateral decisions, which are counterproductive for Hindustani music.

1

Riding the Airwaves

The degree of state patronage for the arts largely depends on the economic prosperity of a country. This comes as a stark reminder in the case of a developing country such as ours, which faces glaring problems requiring immediate attention, such as the agrarian crisis and large-scale unemployment. Besides, Hindustani music is only a segment of the arts in India, and it would be natural to expect it to receive only a small part of the total funds disbursed for the propagation of culture. But the constant affirmation of the state's responsibility towards its culture and arts through the aims and objectives of its constituent institutions leads one to examine, in some detail, the present state of policy that concerns Hindustani music, directly or indirectly.

Given the extent to which public radio and television networks have spread Hindustani music, it would not be an exaggeration to say that they have democratized access to it far more than any other government-run institution. I have therefore chosen to look at policies that have guided their working before examining other media.

All India Radio (AIR), or Akashvani, and Doordarshan (DD) were earlier under the Ministry of Information and Broadcasting. They became a part of Prasar Bharati, the country's public service broadcaster and a statutory autonomous body established in 1997, under the Prasar Bharati (Broadcasting Corporation of India), Act of 1990.[1] Both units continued to feature Hindustani music recitals under the new formation. In his address at a seminar held in 2012, Rajiv Takru, additional secretary in the information and broadcasting ministry and chief executive officer of Prasar Bharati at that time, stated that AIR and DD genuinely promoted music without any profit motive. He added:

> We present programmes, which would never generate profit if we had to do them commercially. As a matter of fact, 80–90 per cent of our effort, time and resources are put into [the] generation of material into creation of archives, which under no circumstances can ever be called commercially viable . . . may be in the next couple of years, we would have a niche channel operating on All India Radio . . . for various categories of Indian classical music depending on the nature of the audience we are looking at. Now it would be foolish of me if I was to expect that these niche channels are ever going to make a profit or that I am ever going to run it commercially – no, but this is [under] taken by All India Radio as part of their public service mandate.[2]

Evidently, Takru had arrived at the conclusion that channels featuring art music were not commercially viable and that they would never make profits. He felt the government was not given due recognition for its selfless role:

> We do not work for profit; we [don't] care a hoot if we make money. We are not particularly bothered about not making any

money since [the] government is funding us very substantially and I think [the] government gets far less credit than it really deserves in these matters.[3]

But this purported government largesse to Prasar Bharati did not seem to reflect in its administration and financial status. For one, despite the autonomy assured to the corporation by the act, it is obvious that it has always been controlled by the central government as per the powers bestowed upon it in Chapter IV of the act.[4] This seems to have been a major source of annoyance and hindrance to the corporation, as is clear in the candid comments made in many publications by Jawhar Sircar, the chief executive officer of the corporation from 2012 to 2016 and former secretary, Ministry of Culture, Government of India, from 2008 to 2012.[5] Lack of funds, limited share of the revenue for software development and problems concerning recruitment of staff were some of the major areas of concern when Sircar took the reins at the corporation.[6] Upset with the twisted equation with the government, Sircar admitted, 'Prasar Bharati is also a classic case of myopic handling of a public institution by [the] government, and evidence on "how not to govern".'[7] He was hopeful that the new government voted into power in 2014 would bring about a transformation and improve the quality of programming.[8] But despite the change in the Centre, he accepted that the quality of content on AIR and DD had declined, and that special efforts were needed to reach out to young listeners, who were a significant part of the population, in order to know and cater to their tastes.[9] Commenting on the controversy that played out in February–March 2018 between the information and broadcasting ministry and Prasar Bharati over the payment of dues to a private company, Sircar has been even more vociferous in his castigation of the ministry.[10] Even Mrinal Pande, noted author and former chairperson of Prasar Bharati, has unequivocally stated that the information and broadcasting ministry exercises control over

Prasar Bharati, despite the autonomy granted to it by the 1990 act.[11] Perhaps, it is for this reason that even the presence of an eminent person like Pande, who is an art music aficionado, on the Prasar Bharati Board does not really help in changing policy to make a positive impact on the spread of Hindustani music through national media units.

The lack of government performance is not altogether surprising since culture comes sixth in the list along with sports, games and youth affairs, from among the eight objectives enumerated on the Prasar Bharati website.[12] One can only wonder why culture is mentioned so low in the order, when Chapter II, Sub-section 12 of the Prasar Bharati Act lists it as fourth among sixteen objectives.[13]

Akashvani

Organized broadcasting came into existence with the inauguration of the first station of the Indian Broadcasting Company in Bombay by Lord Irwin on 23 July 1927. The Calcutta station was inaugurated on 26 August 1927. In April 1930, the Indian Broadcasting Service, under the Department of Industries and Labour, commenced operations on an experimental basis. Lionel Fielden was appointed the first controller of broadcasting in August 1935 and it was under his initiative that the Indian State Broadcasting Service became AIR on 8 June 1936. AIR was brought under the Department of Communications in 1937 and, four years later, became a part of the Department of Information, and Broadcasting.[14]

Hindustani music was broadcast even before the establishment of AIR through radio stations set up by private businessmen. The Bombay Radio Station, established in 1925 by the Chenoi brothers, noted businessmen, was inaugurated with a vocal recital by Faiyaz Khan (1881–1950), iconic vocalist and doyen of the Agra gharana.[15] Beenkaar Murad Khan, also broadcast on the same radio station in 1928.[16]

But these were exceptional cases, as many senior musicians refused to broadcast their music. This attitude continued even after the establishment of AIR and was in some ways similar to the reactions in the early days of the gramophone, when they feared that they would lose their voices once they were recorded. The constraints on the duration of performances placed by the new technology may have also prompted them to stay away. The ease with which an uninitiated audience would have access to their repertoire through such recordings could have been another contributory factor. Broadcasting of Hindustani music saw similar hesitation or outright refusal from many musicians. Consequently, most music broadcasts featured performers from the salon district, so much so that the Delhi radio station was nicknamed 'Sarkari Chawri Bazaar', after the well-known street where hereditary women performers pursued their profession.[17]

With the passage of time, more musicians agreed to broadcast from different stations of AIR. Faiyaz Khan performed from Mumbai, Delhi, Kolkata and Lucknow AIR stations and Mushtaq Hussein Khan (1880–1974), the Rampur–Sahaswan gharana maestro, performed from many stations of AIR, although he was heard most frequently from Lucknow, Allahabad and Delhi.[18] Broadcasts were also scheduled to mark significant events. For instance, vocalist Dattatreya Vishnu Paluskar (1921–1955), son of music educationist and vocalist Vishnu Digambar Paluskar was featured in his first radio concert held at the Mumbai station in 1938 to commemorate his father.[19] From January 1938, broadcasts of live concerts were organized, which included the Abdul Karim Khan Anniversary from Miraj, relays from the Wagle Memorial Hall and a programme held by Bombay Music Circle, featuring eminent vocalists Omkarnath Thakur (1897–1967) and Abdul Karim Khan of Delhi (not to be confused with Abdul Karim Khan of the Kirana Gharana).[20] In Mumbai, special programmes featuring orchestral recitals by students of the School of Indian Music, an institution set up by scholar musician B.R. Deodhar (1901–1990), were recorded three to four times each year for eight to ten years.[21]

It was obvious that Indian music was not broadcast on AIR as part of an overarching policy geared towards its promotion. In fact, Fielden had misconceptions about Indian music. He believed that it was primarily pursued by 'prostitutes and mirasis' and that this led to a general feeling that the music was in itself immoral; that there were no universally accepted standards for compositions, voice production and the art of singing; that the schools of Indian music were rigid with regard to change or progress, which, according to him, had been introduced by gramophone records, films and orchestras; that there was no distinction between 'classical' and 'light'.[22]

But even though music broadcasts were treated merely as a means of popular entertainment, they were too important for the government to ignore, as was obvious from Fielden's remarks:

> Music, which must necessarily fill about seven–eighths of any broadcasting programme, is naturally a factor of considerable importance. It may be said that music is, to some extent, 'padding', because it does not instruct or inform, and that it is, therefore, actually of less significance in broadcasting than talks or news. Nevertheless, it is obvious that for a large percentage of listeners, music will be the chief source of entertainment and possibly also the general factor governing popularity or unpopularity.[23]

During the early phase of AIR, fees and duration of broadcast were directly negotiated between the local station and the performer. Distinguished musicians were paid a fee of approximately ₹100 and, in exceptional cases, they received more than ₹150. Each year, every radio station prepared a list of approved performers indicating their fee and gradation, and this list was circulated among all stations. Stations tried to maintain uniform standards and booked performers from other zones as well.[24] Apart from notable professional musicians, talented youngsters were also encouraged to broadcast. Auditions were arranged by the programme assistant in charge of music and heard by one senior officer, like the assistant station director or the station director.[25]

Interestingly, even in the early years of AIR, Fielden mentioned that the younger generation found greater pleasure in films and gramophone recordings.[26] Supporting the broadcast of art music, he believed that variety had to be introduced to widen the scope of listeners' tastes. He stated:

> Thus we find, in most broadcasting organizations, that classical music gains a place which a majority vote would not actually give it and it is undoubtedly true that the taste for classical music has, in many countries, been considerably strengthened by this policy.[27]

I must add a rider, though, that it is unclear whether Fielden's remarks in this context pertain only to Western art music or if they were directed to Indian art music too.

The length of performances was pre-determined by the duration of the broadcasted programme and musicians had to modify their recitals to meet this limit. As per details provided by Fielden about the length of transmission in 1937–38 for many types of programmes, Indian vocal music enjoyed the maximum time, followed by European instrumental music. Indian instrumental music was at the sixth position, followed by European vocal music. In 1938–39, Indian vocal music continued to enjoy maximum transmission, but Indian instrumental music had risen to the fourth position, and European instrumental music and vocal music were at the fifth and eighth positions, respectively.[28] The bias towards vocal music seems to have reflected a similar tendency seen in live concerts around this time.

Fielden was keen to retain the services of regular ensembles for Indian music. He noted:

Three to four Indian musicians must be engaged every day to provide a modicum of variety, their fees ranging from Rs. 20 to Rs. 300 per artist. A European orchestra which fills an hour or so, may cost anything from Rs. 50 to Rs. 150. Indian orchestras have to be maintained at all stations for accompaniments, rehearsals and for performance. Such orchestras consist of 8 to 15 instrumentalists and cost on the average Rs. 500 to Rs. 1,000 a month or Rs. 17 to Rs. 34 a day.[29]

Apart from the policy to retain an in-house orchestra, the Mumbai station also featured B.R. Deodhar's orchestra every Sunday.[30] The engagement of Indian orchestras was encouraged by Fielden, notwithstanding the concept of orchestral music being a Western one. Contrary to this, he was against the inclusion of the harmonium on radio broadcasts and banned the instrument from AIR broadcasts after 1 March 1940. Although the issue had been discussed at the Station Directors Conference in 1939, Fielden took this initiative after John Foulds (1880–1939), a composer heading the Western music section of the Delhi station of the AIR in the 1930s, stated in an article that the harmonium was not appropriate for Indian music as it could not produce the microtones that were integral to this system of music.[31]

In the decades following Independence, broadcasts of Hindustani music attracted more listeners across several regions as the number of radio stations rose. By August 1947, the AIR network had nine stations at Delhi, Calcutta, Bombay, Madras, Lucknow, Tiruchirapalli, Lahore, Peshawar, and Dacca. Low-power radio stations in the princely states of Mysore, Trivandrum, Hyderabad, Aurangabad and Baroda were taken over by AIR when they were integrated with India and became a part of the AIR network by 1950.[32] At that time, there were 2.5 lakh receiver sets for a population that exceeded 325 million. By 1961, the number of radio stations trebled.[33]

Hindustani music certainly benefitted with the spread of broadcasting across the country. The tenure of B.V. Keskar (1903– 1984) as minister of information and broadcasting from 1952 to 1962 was particularly relevant to the status that this system of music and its performers achieved on AIR. For Keskar, film music was alien to Indian culture and was an 'exotic cocktail' of many kinds of music with limited appeal.[34] He strongly believed in a constant endeavour to accord classical music its rightful place in Indian society. Having studied Hindustani music, Keskar was keen on promoting it on radio, particularly because he believed the musical heritage of India had been adversely affected due to Muslim rulers and Muslim musicians, a sentiment that had been expressed since the late nineteenth century by individuals within the Indian intelligentsia, who had worked towards establishing Indian art music as a symbol of an ancient Hindu-Sanskritic past.[35]

Keskar's blinkered attitude towards film and art music impacted AIR's policy and gave Hindustani music a boost during his tenure as minister. He inducted respected writers, poets, musicians and dramatists on staff-artistes' contracts and appointed them as 'producers' in AIR, instead of restricting them to the earlier post of 'performers'.[36] The first National Programme of Music was broadcast on 20 July 1952 and continues to be broadcast every weekend even to this day. In October 1952, the National Orchestra of AIR was set up in Delhi, with Ravi Shankar as conductor. T.K. Jairama Iyer joined as the second conductor. The first Radio Sangeet Sammelan was broadcast in October 1955 and continues to be an annual feature even till today.[37]

But Keskar's term was also vitiated by the new policy that sought to grade musicians irrespective of their public stature. According to Jawhar Sircar, this policy initiated by Keskar was to enable the

State to 'take over the role of princely patrons and ensure fair play, through a system of "grading" artists to ensure that the best received their just dues'.[38] In September 1952, at Mumbai, 400 musicians from western India were required to undergo audition tests in the period of a week.[39] But the performers considered the procedure followed by the specially appointed audition panel, headed by noted scholar-musician S.N. Ratanjankar (1900–1974), as arbitrary and disrespectful. They registered their protest through a countrywide agitation with Mumbai at its epicentre. A musicians' organization called Bharatiya Sangit Kalakar Mandal was set up in 1953, with eminent vocalist Vilayat Hussain Khan (1895–1962), as its president, vocalist Kausalya Manjeshwar (1922–2007) as secretary, and businessman and sitar player Arvind Parikh as joint secretary. A decision was taken to stop broadcasting and to picket outside the Mumbai radio station until the policy was replaced with one that treated musicians with respect. The agitation ended in 1955 and a settlement was reached. The audition policy was altered to incorporate a screening process, which was not demeaning to performers.[40] This agitation aside, many praised AIR for rendering yeoman's service to Hindustani music. But there have been mixed responses from some quarters. Writing in the 1940s, commentator S.K. Chaubey discussed the potential of the broadcasting medium and its relevance to art music:

It can teach music to its listeners and help them to appreciate it better. It can engage first-rate musicians whose duty would be to train a small group of promising and talented musicians and also broadcast special music on special occasions according to an intelligent plan. It can do immense propaganda for it and also raise public opinion on this issue.[41]

But Chaubey found AIR wanting in its contribution to art music:

I grant that the A.I.R. has not failed to popularize Indian music and Indian musicians. Apart from making them presentable, it has entertained its listeners too. But this is hardly satisfactory. The Radio in India has made no solid contribution to the development and progress of Indian music. Like the film company, the Radio knows how to entertain its listeners. But in doing so it shapes their likes and dislikes. It teaches them to develop a habitual indifference towards classical music. It does not care for that negligible minority which shouts the slogans of classical music.[42]

Chaubey did not believe that a commercially motivated AIR could do justice to art music:

On the whole, Radio music is detrimental to taste and judgement. In its actual working, it is a free innovator indifferent to the voice of the tradition and the genius of our music. . . . It treats music as a marketable commodity whether it is classical or popular. With its limited mental equipment, it widely avoids making excursions into the realm of higher music.[43]

There were other voices, too, that were critical of the quality of music. In 1952, a source assuming the name 'Lancet' in a letter to the *Times of India* lamented the adverse impact that the quality of broadcasts had on a specific musical form:

A good deal of the classical music at present broadcast from A.I.R. is of such poor quality that it does the khyal no credit. Singers who have no right before the microphone have to be booked again and again to keep up at least the semblance of variety – in artists, that is.[44]

Correspondence exchanged at the ministerial level in February 1947 between Sardar Vallabhbhai Patel (1875–1950), the minister for information and broadcasting and for home in the Interim Government, and Maulana Abul Kalam Azad (1888–1958) the minister for education, exhibit similar worries. Commenting on music broadcasts on AIR, Azad wrote:

> You perhaps do not know that I have always taken a keen interest in Indian music and at one time practised it myself. It has, therefore, been a shock to me to find that the standard of music of All India Radio broadcast is extremely poor. I have always felt that All India Radio should set the standard in Indian music and lead to its continual improvement. Instead, the present programmes have an opposite effect and lead one to suspect that the artistes are sometimes chosen not on grounds of merit.[45]

Azad offered to advise the secretary of broadcasting in the matter.[46] Patel's response to Azad's comments was equally forthright when he stated:

> While I make no apology for such defects as exist in the quality of these broadcasts, I think it would be a mistake to ignore the patent fact that the artistic talent at the disposal of each radio station is limited, and that they have to make the best of whatever talent is available to them. We have also to take note of the fact that the remuneration which we can give to these artistes is not sufficiently attractive, and having regard to the present financial difficulties of which you are no doubt aware, it does not seem possible to make any improvement in that respect.[47]

To many, the special interest shown in daily music programmes at a ministerial level and the prompt response directly from the minister of information and broadcasting would appear as odd. Patel's response shows that the remuneration to performers was not as good as desired due to the inadequacy of financial resources. But more relevant to our times is the fact that the problem of insufficient fees is not just an issue of the past, but continues to be a sore point among musicians even today, though spoken about only in closed circles.

With this as a brief historical backdrop to the role of AIR in broadcasting Hindustani music, it would be worthwhile to turn to the present situation.

According to its website, since its inception, AIR has been informing, educating and entertaining the masses. The website mentions the promotion of the nation's composite culture as one of its key objectives.[48] With a network of 262 radio stations, AIR is today accessible to almost the entire population of the country and heard in nearly 92 per cent of the total area. AIR operates eighteen FM stereo channels called AIR FM Rainbow, which target urban audiences, and four more FM channels called AIR FM Gold, which broadcast news and entertainment programmes from Delhi, Kolkata, Chennai and Mumbai.[49] The website states that AIR plays a very important role in the propagation and preservation of classical music.[50] AIR also organizes annual music competitions for young performers.[51]

Despite the extent of radio coverage across the length and breadth of the country and the avowed objective of promoting culture in general and art music in particular, there has been a sharp decline in the broadcasts of Hindustani music in the past few years. In 2012, Leeladhar Mandloi, director general of AIR, while addressing a seminar explained that AIR had to contend with a multitude of musical forms for which it had already allocated 40 per cent of the transmission time. The increase in the number of performers and the need to include all kinds of cultural programmes without restricting broadcasts to music recordings was a challenging task, even if there were a few channels exclusively dedicated to music.[52] He mentioned that AIR had to work within strict parameters and therefore could not accommodate certain professional terms that

were demanded by top-notch performers, who he would have liked
to invite for radio broadcasts. Instead, he put the ball in the court of
these musicians, exhorting them to relax their terms and treat the
promotion of art music as a joint responsibility by accepting the
contractual arrangement provided by AIR.[53]

It may be appropriate to point out that Vividh Bharati, a
commercial service of AIR launched in 1957 known for its
broadcasts of old and new Hindi film songs in a variety of
programmes, had also included limited broadcasts of art music
within the list of specially curated programmes.[54] The two main
programmes that included such broadcasts were *Sangeet Sarita* and
Anuranjani. Of these, *Sangeet Sarita* was particularly popular, but
the number of new episodes for this programme declined. Mandloi
explained that the programme featured 250 episodes, after which
it had to be wrapped up because, according to him, 'classical music
is not something like *Saas Bhi Kabhi Bahu Thi*. It has to come to an
end.'[55] He was referring to the multi-episode soap opera that had
been telecast on a privately owned television channel over a very
long period of time.

To many, Mandloi's response to the concerns voiced by
musicians and music lovers may appear insensitive. Indeed, some
believe that this insensitivity is exhibited by other officials in the
organization too. Bhaskar Chandavarkar (1936–2009), eminent
music composer and sitar player, stated:

> The officials who manage the media establishment are often
> oblivious of the problems that arise out the [sic] control over
> the trade of music. Those people who were entrusted with the
> responsibility of spreading the art ought to be broad-minded enough
> to acknowledge the need for artiste's freedom and be caring towards
> the future of music. Unfortunately, most of them have not been so.
> It is possible therefore that some irrevocable changes in the field of
> music have set in and all these changes are not necessarily good.[56]

Setting aside individual opinions, the current situation may be understood by examining some facts. Data collected from a limited survey carried out in Mumbai between 6.30 a.m. and 12 midnight during the period 4 May to 11 May 2016 of broadcasts on AIR Marathi, AIR Vividh Bharati, AIR FM Rainbow, AIR FM Gold through the AIR mobile app, Mumbai FM Radio and AIR website brought to light the following facts:

a. A total of 859 minutes (14 hours and 19 minutes) of art music was broadcast during this period, with an average 105.5 minutes of art music relayed on AIR Marathi and 15 minutes on Vividh Bharati.

b. There were no art music broadcasts on AIR FM channels during this period.

c. The average share of art music broadcast was about 7.45 per cent in 24 hours.

d. Art music programmes were usually relayed at night after 9.30 p.m. Fewer programmes were relayed during the mornings and afternoons.

e. At times, broadcasts ended abruptly to accommodate programmes that were to follow.

f. The broadcasts generally adhered to the Hindustani music convention of presenting specific raags at several times of the day and night.[57]

A similar survey was carried out in Mumbai almost a year later, from 17 March to 23 March 2017, from 6 a.m. to 12 midnight. In the period between the two surveys, AIR launched a 24x7 channel called 'Raagam'. According to the Prasar Bharati Annual Report of 2015–2016, this channel devoted entirely to Hindustani and Carnatic music was launched on 26 January 2016 and is available on Direct-To-Home (DTH) services as well as through the mobile app and via web streaming. The report states that the channel would include recorded material from all major regional stations and would feature old masters and contemporary luminaries.[58] The survey, as a result, monitored AIR Raagam in addition to AIR

Marathi and AIR Vividh Bharati. This survey brought to light the following facts:

a. A total of 6228 minutes (approximately 104 hours) of art music was broadcast during this period.
b. Every three hours, AIR Raagam broadcast Hindustani music for one hour and Carnatic music for two hours. Hence, approximately eight hours of Hindustani music and fourteen to sixteen hours of Carnatic music was broadcast in a day. Religious music based on Hindustani or Carnatic music was broadcast between 6 a.m. and 8 a.m.
c. AIR Marathi broadcast Hindustani music every night between 10 p.m. and 12 midnight.
d. AIR Vividh Bharati broadcast Hindustani music for 15 minutes in the morning from 7.30 a.m. to 7.45 a.m.
e. Out of all the channels monitored, AIR Raagam was found to be the most useful channel for students, listeners and connoisseurs of art music. But despite being called a 24x7 art music channel, it also broadcast regional devotional music.[59]

Many of the musicians and listeners I have interacted with have rued the fact that Hindustani music broadcasts have reduced over the years. This has also been my own experience as a listener since the 1970s and as a performer since the late 1980s until now. In light of what seems to be a desperate situation for Hindustani music broadcasts on AIR, musicians who had earlier regarded AIR as a prime avenue of spreading their music, are now disappointed that the institution is not as supportive as it was earlier.

There was also a time when musicians could avail of recording opportunities outside the jurisdiction of their home station and across two or three cities. Such opportunities were called chain bookings. These were stopped several years ago, probably because of the increase in the number of musicians in other cities too. But the reduction in the number of periodic recordings within one's own city or town is not an encouraging sign. The increase in fees over time provides little solace in this situation.

Furthermore, there have been no changes in the contractual terms offered by AIR. They remain one-sided, favouring the broadcaster, with no mention of the organization's obligations or the rights of the musicians. Clause 5 of the conditions referred to in the offer of engagement is an example of this inequitable arrangement:

> All India Radio shall have the absolute right of rejection of all or any part of the entertainment submitted by the Artist and shall not be called upon to give any reasons for any such rejection. Should the Station Director reject all or any part of such entertainment the Artist shall with all despatch submit other matter or material in place of that rejected for the approval of All India Radio.[60]

Successive governments have seen legal luminaries holding ministerial positions in the Central Cabinet, but no one seems to have found it necessary to revisit these terms and amend them in keeping with current international standards. This is also completely at variance with the range of copyright laws in India, which suitably empower artistes. It would seem, therefore, that while the law empowers artistes, the public broadcaster divests them of their rights. The sad truth is that even musicians are blissfully unaware of the terms that they are offered, and they often accept the contracts. Understandably, caught as they are in a situation that does not augur well for bright career prospects, an opportunity to broadcast and earn a recording fee is probably what matters most to them.

Notwithstanding the gradation policy that was introduced after the historic musicians' agitation in the 1950s and the new gradation policy that was initiated in 2014, rumours of nepotism and corrupt practices continue in hushed tones among candidates aspiring for higher grades.[61] Musicians who have attained seniority in age and experience feel belittled to have to apply for upgradation, particularly to the top grade. We cannot circumvent a system that has been put in place, but some believe that AIR needs to revisit the system to allow for upgradation without evaluating performers afresh. Most of all, some feel that there is a need to establish transparency in the process of choosing and appointing members of the audition committees at the local and central levels.

There is no doubt that AIR's policy to pay equal fees to soloists and accompanists placed in the same grade has brought about a change in the situation in live concerts held outside its ambit. In the latter case, payments to soloists and accompanists, who may enjoy the same public stature as performers, almost always differ. But parity of gradation and fees between individual disciplines are also causes for concern. For instance, harmonium players have for many years faced an uphill task due to unequal terms that they were offered with regard to their fees and opportunities to broadcast as soloists. The ban imposed on harmonium in all radio broadcasts, a decision taken during the pre-Independence days, continued even after Independence. This policy was in effect for several decades thereafter, although the instrument gained acceptance in live concerts and commercial recordings. The ban was opposed in some quarters, but this was not a concerted effort. A petition was filed in court to get the ban lifted through legal channels. In Mumbai, the Dadar Matunga Cultural Centre, a music club established in 1953, took an active part in the agitation against this ban.[62] Constant arguments among those outside the official circles for and against the instrument led AIR to organize a special seminar focusing on the different aspects of the harmonium.[63] Circumstances have fortunately changed over the years, though not entirely so. The harmonium is used regularly in broadcasts and harmonium players are now graded like other musicians. A solo recital by Bengaluru-based harmonium player Ravindra Katoti was broadcast on the National Programme of Music on 1 April 2018.[64] It is unclear if this is a policy decision to broadcast harmonium solo recitals as a regular feature in the future. For now, this does not seem to be the case.

Tabla solo recitals are not featured for the same duration as broadcasts of vocal music and other instrumental music on the National Programme of Music. A tabla player has to share the total duration of ninety minutes with another soloist. This, despite the fact that tabla solo recitals in live concerts extend well over an hour or two and are received well by audiences.

Beyond the list of graded artistes, in 2004, AIR recognized twenty-three musicians as 'national artistes' for 'their outstanding contribution to the cause and promotion of Indian Music and for their long association with All India Radio'.[65] Nine of these were performers of Hindustani music. Of these nine, seven died between then and now, and only two musicians from the Hindustani stream now enjoy 'national artiste' status. The glaring omissions in the original list of nationally and internationally renowned musicians are only accentuated with the passage of time, as the list has not been updated since then.

The number of musicians on the staff of AIR, who would provide musical accompaniment to graded artistes engaged on contractual terms, has drastically reduced. There does not seem to be a desire to make fresh appointments. Instead, AIR is now hiring non-staff musicians on contractual basis to play the role of accompanists. Thus, AIR is no more an organization that provides employment to a significant number of musicians across the country.[66]

On the technology front, computer software currently available should improve the recording and broadcast quality drastically, especially since AIR has to compete with other broadcasting networks. But software has to be combined with the latest recording equipment. It may surprise many to learn that AIR has never had any posts for sound engineers. Technicians or musicians on the staff who learn to record while on the job play the role that would conventionally be performed by sound engineers.[67]

Given the present conditions, music lovers who tune in regularly to radio broadcasts are disappointed by the downturn. In this context, it would be appropriate to study AIR's efforts at community outreach, specifically popularizing Hindustani music. AIR has a 'listener's corner' on its website, probably to address this requirement. Previous feedback was not readily available when the web link was accessed.[68] According to the Prasar Bharati Annual Report of 2014–2015, a director for audience research assists the director general in 'carrying out feedback studies on the programmes broadcast by various stations of All India Radio'.[69] The findings of this audience research are, disappointingly, not made public on the AIR website. We wonder if such information can be procured only in answer to questions under the Right To Information (RTI) Act.[70] It appears from the last two Prasar Bharati Annual Reports that no radio audience surveys for Hindustani music were conducted by the audience research unit in 2014–2015 and 2015–2016.[71] If this was accomplished in as early as May 1938 under the British colonial government, when an exhaustive questionnaire relating to listeners' musical preferences was issued to 17,000 listeners in the Bombay Presidency, it seems surprising that a regular line of contact between the public and a public service organization, particularly between listeners and a public broadcaster, is not suitably established in an age when superior technology is at our disposal.[72]

The absence of effective community outreach is also noticeable in the lack of publicity for Hindustani music programmes. Indian broadcasting since its inception had seen print publications like the *India Radio Times* and the *Indian Listener*, the latter also published in regional languages, carrying listings of forthcoming broadcasts.[73] Similar information was made available in newspapers until a few decades ago. Despite the AIR's presence on social media in present times, its complete listings are not readily available, neither on social media nor through conventional media.[74]

In his address mentioned earlier, Mandloi also revealed that the radio archives had a treasure trove of 178 radio-autobiographies of different artistes, including those of eighty-six musicians. The duration of each of these recordings was between three to six hours.[75] He added that AIR had marketed more than a hundred audio CDs, but admitted that an effective marketing system was lacking. He believed that a partnership with private distributors was required for such a project to succeed, but that the terms and conditions had to be worked out.[76] Despite this, he was optimistic that more than sixty audio CDs featuring noted musicians would be released that year.[77]

The lack of a successful marketing system for the archival recordings that have been made available on CDs has been recognized not only by Mandloi, but also in the Prasar Bharati Annual Report for 2015–2016.[78] The report states that sales counters were opened in one hundred AIR stations and in many of the Doordarshan Kendras. However, I have found during several visits to the stations in Mumbai that these counters are either not stocked or not operated properly.[79]

Doordarshan

Another public service broadcaster and a division of Prasar Bharati, Doordarshan (DD) began its experimental telecast in 1959, but daily transmission began only in 1965. By 1975, seven Indian cities had television service and DD was the sole provider of this service in the country. DD became a national broadcaster in 1982, the year colour television was introduced in India. A host of entertainment programmes and serials were telecast during the 1980s. According to the official DD website, there are sixty-seven DD studios producing programmes. DD reaches more than 90 per cent of the total population and programmes are developed for national, regional and local audiences.[80]

Hindustani music was featured on DD soon after its inception, either in the form of recitals with or without an audience, in an interview-cum-demonstration format, or as thematic programmes.[81] For years, a National Programme of Music, similar to the one broadcast on AIR, was telecast on DD, in addition to other Hindustani music performances recorded specifically for regional stations.[82]

In the early 1990s, DD telecast Hindustani music programmes in the mornings using the newly introduced chroma technology. These short recitals, each lasting a few minutes, were recorded originally against a plain backdrop, which was then replaced with other images to create what could be considered early incarnations of music videos. The result was often far from what may have been desired, as random images and stock shots were chosen to populate the backdrop, all of which had little or nothing to do with the actual recital.[83] In 1995, DD telecast a thirty-nine-episode programme entitled *Ragrang*, which sought to acquaint viewers with basic knowledge of raags.[84]

Fortunately for performers, grades awarded by AIR are recognized by DD and the fees are higher than those paid by AIR. But there has also been a decline in Hindustani music recitals on DD, as has been the case with AIR. There have been occasions when authorities believed that a conventional performance did not have the potential of reaching a wider audience and hence, fusion items or ensembles involving Hindustani, Carnatic and/or Western music were considered a necessary addition. It has been my experience that it is not usually left to the performers to decide whether or not they wish to incorporate these elements in their performances.

In January 2002, the DD Bharati channel was launched 'as a niche channel for culture, health and children, to preserve Indian culture with authenticity and to present it to the wider public'.[85] But barring a few exceptions, the lack of new programmes and financial resources forced the channel to fall back on featuring recordings from the DD archives.[86] In a bid to resolve such issues, DD Bharati partnered with several institutions 'to acquire and premiere programmes available in their archives, after making very judicious selection keeping the character of the channel in view. Under these partnerships, DD Bharati has the copyright to air various events organized by the partner institutions.'[87] Thus, we often see repeat telecasts of music festivals held by different organizations across the country. However, the agreements between DD Bharati and non-government organizations often do not take into account the performers' rights as guaranteed by the Indian Copyright Act, which expressly require the permission of the performers for any recording of the performance, and for the broadcast or telecast of the same, unless the recording and/or broadcast is done within limits permissible by the law. In the absence of requisite permissions from the performers, these recordings are, in effect, unlawful and illegally telecast. Strangely, neither the channel nor anyone at the ministerial level nor musicians, barring some, seem to have challenged this blatant violation of laws.[88] I have had personal experience in this regard and the matter was resolved in favour of all performers, including me, only after several weeks of communication with the authorities.[89]

The recording and telecast qualities of many concerts that are telecast live or recorded for future telecast, like those which are held during the annual Akashvani Sangeet Sammelans, leave much to be desired.

Thus, quite like AIR, the current situation at DD with regard to Hindustani music does not appear encouraging for the present generation of performers. There are few opportunities to record and DD does not provide regular employment opportunities for musicians, as they did earlier. DD Bharati continues to feature Hindustani music, but most of the programmes are repeat telecasts of earlier recordings.[90] The programme schedule does not seem to respect the age-old convention of presenting specific raags at certain times through the twenty-four-hour cycle while scheduling these telecasts, with the result that a morning raag is often heard at night.[91] Propagation of this music is done by way of publishing archival recordings, but even these are not readily available in the market.[92]

Films Division of India

Though not a broadcasting or telecasting network, the Films Division of India is a media unit that falls under the jurisdiction of the Ministry of Information and Broadcasting and is relevant to this discussion due to its engagement with Hindustani music.[93] The Films Division was established in 1948 as the primary film-related organization of the Government of India. It has in its possession over 8,000 titles, including news clips, documentaries, short films and animation films.[94] Some of these films are documentaries on the lives of famous Hindustani musicians and on other aspects of this style of music. Over time, these films have been telecast on national and local television channels, and have been screened by many educational institutions and non-government organizations across the country. They are also available commercially.[95]

The Films Division of India had a few musicians on its staff to facilitate recordings of background music for in-house films. Among these, some Hindustani musicians were engaged as music directors and performers. This practice has been discontinued. Very few in-house films are being produced today and the music is recorded elsewhere.[96]

Rajya Sabha TV

Before concluding this chapter, I would be remiss not to include information related to a programme telecast on the Rajya Sabha TV channel. Unlike the media units discussed earlier that fall within the ambit of the Ministry of Information and Broadcasting, this channel is owned and operated by the Rajya Sabha or the Upper House of the Indian Parliament. Its main focus is to provide live coverage of the Rajya Sabha proceedings.[97] But it also includes some discussions and chat shows. Among these and relevant to Hindustani music is a programme called *Shakhsiyat*, which invites performers to talk about their musical journey and demonstrate some of their music. These interviews are later made available by Rajya Sabha TV on its YouTube channel.[98]

2

From Facilitating Culture to Governing It

A part from the role of radio and television networks in the propagation of Hindustani music, the years immediately after Independence were marked by the state's proactive role in establishing many cultural institutions. Ever since, the state has been seen as a facilitator of cultural activities rather than a decision-maker in framing cultural policy. The *Approach Paper on the National Policy of Culture* of 1992 recommended that the state should only play 'a catalytic role in the development and progress of culture'.[1] Ten years later, Jawhar Sircar, secretary, Ministry of Culture, and chairman, Working Group for XII Five Year Plan, drew attention to the importance of culture in all developmental activities and stated that it should not be treated as a marginal sector. He said that the state should not guide culture and should instead make infrastructural facilities available to accelerate cultural activity.[2] But since autonomous cultural institutions formed by the state draw their funds from the ministries in the government, it means that the government is in a position to decide the manner and scope of activities planned and executed by these institutions.

The stated mission of the Ministry of Culture is 'to preserve, promote and disseminate all forms of art and culture'.[3] With this as its mandate, the ministry offers many schemes for sanctioning grants, some of which also relate to Hindustani music. For example, grants have been provided for projects concerning intangible heritage, for supporting repertories or individual young performers, for fellowships to senior and junior scholars, and for music festivals organized by private and public trusts, and other non-government organizations.[4] In its mission statement for National Mission on Cultural Mapping and Roadmap, the ministry records the shortcomings experienced in these schemes, such as the absence of comprehensive cultural mapping data and a systematic database of artistes. The statement mentions that schemes drawn up by the ministry are not linked to a database, because of which there is no rational approach to the sanction of grants.[5] Therefore, government resources, already scarce, are not adequately utilized. While the cultural mapping project envisaged and described in this document is ambitious and may encounter problems which are often seen in bureaucratic set-ups, it would be interesting to see the manner in which the programme evolves and the ways in which stakeholders are brought on board as domain experts, and to provide information and feedback.[6]

It would be appropriate to examine the working of autonomous bodies under the Ministry of Culture, which relate to Hindustani music.

Sangeet Natak Akademi

Created in 1952 by a resolution of the Ministry of Education, the Sangeet Natak Akademi (SNA) became functional the following year and was registered as a society in 1961.[7]

In his opening address at the inauguration of the SNA, Maulana Abul Kalam Azad, the union minister for education, said:

> India's precious heritage of music, drama and dance is one which we must cherish and develop. We must do so not only for our own sake but also as our contribution to the cultural heritage of mankind. Nowhere is it truer than in the field of art that to sustain means to create. Traditions cannot be preserved but can only be created afresh. It will be the aim of this Akademi to preserve our traditions by offering them an institutional form . . . [8]

Azad's statement appears contradictory in its assertion that traditions cannot be 'preserved' per se, but that SNA can accomplish the task by institutionalizing them. The important question is whether traditions should be 'preserved' in the first place, no matter by which entity, as the idea of preservation does not merely suggest sustenance but also implies maintaining status quo, an idea that is obviously opposed to creativity expected of any arts practice.

Be that as it may, SNA prides itself as being 'the apex body of the performing arts in the country, preserving and promoting the vast intangible heritage of India's diverse culture expressed in the forms of music, dance and drama'.[9] As per this declaration of its role as the premier institution for the performing arts in the country, SNA states that it 'renders advice and assistance to the Government of India in the task of formulating and implementing policies and programmes in the field' and that it promotes cultural interaction between different parts of the country, and between India and the rest of the world.[10] Among the objectives listed in its constitution, SNA mentions that it wishes 'to take suitable steps for the maintenance of proper and adequate standards of education in music, dance and drama, and with that object to organize research in the teaching of the said subjects' and 'to foster cultural contacts between the different regions of the country and also with other countries in the fields of music, dance and drama'.[11]

According to this mandate SNA is a facilitator of activities undertaken in the fields of music, dance and drama. It is also supposed to advise the government on matters related to the shaping of cultural policy. For staunch proponents of freedom of speech and expression, the government's role in formulating culture policy would be questionable in the first place. Rather, according to its role believed to have been adopted immediately after Independence and as prescribed in official documents mentioned earlier, it was to be restricted to facilitating institutions like SNA. But SNA, while being an 'autonomous' body, works within the ambit of the Ministry of Culture, and is fully funded by the government for the schemes and programmes it implements. This clearly shows the government's hold over it and the lack of total independence that was possibly imagined when it was founded.

SNA has been granted the primary status in representing all Indian performing arts, a task that is obviously gigantic given the plurality of musical, dance and theatrical forms in our vast country. We can only imagine the conceptual depth that would be required to even attempt this, let alone the wide organizational network necessary for gathering and sifting information related to the performing arts from every nook and corner of the country. Detailed discussions among performers and scholars representing all forms of performing arts would seem necessary. This begs the question whether such a mammoth, continuous and onerous task can be accomplished successfully by a single institution like SNA, and if a larger vision can emerge for the formulation of any institutional policy, if indeed this was expected of SNA in the first place.

SNA has regional branches, a decision that was taken at a fairly early stage. In reply to the recommendation of the estimates committee of the second Lok Sabha in 1958 that state Akademies be set up in order to spread cultural activities throughout the country and that the feasibility of a suitable grants-in-aid for this purpose be examined, the government responded that SNA and the Central government had already communicated with the states, and that it was for the state governments to take necessary action in this regard.[12] The activities of the existing state Akademies and their efficacy would need to be dealt with separately, as this book concentrates on the central Akademi. However, it must be noted that there are some states that still do not have branches of SNA.

The central and state Akademies have numerous committees, which have members from among practitioners and scholars. These are nominated members and do not, therefore, represent the fraternity through an elective process. The criteria for nominating members is not easily accessible and their role in advising SNA regarding matters other than proposing names of potential SNA award winners and Fellows is equally unclear. Can these committees be of a representative nature in the truest democratic tradition through a series of elections, or is this too huge a task, one that is almost unachievable? A report of the High Powered Committee (HPC), set up in 2014 to examine the working of cultural organizations under the Ministry of Culture, had made specific recommendations regarding the representation of states and union territories in central Akademies and the appointment of chairpersons and members of different committees. Sadly, many of the recommendations in the HPC report have yet to be implemented.[13]

The numerous activities of SNA as described on its website include establishing institutions for performing arts, undertaking projects of 'national importance' in the field of performing arts, collaborating with governments and art institutions in the different states and union territories and giving grants-in-aid for research, documentation and publishing to institutions engaged in teaching, performing or promoting music, dance or theatre. SNA also organizes concerts, seminars and conferences.[14]

The publication section of SNA publishes books recommended by the Publication Committee, journals called *Sangeet Natak* and *Sangna* (Hindi) and a biannual magazine called *Rajbhasha*, administers grants-in-aid enabling authors, editors and non-commercial publishers to bring out books and periodicals on performing arts, and processes grants supporting research projects leading to published books. These functions also include the assessment of manuscripts, editing and production of printed material, and sales and management of stocks. In March 2017, SNA had approximately fifty books in print. It also has issues of the journal *Sangeet Natak* dating back to its first issue in 1965. Books and periodicals brought out by other publishers in many Indian languages have also received publication grants from SNA.[15]

SNA undertakes documentation projects and has a large audio-visual archive, believed to be the biggest in the country and a major resource for research scholars. Its reference library has books on performing arts in English, Hindi and some regional languages. It houses a gallery of musical instruments in Rabindra Bhavan, New Delhi.[16] It has also published music from its archives in audio and video formats.[17]

Activities undertaken each year by SNA also include recognizing the contribution of performers and scholars to their disciplines by conferring upon them fellowships and awards.[18]

The brief description provided here shows that SNA has a formidable scope of annual programmes. The annual reports for the past few years have categories which act as templates for all kinds of work undertaken in successive years. The major changes noticeable in these reports are the listings of award winners, grantees, committee members, budgetary allocations and financial reports.[19] Disappointingly, there are no explanatory notes provided to enlighten the reader about the linkages between the overarching vision of SNA and the specific activities that are undertaken annually. In a sense, they would all be within SNA's objective to 'preserve and promote' the performing arts. But more specific information would be required for the projects to be justified. For instance, descriptors like 'Training in Tabla Music' or 'Training in Hindustani Music' used to define the role of grantee institutions are of a general nature and could well be applied to hundreds, if not thousands, of institutions across the country. The number of applicants is provided and so are the numbers of those who were granted aid. But the reasons for granting such aid are missing, thus not giving the reader any clues to the criteria for the selections. More significantly, how are grantees and their projects going to impact the field in a wider context? Deliberations related to these issues have perhaps taken place in committee meetings, but the minutes of these meetings are not publicly accessible, unless probably applications are filed under the RTI Act to the relevant ministry. In an ideal situation, such information, if made easily accessible, could invite comments and suggestions from stakeholders and the general public.

Performances and documentation programmes are held at periodic intervals as is evident from the reports, but reasons for choosing to do one or the other event are not known. Regarding grants made to other institutions for performances, some questions come to mind almost immediately. For example, did an event require specific aid from SNA as it lacked support from elsewhere, or did an event feature repertoire that would otherwise not have been easily accessible elsewhere? How were performers chosen for these events? Were they chosen because of their experience in the field or for the repertoire that they possess, or were they selected due to their previous association with SNA as awardees? The annual reports do not help in answering such questions.

The reports also do not provide any information about the procedure adopted to evaluate the performance of previous grantees and the manner in which their projects have impacted the field. The listings appear to suggest that the role of SNA is to choose potential grantees, provide financial aid and leave it to the grantees to use the amount wisely, however small or large it may be. It is not clear if periodic reports are sought from grantees, but it seems necessary for more to be done in terms of establishing transparency and accountability. It is unfortunate that an institution run on public funds does not make a detailed report easily accessible to explain the logic supporting its decisions while making specific grants. The connection of the original grant proposals to the primary objectives of the institution needs to be clearly established and the proposals need to be made available. This would also be beneficial for potential applicants to understand the scope of the proposals that have been supported by the SNA in the past. Additionally, it would create awareness among potential applicants about ways of articulating their ideas for the SNA grant proposals. This would particularly be useful as the method of writing grant proposals is an area that is often neglected in a system where oral transmission is held paramount.

But if we were to even discount the fact that the inclusion of information related to grants may be beyond the scope of annual reports, this could be uploaded to the official website. In fact, the HPC had recommended the following:

> Lists of all grantees must be placed on the website of the SNA with all relevant details to enable the public to judge the transparency of the process. This will also enable better management of funds.[20]

While describing the treasures in its possession, SNA is candid in its admission that it 'lacked the wherewithal for production and distribution of books on a larger scale, and therefore it has also been isolated from mainstream publishing activity.'[21] It also points out that steps had been taken to improve the production and distribution of books by Ram Niwas Mirdha, chairman of SNA from 2005 to 2010 during the United Progressive Alliance (UPA) government headed by the Indian National Congress.[22]

Among its numerous activities, SNA has set up 'Interpretation Centres' in five schools in Varanasi. This endeavour was a part of a larger project involving the adoption of thirty-two schools by key bodies of the Ministry of Culture following Prime Minister Narendra Modi's speech in Varanasi on 25 December 2014, which stressed the need of acquainting students of schools and colleges with the life and work of eminent personalities of the city, with themes concerning the heritage of Varanasi, and of organizing programmes based on such themes. This was considered an effective mechanism to increase tourist interest in Varanasi and to make students aware of the city's cultural heritage. The project was also envisaged as a means to motivate students 'to aspire for greater heights in their artistic career just like the maestros they have been introduced to through these Interpretation Centres'.[23]

In consonance with the prime minister's idea, SNA held a festival in Varanasi from 25 to 29 December 2014 to highlight the cultural heritage of Varanasi by providing information to schoolchildren about the life and work of eminent personalities of the city in the field of performing. According to the SNA website, of the five schools adopted by the Akademi as Interpretation Centres, three focus on the life and work of eminent personalities from the world of Hindustani music, namely, sitar maestro Ravi Shankar, shehnai virtuoso Bismillah Khan (1916–2006) and tabla exponent Kishan Maharaj (1923–2008). The activities planned for the Interpretation Centres are to include a talent search among students in all forms of performing arts, career counselling, workshops and lecture-demonstrations, screenings of films on eminent performing artistes, visits to historical places, heritage walks and essay competitions focusing on the lives of eminent personalities, with cash prizes for the winners. A scholarship of ₹500 per month has been instituted in the memory of Bismillah Khan for the students who are participating in activities at the centre, and a cultural space or a room was to be created in the school with audio-video equipment and a permanent photo gallery commemorating Bismillah Khan.[24] While this project and the activities envisaged are positive signs in creating artistic awareness among students, we cannot assess the efficacy of these activities in the absence of detailed reports.

In 2014, the HPC clearly stated that SNA needed to review its aims and objectives and it required new vision and mission statements.[25] It said that there was a lack of emphasis on academic and research activities and that funding for such programmes was significantly lower than was the case of performances.[26] A separate study of programmes executed after these recommendations were made would throw light on whether the recommendations of HPC have indeed been implemented in letter and spirit.

Centre for Cultural Resources and Training

The Centre for Cultural Resources and Training (CCRT) was established in 1979 as an autonomous body under the Ministry of Culture to incorporate cultural knowledge in mainstream education. A project initiated by freedom fighter, feminist and expert on India's craft traditions Kamaladevi Chattopadhyay and Kapila Vatsyayan as a commitment to holistic education, CCRT has its headquarters in New Delhi and branches at Udaipur, Hyderabad and Guwahati.[27]

According to its mandate, CCRT has been organizing training programmes for school teachers through workshops, seminars, orientation courses, refresher courses and educational kits. Information about Hindustani music is also shared through these programmes. Under its Cultural Talent Search Scholarship Scheme, CCRT awards scholarships to children in the ten to fourteen age group to study different art forms. Hindustani music features in the list of art forms that can be studied under this scheme. Unlike many art music aficionados and institutions, it is refreshing to note that CCRT does not believe in propagating only Hindustani music in schools. Instead, it includes songs in regional languages which are not necessarily related to this music style, stating that it 'revitalizes the education system by creating an understanding and awareness among teachers, students and educational administrators about the plurality of the regional cultures of India and integrating this knowledge with education.'[28]

CCRT also grants the Young Artiste, Junior and Senior Fellowships, and executes an Arts Management Training Programme and the Cultural Heritage Young Leadership Programme. While the Junior and Senior Fellowships include Hindustani music among other art forms, it is unclear whether the other programmes do the same.[29]

The annual reports of CCRT for the years 2011 to 2016, which provide information about activities undertaken by the organization during this period, include some that are relevant to Hindustani music. They also mention the number of teachers who have participated in CCRT training programmes since its inception, along with a year-wise listing.[30] But there is no assessment data on the CCRT website that may indicate the efficacy of its programmes at the grass-roots level. Thus, it remains to be seen how participants in CCRT programmes have initiated cultural activities, including those concerning Hindustani music, in their respective schools and whether they have successfully integrated cultural knowledge in mainstream education.

Zonal Cultural Centres

In 1985, Rajiv Gandhi, prime minister of India, announced the setting up of seven Zonal Cultural Centres, each zone covering a group of states. The basic objective was to represent cultures specific to each of these zones and to also integrate them into a common composite culture of the nation.[31] The centres were designed to reflect and strengthen the official goal of promoting 'unity in diversity'.

The seven centres set up between 1985 and 1986 by the Ministry of Human Resource Development function presently under the Ministry of Culture. The objective specified that while the cultural diversity of the zones is to be portrayed, the focus has to be on folk and tribal arts, and on preserving and strengthening vanishing art forms.[32] In the past, some zonal centres, as part of the Apna Utsav, a national cultural festival held in Delhi in 1986 by the Government of India, featured Hindustani music.[33] I have also performed in Hindustani music festivals organized by the South Central Zonal Cultural Centre in the late 1980s and mid-1990s. But presently, it appears from information available on the websites of the centres that their programmes do not necessarily include activities related directly to art music systems like Hindustani music, although special programmes have featured genres like kajri and chaiti, which are essentially folk forms but have been incorporated in the Hindustani system.[34]

A three-member committee appointed by the Ministry of Culture in 2010, headed by Mani Shankar Aiyar, member of parliament, Rajya Sabha, to evaluate the functioning of the centres since their inception, observed that the centres were urban-centric and focused on classical arts instead of folk and tribal arts. Identifying, among other things, structural problems and the sidetracking of the main purpose of providing cultural access to all Indians, the committee's report, made public in 2011, favoured the establishment of a separate folk and tribal Akademi on lines similar to the SNA and other institutions.[35] This recommendation implied that an institution like SNA was not in a position to singly represent folk and tribal arts to the fullest, a point that I made earlier in the section on SNA.

Indira Gandhi National Centre for the Arts

An autonomous institution under the Ministry of Culture, the Indira Gandhi National Centre for the Arts (IGNCA) was set up in 1987 as a research and dissemination centre for the arts.[36] It has six divisions, among which Kalanidhi has a reference library which includes books on Hindustani music and a cultural archive that also contains Hindustani music recordings.[37] The Kalamulasastra series, or texts regarded as fundamental to the arts, form a part of the Kala Kosa, or research and publication division of the IGNCA and include texts related to this music.[38]

While the IGNCA can be of great value to scholars, musicians and students working in the field of Hindustani music, there seems to be a lack of awareness about the resources housed here. Outreach programmes that aim at creating awareness among these sections about the resources available would go a long way in making the centre more accessible.

Apart from hosting occasional music performances, lectures and lecture-demonstrations that relate to Hindustani music, IGNCA also organizes a concert series called *Bhinn Shadj*, which includes Hindustani music recitals.[39]

In some cases, activities that are carried out under programmes related to Hindustani music do not reflect the original objectives. For instance, IGNCA's Varanasi Regional Centre established an interpretation centre named after the renowned Banaras gharana exponent Siddheshwari Devi at the Shri Harishchandra Balika Intermediate College. The interpretation centre is part of the larger scheme to set up such centres, as alluded to earlier in the section on SNA. Reports on this centre reveal that apart from a lecture and some performances relevant to this music held during its inaugural function, other activities organized over successive months have been unrelated to why it was set-up in the first place. An event organized by the centre in November 2016 included a mehndi competition, which involved participants decorating their hands with henna and inscribing the words 'matdata jagrukta' (voters' awareness) to create awareness about their rights as voters. Singing competitions were also held in the same month. In December 2016, students participated in solo and group dance competitions and visited a cultural festival held at the Banaras Hindu University. In January 2017, the election awareness campaign continued with students, teaching and non-teaching staff pledging to vote. Routine singing and dancing competitions were also held. February 2017 saw children participate in a cleanliness and tree planting campaign. A cultural programme was held in the same month, which was not associated with the life and work of Siddheshwari Devi. In March 2017, students participated in a cleanliness campaign and attended a discussion held to mark freedom fighter Bhagat Singh's death anniversary. The birth anniversary of B.R. Ambedkar, Dalit leader and chief architect of the Constitution of India, was observed in April 2017.[40] In short, very little was done during this period to acquaint students with the musical legacy of Siddheshwari Devi, which was a significant aspect of Prime Minister Modi's stated purpose behind establishing the interpretation centres.

The National Cultural Audiovisual Archives (NCAA) set up by the culture ministry at IGNCA in 2014 was slated to make 30,000 hours of audio-visual material available in the public domain through its web portal.[41] The NCAA website states:

The project is being implemented by the IGNCA through a Project Management Unit (PMU), under the supervision of a Steering Committee and a National Monitoring Committee.... The PMU coordinates with 26 Partnering Institutions across the country. Selected audiovisual material emanating from these Institutions is envisaged to be digitized by a digitization agency and subsequently submitted to the Project. The PMU, in turn, has created a trusted repository developed by C-DAC Pune, under the National Digital Preservation Programme. The access quality digital files will be made available on the repository for public access and also be given to the Partnering Institutions for in-house access and use. The archival quality files will be stored at IGNCA, New Delhi and IGNCA, Southern Regional Centre, Bengaluru.[42]

The partnering institutions are:

- All India Kashiraj Trust, Varanasi
- Centre for Cultural Resources & Training, New Delhi
- Centre for Indian Classical Dances, Delhi
- Cinema Vision India, Mumbai
- Indian Council for Cultural Relations, New Delhi
- Indira Kala Sangeet Vishwavidyalaya, Khairagarh
- Indira Gandhi National Centre for the Arts, New Delhi
- Indira Gandhi Rashtriya Manav Sangrahalaya, Bhopal
- JD Centre of Art, Bhubaneswar
- Kalakshetra Foundation, Chennai
- Kerala Kalamandalam, Thrissur
- Manav Uttardayitav, Delhi
- Maulana Azad National Urdu University, Hyderabad
- National Archives of India, New Delhi
- National Institute of Design, Ahmedabad
- Natya Shodh Sansthan, Kolkata
- Regional Resources Centre for Folk Performing Arts, Udupi
- Rupayan Sansthan, Jodhpur
- Sahitya Akademi, Delhi
- Samvaad Foundation, Mumbai
- Sangeet Natak Akademi, Delhi
- Sangeet Parishad Kashi, Varanasi
- Saptak Archives, Ahmedabad
- Shri Kashi Sangeet Samaj, Varanasi

- Visva-Bharati University, Santiniketan
- Vyas Sangeet Vidyalaya, Mumbai

This major project includes vital source material pertaining to Hindustani music. Digitized recordings have already been shared on the NCAA website. But some important questions need to be asked with regard to the manner in which this project has been undertaken. Some of these are:

1. The NCAA Project Report for the period 2014–2017 mentions that due diligence has been done with regard to the intellectual property rights (IPRs) for the material.[43] Without reducing the importance of archives in maintaining artistic works, we would imagine that on an ethical and legal level, representation of the artiste fraternity on the committees that have been heading this project would have been done to establish transparency and credibility of the process. Was there such representation on these committees? Were artistes consulted before making their work available for public access? Were written permissions sought from them when these recordings were originally made and was there a clause that allowed the institution to share their work without further permissions?

2. How was the material that needed to be digitized and made open for public access selected? Was all the material digitized, or were specific choices made?

3. What kind of expertise was required for dealing with Hindustani music? Were the people involved in the project qualified experts in the field of music and archiving? In other words, were some qualifications required for this purpose, or was it only experience that counted?

4. Did partnering institutions benefit commercially in any way in the process of sharing the original material that was in their possession? Was there any commercial transaction with artistes for the distribution of their work?

The answers to many of the questions listed in the first point are in the negative, at least in cases pertaining to Hindustani musicians. For the other questions, answers are not readily available, leaving a feeling of distrust in the air. Perhaps representation from stakeholders of the Hindustani system on the committees related to the NCAA project, on the IGNCA Board of Trustees and the Executive Committee could help in ensuring that policy decisions of the institution take cognisance of the needs of the practitioners and their sphere of artistic activity.[44] In June 2018, I wrote to Irfan Zuberi, project manager of the NCAA project, in an attempt to find answers to these and allied questions. I received specific answers only in November 2018, after I exchanged Twitter messages with him.[45] Many of the answers contained information that was already available on the official website. I was informed that there was no commercial transaction with the partnering institutions. Answers to other questions left much to be desired.[46]

National Culture Fund

The National Culture Fund was founded as a trust in 1996 in an attempt to establish a partnership between the government and private institutions and individuals for providing financial support to cultural activities. Donations to the fund are eligible for income tax benefits.[47]

The fund offers grants to projects related to tangible and intangible heritage. Whether it is to document endangered forms of cultural expression or to support new work or even create employment opportunities, all of which are the stated objectives, there is much that can be accomplished in the Hindustani music sphere with help from the fund. But the fund does not seem to have supported any project so far which has a direct link with Hindustani music, as is evident from annual reports that are available on the site for the period 2005 to 2012. No reports for the period after 2012 are available.[48] Significantly, the council of the National Culture Fund has no representation from the world of performing arts, let alone Hindustani music.[49]

High-Powered Committee

The report of the High-Powered Committee (HPC) set up in 2014 questioned the state machinery's ability to address concerns related to creativity, patronage and accountability. It said:

> No culture has survived without patronage. In the past, such support came from royalty and the nobility. In modern society, it must come from the Government of the day. But is the State machinery able to appreciate the nuances of creativity, and to encourage, and harmonise, the many voices of human endeavour? The representatives of Government often believe that theirs is the power and the right to receive obeisance.[50]

The HPC favoured the existence of a ministry to supervise the administration of culture by acting as a coordinator of cultural expression and a catalyst of its dissemination through sponsorship of artistic activities. While it felt that the ministry was capable of accomplishing this role to some extent, it also said that the ministry acted more in the nature of a 'controller rather than a facilitator'.[51]

The HPC also stated that the ministry should guide people towards higher artistic expression and actively distinguish between mediocrity and excellence in such expression, protect tangible and intangible heritage through research and documentation, as well as encourage new creative pursuits.[52] It felt that the Ministry of Culture was incapable of achieving these goals due to a variety of reasons ranging from being ill-equipped to look beyond bureaucratic activities and engage with intellectual and intangible matters to being completely burdened by the weight of the number of institutions and activities under its helm and being inflexible in financial and administrative matters.[53]

The HPC stated in no uncertain terms that the recommendations of similar committees set up in the past had not impacted in any significant manner the working of the bureaucracy and institutions.[54]

We would imagine that the choice to have the state function only as a facilitator would empower stakeholders to take policy decisions. But the absence of any musicians on the experts' panel in the sub-group dedicated to performing arts during the preparation of the Report of the Working Group on Art and Culture for the Twelfth Five-Year Plan (2012–2017) seems to imply that musicians do not seem to be considered as important stakeholders.[55]

The HPC had pointed out several problems related to administrative procedures in the ministry related to the sanctioning process of grants, the delays in releasing funds and that the ministry had too many institutions to look after and there was a lack of cooperation among them.[56] It recommended that the activities of these institutions should be constantly reviewed.[57] The mission statement seems to suggest that matters are much the same as they were when the HPC made its recommendations.

3

Civil Society and Corporate Patronage

Irrespective of government support to Hindustani music or the lack of it, civil society has patronized concerts through subscription-based music clubs and music circles. Generally speaking, the clubs included music education as one of their objectives and often engaged teachers for this purpose. Music circles, on the other hand, focused on performance and organized concerts at regular intervals. Since the last quarter of the nineteenth century and through the twentieth century, the numbers of such organizations gradually increased. Nineteenth-century western India saw the birth of clubs, like the Bombay-based Parsi Gayan Uttejak Mandali, started in 1870 exclusively for promoting music education and performance among Parsis, and the Poona Gayan Samaj founded in 1874 with branches in Bombay, Madras, Baroda, Wadhwan, Bhavnagar and Kolhapur. After that, in colonial Bombay alone, clubs like Arya Gayan Rakshak Mandali, Shripad Sangit Shala, Albert Music Club, Saraswat Gayan Samaj and Trinity Club, and music circles like Bombay Music Circle, Musical Arts

Society, Bhartiya Sangeet Samiti, Gandharva Sangeet Mandal, Agra Gharana Sangeet Samiti and the Sangeet Niketan Suburban Music Circle were established.[1] Calcutta too saw the formation of similar organizations.[2] Independent ticketed concerts were held to draw larger audiences through clubs like the Parsi Gayan Uttejak Mandali and even by individual musicians like Vishnu Digambar Paluskar and Abdul Karim Khan. Paluskar's first ticketed concert was held at Rajkot in 1897 and Abdul Karim Khan's at Poona in 1909.[3]

Early public concerts received mixed responses. They democratized the listening experience to a certain degree as they reached out to largely middle-class audience and to that extent, moved Hindustani music performances out of their isolated and elitist existence in princely courts and aristocratic homes. Not all in the audience may have been equally initiated into the subtleties of the music, but reminiscences of senior patrons indicate that these concerts drew many discerning listeners. Dinker Manjeshwar, a music aficionado since the 1930s, recounted that those desiring to join the Bombay Music Circle were tested for their musical literacy before they could be enrolled as members.[4] Scholar-musician Ashok Ranade has also noted similarly, 'Music circles provided more discriminate audiences. They were useful since they allowed freedom to the artiste to prove his talent.'[5] On many occasions, reputed musicians would also be present in the audience, thus providing an inspiring and challenging concert atmosphere.

With this brief description as a background, I would now like to examine civil society institutions in the present context.

Music Circles

Hindustani music concerts nowadays take place all through the year in small venues which accommodate around 100–300 people. They are organized by music circles established in different cities and towns and run on periodic or life subscriptions. The activities of these music circles are similar to those undertaken by older music clubs and circles, some of which were established in the nineteenth century. But their long-term vision differs to an extent from their forerunners. To quote an example, the Poona Gayan Samaj, established in 1874, included among its chief objectives the setting up of a platform for musical performances in order to provide musicians with financial support and to bring them respectability in the society. At a social level, the samaj sought to bring a closer interaction among its members and entertain them with music performances. The nationalistic sentiment that motivated the founders of the samaj was evident when they stressed the indigenous identity of the music they were propagating and the need to continue its existing character.[6] The Samaj was operating at a time when music was performed primarily by hereditary musicians.

But the demographics of the performers have changed vastly over the past few decades, with a significant number of first-generation musicians having taken to the concert stage. Given this change, it is not surprising that music circles today have a different vision. This is evident in the case of the Suburban Music Circle, founded in 1937, and the oldest music circle operational in Mumbai at present. The circle lists the following aims and objectives:

- To cultivate a taste for an appreciation of [sic] the scientific system of Indian Music by holding concerts, lectures and demonstrations.
- To conduct other activities imparting knowledge of Indian music and help in its propagation.
- To conduct programmes that serve as a platform for young talent and youth pursuing Indian Classical Music.[7]

Broadly, the Suburban Music Circle shares the sense of music history that the nineteenth century music clubs had when it considers Hindustani music to be 'an ancient art form developed and perfected over centuries' and a scientific system.[8] It believes in the 'promotion and preservation' of this music, as it is 'now losing the interest of newer generations to the more publicised commercial tunes.'[9] The intention to feature young performers on its platform reflects the circle's concern for the present generation of musicians, but the mention of young people veering towards 'commercial tunes', perhaps referring to popular music, seems to be a hurried generalization about musical preferences among the youth and indicates the musical inclinations of the office-bearers.

Unlike the stated objectives of the Poona Gayan Samaj, present-day music circles do not view the improvement of the musician's social and financial status as one of their objectives. Probably this is not seen as a real problem any more, but we cannot escape from the truth that the financial aspect is as important to performers as is the opportunity to perform. The honorarium to musicians has increased over the years. In the 1960s, Vamanrao H. Deshpande stated, 'The fees of these artists before the War were roughly Rs 75/- to Rs 100/-. They have now increased almost twenty times more. Fees in the range of Rs 500/- to 5000/- have become very common.'[10] These amounts would seem unbelievably low today and yet the harsh reality is that honoraria handed out by most music circles today are not significantly larger if we factor in the rate of inflation over the years. In a sense, by performing for such honoraria, musicians are equally serving the cause of promoting Hindustani music as are the music circles, although this fact is never recognized by the latter and other stakeholders in the field.

But there are some musicians who strongly believe that remuneration never was and should never be a consideration for performers. In the words of renowned Kirana gharana vocalist Gangubai Hangal(1913–2009):

The financial factor was not so crucial in my times.... This reaction is strikingly different from that of a contemporary artist who, once he has reached the heights of fame, can strike and bargain at whatever rates he fancies for. This asking price moreover, does not depend upon his real worth as an artist. I have seen organisers who evaluate artists at mere face value. In Calcutta, especially, the asking rate of the artist often determines his value. . . . Such evaluation is really beyond my understanding.[11]

Hangal's assertion highlights that fees demanded or commanded by performers often do not represent their artistic ability. But we cannot dismiss the reality that musicians are also affected by the rising costs of living like other sections of society.

At the same time, it must be acknowledged that music circles also encounter challenges. Old music circles are gradually losing ground due to lack of financial resources, and sustenance for the new ones established in distant suburban areas of big cities and towns has been a major concern. The experience of the Suburban Music Circle may be indicative of the present circumstances. In its annual report of 2016–2017, the circle stated that it had a total of 1036 members, of which seventy-nine were founder-members, 119 were patron members and 838 were life members.[12] The total investments or assets of the circle amounted to ₹30,50,000 as on 31 March 2017, but the decrease in bank interest rate and the rising costs of organizing a concert were highlighted in its report as obstacles in hosting concerts. Members were therefore urged to donate generously to meet the growing expenses.[13] Concert expenses for the financial year ending 31 March 2017 amounted to ₹7,88,263 of which ₹4,52,000 went towards honoraria to performers. The donations for concerts amounted to ₹5,58,620 during this period. To some people, these figures may seem huge, but considering the amounts that are involved in large music festivals, the budget for the Suburban Music Circle seems quite modest. Yet, the circle faces hurdles, as would be the case with most other circles running primarily on subscriptions.[14]

This may appear odd since subscription-based concerts have had a long history dating back to the nineteenth century. Information about the subscription charged by music clubs and circles in the late nineteenth and early twentieth centuries comes as a revelation. The Parsi Gayan Uttejak Mandali mentioned earlier, charged a monthly membership fee of Rs 3 in its first year, a handsome amount as compared to the subscription charged by the Bombay Music Circle in the 1930s.[15] The fee for life membership of the circle was a Rs 100, ordinary members had to pay a quarterly fee of Rs 3 and guests were charged a fee of Rs 1.50 per month. Of course, the mandali was also a teaching institution and hence the higher fees were perhaps taking care of the salaries to the teachers on its staff.[16]

But the situation today is vastly different, as expenses required to arrange such concerts have risen exponentially. Music circles are seldom supported by other agencies and have limited resources for conventional publicity campaigns to promote their concerts. Even if such support is available, it is at a miniscule level and not enough to sustain the circle through the year. The uncertainty of audience turnout also renders ticketed entry as an unreliable source of revenue.

To that extent, performers' fees could pose a problem. We would think that the experience of Mumbai's premier music circle, Dadar Matunga Cultural Centre, would be different, but it is not so. Originally set up as the Dadar Matunga Social Club in 1953, the centre is probably one of its kind in the metropolis with a membership of over 1100 and a building complex that includes an air-conditioned auditorium, which is also rented out for weddings and other functions. In most other cases, music circles do not have a building or auditorium and, very often, even have to hire an amplification system, unlike the centre, which has its own infrastructure addressing these requirements. But even in the case of an institution like the centre that seems to be financially stronger than other music circles, performers' honoraria pose a problem. Sharad Sathe, Gwalior gharana vocalist and the president of the centre in

2010, said that negotiating honoraria with younger performers did not pose a problem to the centre.[17] This indicates that the growing number of performers and their desire to procure performance opportunities pushes them into a corner. The high fees charged by celebrated artistes generally kept them out of the ambit of music circles. As Sathe stated, these musicians or 'superstars' as he called them, were less cooperative and their terms and fees running into lakhs of rupees could only be afforded by corporate bodies.[18]

But it must be noted that some better-known artistes have on occasion agreed to perform for music circles for remuneration lower than their normal fees, either to support the circles or because they are inspired to perform for the initiated audiences present in music circle concerts. Some well-known musicians may even be willing to perform for music circles despite the limited remuneration, but they decline their invitations due to the lack of basic amenities, like adequate green rooms and good amplification systems. Music circles claim that they have these facilities, but a closer look at the situation reveals otherwise. To give an example, the people operating the amplification equipment are often far from trained. Very few trained audio engineers are engaged for Hindustani music concerts, irrespective of the scale of the event. There are some exceptions in cases where performers specifically ask for one or the other audio engineer. Surprisingly, this is not seen as an inadequacy by concert organizers, or even by performers. It appears that the quality of sound is the last thing on everyone's minds when it comes to a performance, whereas this should in fact be an integral part of the concert experience.

In spite of the long history of music circles and their contribution to music, the transactions between them and the performers have not been sufficiently systematized in the form of contracts or agreements, which are the norm in almost every other professional field. The mere mention of contracts or agreements encounters a scornful response from office-bearers of many music circles. Instead of a means to establish transparency between the parties, music circles regard a contract as a hindrance or a symbol of commercialism of the performers. Commercialism is, of course, seen as a corrupting influence in the 'spiritual' world of music-making. Talks of contracts also meet with an uncomfortable silence from performers, because most of them regard this as an obstacle to getting concert opportunities. Though correspondence mentioning basic terms of engagement is exchanged, usually permissions for audio and video recording of the concerts or webcasting them are not taken by the organizers.

Efforts have been made in Mumbai to discuss ways in which the performance situation for Hindustani and Carnatic music can be improved. This has been attempted under the banner of Music Forum, a collective of office bearers from music circles, a few performers and representatives from Akashvani, DD and other bodies which have been involved in distributing music. A brainchild of businessman and senior sitar player Arvind Parikh, the Music Forum has largely been a space for discussion due to its voluntary and informal structure.[19] Similar attempts do not seem to have been made over a long span of time in other cities, although offshoots of the Music Forum have been active at certain times in cities like Delhi and Chennai and even in suburban Mumbai. But in matters such as developing and accepting model contract templates, there has been little or no progress. I was also involved in drawing up such templates, but they did not receive the desired response. Hence, they were made available on the internet as freely downloadable documents.[20]

Music Festivals

Apart from the music club and music circle circuit, Hindustani music has also been featured in large music festivals or music conferences. There are references to one such music conference held way back in the 1890s by Shamsher Jang Bahadur, the

Maharaja of Nepal.[21] The Harivallabh Sangeet Sammelan, originally a religious congregation started in 1875, went on to become one of the leading public platforms for Hindustani music performance after 1908 and continues to hold annual music festivals to this day.[22]

These conferences seem to have only featured concerts, unlike the ones held by Vishnu Narayan Bhatkhande and Vishnu Digambar Paluskar, which included discussions on the theory and practice of music, along with performances. Bhatkhande organized all-India music conferences in Baroda, Delhi, Varanasi and Lucknow between the years 1916 and 1925, with financial support from princely patrons and other affluent individuals.[23] Paluskar organized five conferences or Sangeet Parishads between 1918 and 1922, and provincial music conferences in 1928 and 1929, all of which were held in Bombay under the auspices of the Gandharva Mahavidyalaya, a music school he founded at Lahore on 5 May 1901. A branch of the music school was established in Bombay in 1908.[24] The nationalistic and pan-Indian outlook reflected in the deliberations suggests that the conferences organized by Bhatkhande and Paluskar were inspired by contemporary political conferences which were a part of the struggle for Independence.

The number of music conferences increased subsequently, but theoretical discussions did not necessarily feature in later conferences. In Bengal, Bhupendra Ghosh, a zamindar, and Damodardas alias Lalababu Khanna, started the All Bengal Music Conference in Calcutta in 1925.[25] Mumbai continued to have more conferences and, after 1933, music conferences were also held on an annual basis at Allahabad, Lucknow and Kanpur.[26]

As conferences and festivals grew in size, they attracted a wider audience with varying degrees of musical discernment. This was true of audiences even in the first quarter of the twentieth century. Bhatkhande commented then that the modern age was fast-paced and listeners did not have time to enjoy night-long concerts.

These listeners continuously had their eyes on the time and their wristwatches, often also discussing matters relating to finance while the music was in progress.[27]

In the succeeding decades, there were other commentators like Vamanrao Deshpande and S.K. Chaubey, who believed that this change in the concert situation was detrimental to Hindustani music. Deshpande lamented that the financial status of middle-class listeners, regarded as connoisseurs, had worsened in the post-World War II period. They were unable to purchase even cheap tickets, with the result that the music was adapted to meet 'eccentric, wayward and unaesthetic demands of the newly rich.'[28] Chaubey was particularly disparaging about music conferences held in the 1940s. The following passage is reproduced here in its entirety as it best reflects his sentiments:

An All Indian music conference, today, is neither representative in character nor symbolic of the spirit of classical music. It is neither music nor conference. It is a pompous show organized by some influential organizers who have either power or money at their command. Long-winded patrons and secretaries inaugurate it with long and boring speeches which are exercises in mutual admiration and in which the virtues of our ancient music are described in metaphor, hyperbole and poetic exaggeration. With the veneer of middle class culture is mixed a sufficient quantity of red-tapism and snobbery. In the royal front seats meant for the aristocracy of good taste and good judgement, sit those who either yawn intermittently or gossip quite garrulously in their more lucid intervals. To them music is a luxury, which they think is quite conventional to enjoy once a year. The rest of the audience consists of many mediocre lovers of music whose applause is more worthy than their judgement. The programme is composed of first-rate classical music, third-rate classical music, popular music, unpopular music, no music, classical dances, sacred dances, profane dances, ultra-modern dances, and other items – all printed on fine paper. The listeners constitute a mob, which enjoys adult franchise in the new democracy of music. Every musician has to cater to it.[29]

While the term 'conferences' has gone out of fashion in the past few decades, music festivals spread over two or more days continue to be held in many parts of the country. Most festivals are held during the winter months from November to February. Some of the more popular ones are the Dover Lane Festival in Kolkata, the Indian Music Group Festival at St Xavier's College in Mumbai and the Shriram Shankarlal Music Festival in Delhi.[30] There are others that focus on raags conventionally prescribed for the monsoon, and are therefore held during the monsoon months, between June and September. Similarly, a few music festivals are held to celebrate Basant, or the spring season, and feature seasonal raags prescribed for this period. Some festivals commemorate the memory of one or more maestros from the past. These include the famous Sawai Gandharva Bhimsen Music Festival in Pune, commemorating Kirana exponent Rambhau Kundgolkar alias Sawai Gandharva (1886–1952) and his iconic disciple Bhimsen Joshi (1922–2011), Vishnu Digambar Paluskar Festival held in Delhi in the memory of Vishnu Digambar Paluskar, and Abbaji—A Homage to Ustad Allarakha (1919–2000), a festival held in Mumbai as a tribute to the renowned tabla maestro.[31] Many state governments have also organized festivals which include Hindustani music. Some of these festivals have segments featuring music from other parts of the world or Carnatic music, in addition to the regular programmes of Hindustani music.

Audiences in these festivals have grown over time and in some cases have reached astonishing figures of 15,000 to 20,000 listeners. Obviously, they include increasing numbers of uninitiated listeners, leading to criticism from some quarters. Ashok Da. Ranade stated,

Many public concerts today provide indiscriminate audiences. The artist has therefore to decide on the 'menu' and hence the dependence on successful music. Music which had succeeded on earlier occasions, or music which has been recorded and proved successful – will be repeated! This is expected to ensure them against failure! A real problem for 'creative music'! Experimentation is avoided by the artist because of this fear.[32]

Ranade regarded the public concert as a 'commodity exchange' rather than patronage to the art:

This is a different type of audience. The audiences were aware they have paid for their entertainment and naturally failure in that concert meant right of resentment of the audience. This is a commodity exchange and not an act of patronage. This type of 'patronage' affected performances. The audience oriented the music, artists started moulding the form of music, the ragas which they presented and the time frames of presentation. This was music for the 'indiscriminate' audiences.[33]

Those concerned about the present scenario believe that performers have to be more responsible in guiding audience tastes. Music critic Mohan Nadkarni (1922–2014) summed it up as follows:

We live in a [sic] era of mass culture values where the greatness of a performing artist is evaluated not in terms of the quality of his contribution to the art but his box office taking or, rather, his ability to please the teeming crowds. Crowds, indeed, they are not audiences of the years gone by. At a time when the laws of demand and supply have undergone a frightful change, it is perhaps inevitable that performing artistes big or small, seek an easy way of survival and choose to be completely oblivious of their responsibility to their inheritance or to their new class of patrons.[34]

Vocalist Gangubai Hangal pointed to another reason for present-day musicians not having a good rapport with audiences. Blaming the modern concert proscenium for this state of affairs, she said:

> The music conferences (sangeet sammelan) of olden days were also quite different. Performances at the music conferences were a hallmark of all that was novel and significant in the field of music. The modern conferences have become impersonal and artists appear to be quite indifferent to audience-response as well as to their own performance. The same impersonality and lack of rapport with audience is also evident in the present day concerts. The singer who sits on a stage has little or no connection with the large crowds packed inside a dark auditorium.[35]

But there are others who believe that since people flock to concerts, it proves that music is flourishing across the country. According to santoor maestro Shivkumar Sharma:

> Indian classical music is happening all over the country. Big music festivals and monthly concerts are happening, most significantly in schools, colleges and other institutions.[36]

Regarding the demographics of the audience, Sharma states:

> There is a change. Fifty years ago, there was a lesser number of listeners of classical music and a majority of them were in their 40s or above. Today there is a much, much bigger audience, although not as knowledgeable as in the past. But there is a large number of young listeners being added.[37]

While acknowledging that contemporary listeners may not be as informed as in the past, Sharma celebrates the fact that audience turnout is significantly larger today than ever before and that the number of young listeners is increasing. Arguably, this is an anecdotal reference and one that may be applicable only to concerts featuring specific performers, but it is a viewpoint that cannot be ignored completely.

Corporate Patronage

The merits and demerits of large audiences aside, it is clear that music festivals have become popular. The magnitude of these festivals requires huge finances, the major part coming from corporate patrons. This phenomenon is not entirely new. An earlier version of such patronage existed in the nineteenth century when members of the commercial and industrial elite hosted private concerts at their homes. Audiences were restricted to family members, friends and business associates.[38]

In the twentieth century, sponsorships from business houses to large festivals of music became a reality. While these sponsorships may have been provided due to the personal relations between the concert organizers or their representatives with the business houses, the corporate's support was not charity or philanthropy which was merely acknowledged by mentioning the names of the benefactors. Instead, they marketed their products through advertisements published in souvenirs expressly printed for the festivals. Some patrons chose to provide monetary help without any advertisements, but these were exceptions.

After the 1970s, corporate sponsorship became an integral a part of large festivals, often with single sponsors like Aditya Birla Group, Britannia Industries Limited or Citibank backing entire festivals.[39] The ITC Sangeet Sammelans sponsored by the Indian Tobacco Company (ITC) since 1971 made a great impact, but a few other cigarette and liquor companies began sponsoring Hindustani music concerts, probably to resort to surrogate advertising after they faced legal restrictions on advertising their brands in newspapers, magazines and television.[40] In 1995, a music festival sponsored by Kalyani Black Label, a liquor company, was held at Siri Fort, New Delhi. The music from this festival is still available as concert recordings, which were published for commercial circulation.[41] The involvement of the ITC in the propagation of Hindustani music has been longer and has had a more enduring effect through the Sangeet Research Academy (ITC-SRA), a teaching institution that it founded. The activities of the ITC-SRA will be discussed in greater detail later in the chapter on music education.

The complexion of corporate patronage of live concerts has changed today. This is probably because there are very few sponsors willing to take care of all the expenses on their own. The expenses for concerts include fees to the artistes and to management agencies; costs for hiring the venue, sound and lighting equipment; fees for procuring licences and permissions from numerous authorities; payment for publicity in the print and electronic media and on ground; travel and hospitality; and so on. Given the extent of such expenses, there are very few events which have single sponsors. Instead, multiple sponsors are brought on board and hotels, airlines, radio and television channels and similar agencies are all sourced as partners. Many of them may give little or no money directly, but provide their services like hotel rooms or travel arrangements without charge. In return, their names and logos appear on all publicity material as acknowledgement. There is only a notional monetary exchange, as the arrangement is a form of a barter between the organizers and the partners.

Multiple sponsors and partners bring multiple demands, especially for the best branding opportunities in the publicity material during the event and in any audio-video broadcast of the event, live or recorded. Marketing teams of the sponsors make tough demands for their banners and hoardings on the backdrop, on the wings on either side of the stage, in the foyer, at the ticket window and at other such strategic places. Far from being subtle, corporate branding is in-your-face at these concerts.

Sponsors and partners may also demand free passes to the event for their clients, associates or staff. But many a time these seats, located at premium positions, remain empty. This is disconcerting for everyone, most of all for the performers and those connoisseurs who cannot afford highly priced tickets.

Apart from sponsoring individual concerts or festivals of music, corporate patrons often sponsor music concerts for in-house corporate events for select audience of 50–100, consisting of senior managers, employees, associates, clients or prospective clients. Generally, such events are held in a five-star hotel. In a sense, the corporate event is a larger version of the concerts held by patrons at their homes several decades ago. The significant difference, apart from the change in venue, is that the earlier concerts saw a personal rapport between the patrons and musicians. The corporate event, on the other hand, is an impersonal and professional arrangement, which is bound by constraints of time and space. The performance cannot be very lengthy and has to often provide enough musical variety to entertain the largely uninitiated listeners. Often, Hindustani musicians are invited to perform, but are asked to present 'fusion' music, which is considered to be an energetic, foot-tapping and attractive alternative to the slow and traditional renditions. There are also several corporate events, which include music as entertainment followed by cocktails and dinner. In such cases, the audience is often seated around dinner tables. Though service at the tables may begin only after the concert finishes, many musicians find this environment not conducive for performances. But fees higher than what they would usually be paid for conventional concerts prompts them to compromise.

Large companies conduct many philanthropic activities, some of which benefit Hindustani music in a sporadic manner. Schedule VII of the Companies Act, 2013, mandates that companies with specified or higher turnover have to spend a portion of their net profits on Corporate Social Responsibility (CSR) activities. Clause

(v) of Schedule VII expressly lists 'protection of national heritage, art and culture including restoration of buildings and sites of historical importance and works of art; setting up public libraries; promotion and development of traditional art and handicrafts' as some of the CSR activities. We may expect this would motivate at least some companies to set aside funds for promotion of Hindustani music.[42] It would be in keeping with the objectives of CSR to support music circles which have continued their work without any major financial backing. A separate study would have to be undertaken to determine the number of companies supporting Hindustani music under the CSR provisions. This kind of support may be quite distinct from the marketing and branding exercises which come with corporate sponsorship.

While corporate patronage has been given to single concerts or to music festivals that are held periodically, it is seldom that such funding is provided for developing infrastructure which is sorely needed for Hindustani music concerts. Unlike the developed countries, patrons in India have seldom funded the planning and construction of good performance venues solely devoted to this music or to music per se.[43] Erecting an air-conditioned auditorium to seat a fixed number of people is clearly not enough. The acoustic treatment of the performance space, the placement of the public address console board, stage monitors, speakers and related equipment, the lighting arrangement, and facilities in the green rooms and the extended backstage area, are of paramount importance for the success of a concert. A singular example of the presence of such funding in Mumbai would be the venues which form part of the National Centre for the Performing Arts (NCPA), supported by the Tata group well before CSR became popular.[44] It must be added that acoustic arrangements in concert halls need to factor in performances of diverse forms of music. Unfortunately, this aspect is lacking in most venues across the country, with the result that performers of Hindustani music are often frustrated with the acoustics in big and small venues. This adds to the noise created by high decibel levels of the amplification system, leaving audiences unsatisfied and at times angry as well. Mention must be made of the support given to Hindustani music by Brooke Bond Taj Mahal Tea House through its Taj Mahal Tea House Sessions. But this is once again not a special venue constructed for the purpose of hosting such concerts.[45]

Corporate patronage to Hindustani music has and will always be an uncertain area, as it depends largely on the company's financial status and its ability and willingness to extend funds as sponsorship or as CSR activity. Corporate sponsorship also exists in the area of mechanical reproduction of music. This has been in the nature of a business enterprise with an eye on revenues and profits, rather than philanthropy as its chief motive. Indian businesses have been investing in the recording industry since the early twentieth century and to a greater extent in the post-Independence era.[46]

In the 1990s, corporate houses that had business interests far removed from the music world started record labels to take advantage of the purchasing power of the new middle class. Though Hindustani music was not as popular and commercially fruitful as film music, new labels also decided to have a catalogue dedicated to this category, perhaps due to its long shelf life.

The competitiveness between new record labels was reflected in the race for novelty and branding of musical products, and this impacted the manner in which the music was recorded and marketed during this period. Music Today, a label established by the India Today group, was a major player in the recording industry. The label published its raag series which contained collections of raags prescribed for each part of the twenty-four-hour diurnal-nocturnal cycle. This was in keeping with the Hindustani musical tradition which required raags to be played at specific times of the day. The collections were titled morning raags, afternoon raags, evening raags and night raags. The company also released the Maestro's Choice series and a separate series focusing on other musical genres from the Hindustani system like tarana, thumri-dadra, chaiti, kajri and holi. Well-known musicians from the Hindustani stream composed for a series featuring specially created thematic music to evoke elements from nature like mountains and rivers.[47]

Times Music, set up by Bennett Coleman and Co. Ltd, also began different series, including a separate collection of music therapy albums featuring Hindustani music.[48] There were several other labels which emerged and each of them included Hindustani music in their catalogue.

The new record labels came as a blessing to musicians who were featured in the recordings made during the 1990s, as they generated wider listenership for their music. It would not be an exaggeration to say that these recordings have moulded the musical sensibilities of many listeners who are now in their forties and fifties. The income that these recordings brought to the musicians was in the nature of a one-time lump sum payment, which was often more than what they could have hoped to get through a royalty arrangement with the publishers.

The growth in the recording industry also created new job opportunities. Record labels engaged young people as members of their Artistes and Repertoire (A&R) team, which chose the musicians they wished to record, discussed with them matters concerning repertoire that was to be recorded and finalized professional terms. Record labels had A&R representatives for Hindustani music recordings too. Some of them did not have the in-depth musical knowledge required to discuss with musicians the creative content to be recorded and published. But record labels also hired some who were more knowledgeable or were practicing musicians to oversee these recordings.[49]

Breaking away from the conventional record label model of working in a studio situation, Music Today ventured into organizing an annual live music festival in Delhi called Swar Utsav in the year 2000. The music was recorded and edited versions were commercially published, thus presenting a series of live concert recordings, which had a distinct flavour to them as compared to the music recorded in a controlled studio environment. A separate team from the record label usually handled these live events.[50]

Over the years, there has been a transition from earlier analogue audio formats like vinyl discs and cassettes to digital formats like compact discs and computer files that can be shared, but video publications of Hindustani music tradition have taken a back seat. Not many DVDs featuring this music tradition have been published and those available are often of indifferent quality. Due to this, Hindustani music has not been able to satisfy the expectations of almost two generations of listeners, who have otherwise grown accustomed to multi-sensory stimuli through audio and video formats. Clearly, the involvement of corporates in the recording industry has not helped in this context.

Private Channels since the 1990s

The 1990s saw the rise of private players in Indian broadcasting. Beginning in 1991 with the Satellite Television Asian Region (Star) TV network based in Hong Kong, the number of private cable and television channels grew and their reach across India increased exponentially.[51] We would assume that Hindustani music programmes would be included on these channels, but there have been only rare cases of this. The bulk of Hindustani music broadcasts and telecasts continue, howsoever erratic they may be, on public media channels.

The Star TV channel stands out in its decision to feature a series on Hindustani music called *Ninaad* in the 1990s, scheduled for an early morning slot of forty-five minutes. The first season of this series had thirty episodes, followed by another thirty in a second season.[52] Even though the series was not telecast at prime time, it was popular with music lovers. A thirteen-part biopic series focusing on the lives of celebrated musicians from the world of Indian art music titled *Sadhana* was also telecast on the same channel in the 1990s. This was telecast at prime time.[53]

The Music Asia channel, a part of the Zee network, recorded two hundred episodes focusing on art music, most of which were telecast. Similarly, other private channels like Sahara TV and Home TV also had special programmes related to art music.[54] Telecasts of Hindustani music on private channels were discontinued in the new millennium, probably due to the lack of revenues from such programmes. Since 2013, a subscription-based private channel called Insync telecasts diverse forms of music including Hindustani music.[55] Musicians featured in programmes telecast on these private channels have benefitted from the wide exposure they received, but their honoraria was minimal or, as in some cases, very poor. Art Talk, a chat show hosted on News X is one of the rare programmes that features performers of Hindustani music.[56]

With regard to radio, Hindustani music does not find a place on private FM channels, as they have focused primarily on film and non-film popular music. A rare exception in this context was Worldspace, a satellite radio network providing services to several parts of the world.[57] Working on a subscription model, Worldspace had several Indian subscribers, which included many avid art music listeners. Beginning in the year 2000, Worldspace gradually increased its daily programmes of art music from two hours to four and then to eight hours. Eventually, a twenty-four-hour station called Radio Gandharv was dedicated to Hindustani music. This being a subscription-based model, music lovers had to pay a fee to subscribe to this station. Unluckily, Worldspace stopped operations in India in 2009. But during the time that it existed, listeners from Pakistan could also access music from India.[58] Here too, musicians gained wide exposure, but information related to the fees or royalties they received for the broadcast of music that was published by them or was owned by them and not by record labels, is difficult to come by.

Event Management

Live concerts with major corporate backing in the 1990s began a new phenomenon in Hindustani music. Large concerts, festivals or corporate events began to be managed by event management companies or individual event managers, who undertook to execute complete logistics for such events.

The event management industry has grown with the passage of time. Today, event managers represent their clients, whether corporate, government or non-government entities, when they liaise with performers to engage them for concerts. They discuss and finalize professional terms with the performers and identify a theme for the concert, if this is desired by the clients. On the production side, they liaise with venues and vendors for sound and light equipment, and also supervise publicity of the event.

The involvement of event managers reduces the pressure on the organizers and helps in smooth arrangements even for large events. In some cases, they even assure clients about their ability to market the event and bring on board sponsors and partners. Payment to the event manager is calculated as a percentage of the total cost of the event. Consequently, to serve their individual goals, the event manager and organizers try to maximize and minimize costs, respectively. In such a situation, performers seldom receive the fees they would like.

Event managers have become a powerful entity, as their presence on the performance scene and their close proximity to sponsors can impact the careers of the musicians they choose to promote.

Some event managers style themselves as curators and conceptualizers of events. They structure and market specific themes, and approach potential sponsors and partners to find support for these themes. Event managers and listeners often believe that the idea of producing thematic programmes is new. But cases from the past indicate that thematic presentations took place long before event managers came into existence. For example, the Agra Gharana Sangeet Samiti educated listeners in Mumbai about the subtleties of several raags through explanations and demonstrations presented by scholar-musicians like Agra gharana maestro Vilayat Hussain Khan in special programmes organized especially for this purpose way back in the 1940s.[59]

The industry has become large enough for event management courses to have been introduced in many private colleges and universities across India.[60] These courses do not seem to address the specific needs of music events, particularly those that are outside the realm of popular music. As a result, we do not find many domain experts in the management of music programmes; an event manager or an event the management company could be managing music events as well as seminars, weddings and private parties. There is often a mismatch between the professionalism supposed to be shown by the event manager and the actual production and execution of a music event.

This lack of professionalism is also seen in the contracts between the event manager and the performers. Instead of having separate written contracts with each performer, the event manager often deals only with the main performer. This is done ostensibly because the main performer usually deals with the accompanying musicians directly. This may be true in most cases, but it seems to be the chosen method even when the event manager engages the accompanying musicians. The fact that AIR and DD have invited accompanying musicians directly and not through the main performer, has already established that such negotiations can be conducted by event managers or by other organizers for that matter.

I must also mention that I have been witness to situations where some musicians have also displayed a distinct lack of professionalism even when contractual arrangements were in place. Such musicians feigned ignorance of the terms of contract at the very last minute, and made unreasonable demands on the event managers and organizers.

Artiste Management

The strengthening of corporate links with Hindustani music has also created a professional opportunity in the form of artiste management. This is a relatively recent phenomenon and is more prevalent in the field of rock, pop and film music. Individual managers or representatives of artiste management companies manage rock bands or single performers who have signed up with them.[61] Artiste management in such cases is based on the Western model, which works on the following premises:

1. The artiste is a brand/product/business who seeks to fulfil the needs and wants of a market.
2. This product can work in musical and non-musical situations.
3. The product's work in these musical and non-musical situations has commercial value.

According to Donald S. Passman, author of the superbly crafted and informative book *All You Need to Know About the Music Business*, an artiste should put together a team of experts in order to achieve success in the market. The team should include a personal or artiste manager, a lawyer, a business manager, an agency and groupies.[62]

Passman lists the duties of an artiste manager as follows:

1. Guide major career decisions, such as publishing deals, choice of record labels, etc.
2. Aid the creative process by suggesting band members, producer, photographers, etc.

3. Promote career by coordinating publicity campaign, talking about artist to relevant people.
4. Put together the team mentioned earlier.
5. Coordinate concert tours and liaise with the members of the crew.
6. Ensure the record label promises the best deal and take it to its logical conclusion on the ground through publicity, distribution, etc.
7. Act as a buffer between the artist and others in the business.[63]

Thus, the development of the artiste as a brand or product, locating situations for putting this product in the market (live concerts, recording, film-related work, appearances, etc.), negotiating and determining commercial value, and seeing that this value is collected is what constitutes the artiste manager's job profile.

The manager works on an individual basis or is an employee of a management company. He or she manages the artiste for a fixed period of time, which may be renewed depending upon mutual satisfaction. The period may be determined by the album cycles. The manager is paid a percentage (15–20 per cent, but may be lower) of the net or gross income, that is, after reducing expenses or without doing so, depending upon the contract between the artiste and the manager.

There are several ways of defining the payment terms. The manager or management company may continue to receive the percentage of the earnings from work that occurred during the contractual period, but whose income may have continued after this period, like royalties. According to Passman, artistes must ensure that the manager does not receive double commission in cases where the manager has set up a company for tax purposes or otherwise. In other words, the manager should not draw commission from the company to which the earnings are paid as well as from the artiste who shows himself or herself as an employee of the company.[64]

In the light of Passman's description of an artiste manager's role, it would be interesting to examine whether such conditions exist in the Indian situation. For one, it appears that the Western model treats all kinds of musicians in the same manner. An Indian artiste manager cannot ignore the country's diverse musical landscape with its parallel streams of music-making. Notwithstanding the need for professionalism, discipline and systematization in the overall functioning of each of these streams, it is important to address each artiste's specific needs. There is no escaping the commercial nature of music performance today and it is, therefore, necessary to handle artiste management on a more professional basis. But the specificities of the Hindustani music landscape need to be taken cognizance of, without ignoring aspects of the Western model, which can be modified to the Indian situation.

In Hindustani music, performers in the past were often 'managed' by one of their family members or a close associate. There was no formal contract between the performers and those who managed their professional careers. At times, this informal arrangement would lead to bitterness between the individuals, or between the performers and concert organizers and record labels, when those representing the performers would insist on conditions that the organizers and record labels would look upon as arm-twisting tactics. This would result in mutual distrust.

This ad hoc arrangement between performers and managers seems to continue to this day, often giving rise to misunderstandings and ill-feeling among the parties concerned. Despite that, organizers, record labels and even many musicians, view the concept of artiste management with suspicion and treat performers having artiste managers as ones who have sold out to crass commercialism. But, in the interest of avoiding any misunderstandings, it is necessary to professionalize the arrangements.

4

Personalized and Institutionalized Education

Until the second half of the nineteenth century, Hindustani music was primarily taught in families of hereditary musicians and courtesans. There were exceptions when some patrons learnt the art, but they did not pursue it professionally. The guru–shishya parampara, or the master-disciple tradition, that focused on oral transmission of knowledge through successive generations was the chosen form of imparting music education at that time. Texts, if at all used, were maintained and employed only as supplementary reference material. In most cases, teaching was a male bastion and the shishya, whether male or female, had to be subservient to the guru in order to be able to imbibe knowledge. Thus, the guru played a key role, as it was he who handed down musical knowledge to the shishya and added his wisdom to it.

Most shishyas did not pay any tuition fee to the guru and would often stay with him during the tutelage period. They had to, therefore, prove their merit to the guru and serve him by performing menial tasks and undertaking household chores. They were not encouraged or permitted to ask the guru any questions. Instead, they had to wait for his decision to explain or unravel the mysteries of traditional knowledge.

The transformation in pedagogy since the last quarter of the nineteenth century and more so in the early twentieth century laid the foundation of present-day institutionalized music education. There is now a wide array of possibilities to learn Hindustani music. From the traditional guru–shishya parampara to music schools and universities to online e-learning platforms, there are avenues of learning which cater to all kinds of students with varied aspirations and requirements.

Guru–Shishya Parampara

The training format followed in the guru–shishya parampara continues to be preferred by those who wish to pursue Hindustani music as a profession. Much has changed in the traditional pattern. The obvious challenges that individuals had to encounter and surpass before they could be accepted as disciples and the menial tasks that they had to perform as service to the guru are perhaps not so common now. Service to the guru remains an unwritten commitment, but it is tempered by the ways of the world that the guru and shishya inhabit. Thus, menial service has given way to errands run for the guru and his or her family.[1]

This transition has taken place over time due to a variety of reasons. Easier mobility and access to more than one guru in large cities has reduced the pressure on disciples to choose a particular guru. Those who have made definite stylistic choices narrow their focus to one guru. The guru is equally aware of the changing times and the sense of empowerment disciples may feel due to material benefits available in large cities that enable them to be less dependent on the guru.

The young students struggle to make ends meet, particularly those who have migrated from smaller towns to big cities. With the passage of time, they begin to adapt to the living and working conditions in the city. This means that they have to find ways to survive in these urban centres in order to continue their training and to gradually start pursuing a career in music.

These pressures adversely impact the length of time that they can devote to taaleem or training sessions. Gurus too experience similar material pressures and do not, therefore, find time to focus only on a few students training to be professionals. They are compelled to teach laypersons to earn tuition fees, since they often do not charge a fee from those wanting to train as professionals. For gurus who do not have regular performing careers or do not have alternate means of livelihood, tuition fees become their sole avenue of earning money. In such cases, they may take tuition fees from shishyas as well. Thus, the guru–shishya association continues to be a relationship even now, rather than a commercial transaction, but there are examples of the latter too. This change was seen since the late nineteenth century.[2]

Some may argue that the transformation of the guru–shishya relationship into a commercial transaction has led to the breakdown of this loyalties and has replaced them with a degree of consumerism. While this may be true to an extent, it would be far-fetched to believe that this is the sole reason for the decline of this ideology, as gharana loyalties have often waned due to the eclectic choices made by musicians in drawing upon varied aesthetic influences. Those espousing this argument suggest that the very inclusion of a commercial transaction into a 'pious' activity like teaching music is unethical.

Apart from financial compulsions that have impacted the guru–shishya parampara, changes have also been experienced in the musical perspective that formed the basis of this system of teaching. Conventionally, disciples were taught within the parameters of specific musical styles, which crystallized into the gharanas, although an eclectic approach to learning began as early as the nineteenth century. The reasons for this approach could have been many, some of which could have been pragmatic. For instance, the peripatetic nature of a professional musician's life resulted in disciples learning from different gurus, who did short stints in their city or town. But there were also others who were driven by an artistic urge and curiosity to imbibe multiple musical influences.[3]

The fervour to draw from a broad and diverse range of sources is more real than ever before. It is not necessarily dependent on training gained from multiple gurus, as technology now enables disciples to listen and learn from a variety of sources available on multiple formats, particularly on the internet. There are also cases of disciples training with more than one guru at different times of the day or week. They are prompted in this direction due to a desire to add variety and build a large concert repertoire or the urge to adopt specific musical devices and techniques. Disciples now also have a sense of entitlement as a result of information being accessible on the internet at the click of a button. They have no qualms about changing gurus or learning from more than one at the same time. This approach is different from earlier, when disciples did not learn from multiple gurus at the same time. They trained under them in different phases of their musical journey, as the convention required disciples to seek permission from the existing guru to move to another. This is not necessarily done today with the result that the absence of such courtesies creates animosity between gurus and disciples.

Other than gurus, there are innumerable teachers who teach amateurs on a regular basis and charge fees. Called 'private tuitions', such sessions are held at the home of the teacher or student. In some cases, groups of students are taught together. While many of these teachers may have been trained well and are conscientious instructors, there is no hiding the truth that substandard teachers have been active too.

Music Schools

Beyond the sphere of individual instruction is an entire network of institutionalized music education, the strength and reach of which would appear to give positive signals for the future of Hindustani music. Over a period of about 125 years or so, this network has gone through several phases. From music clubs to music schools, from music included in regular schools to departments of music in universities, institutionalized education has reached virtually every nook and corner of the country and has even reached foreign shores.[4]

Vishnu Digambar Paluskar's Gandharva Mahavidyalaya (GM) has metamorphosed into a gigantic machine which churns out thousands of diploma and degree holders in diverse streams of music. To put it in a historical context, GM was one of the foremost institutions to offer music training to amateurs on a mass scale, crossing barriers of religion, caste and gender, since the early twentieth century. Classes at GM were conducted regularly and punctually. A graded syllabus supplemented with textbooks that did not profess allegiance to any particular gharana ensured standardized training. GM evaluated students and awarded its own diploma and degree certificates.[5]

After the demise of Paluskar, his disciples, Narayanrao Khare, V.A. Kashalkar, Shankarrao Vyas and V.N. Patwardhan convened a meeting in Ahmedabad in December 1931. It was decided to establish an organization called Gandharva Mahavidyalaya Mandal to perpetuate Paluskar's work after his death. The headquarters was based in Mumbai.[6] To begin with, schools established by Paluskar's disciples across the country were affiliated to the mandal. Several students appeared for examinations held according to the mandal's syllabus and certificates awarded to successful candidates were recognized by many universities and educational bodies. In 1947, the mandal also began the publication of *Sangeet Kala Vihar*, a bilingual monthly magazine in Hindi and Marathi, to inform affiliated institutions, music teachers, students and music lovers about the activities undertaken by the mandal, including details about examinations.[7]

Presently, the GM Mandal has its headquarters in Navi Mumbai. It has 1200 affiliated institutions and approximately 800 examination centres across the country. Each year, more than one lakh students appear for examinations held for different levels, ranging from the initial years to the final stage, considered as the doctoral level.[8] The total proposed expenditure towards the examination department, convocation and examination committee for the year 2017–2018 was more than Rs 3 crore.[9]

In the absence of any empirical evidence, it would be impossible to pinpoint reasons for so many students joining music schools and appearing for periodic examinations. We can only surmise that most students are probably interested in learning the basics and continuing as amateurs, rather than pursuing a career in music. Some may have a casual interest in music and consider it to be a leisure activity or a hobby, while others may regard it as a social grace. The possibility of securing a diploma or degree also acts as a catalyst for many, particularly those who wish to flaunt such certificates. Certificates for such extra-curricular activities can also boost the chances of students seeking admission at the undergraduate level, where competition for seats in good colleges is intense.

Aside from these amateurs, there are also those who wish to secure certificates which would enable them to teach music in regular schools, as this is a condition for getting a job in schools. There are others who wish to get the certificates to allow them to set up their own music classes, which can be affiliated to GM for purposes of evaluation.

Irrespective of the reasons for such a large number of admissions to music schools, there is no doubt that institutions like GM offer the opportunity of learning Hindustani music without going through the rigour that is necessary for a would-be professional. Those wanting to become professional musicians shift to the guru–shishya training format, or often start with it.

The GM Mandal has held triennial conferences for music teachers, the first of which was inaugurated in 1952 by Rajendra Prasad, the first president of India. The mandal has also been organizing seminars and workshops periodically since 1975 to enable students to interact with experts in the field. Since these conferences, seminars and workshops are considered beneficial for music teachers and students, the text and recordings of such sessions should be made freely accessible online to encourage a wider discourse, and to help students and the larger community of Hindustani music lovers outside the framework of the mandal and its activities.[10]

The success of the GM Mandal and the increasing number of people wishing to learn in an institutionalized atmosphere has led to a proliferation of music classes. Way back in the 1950s, vocalist and revered guru Vilayat Hussain Khan had concluded that there were approximately 100–125 classes in Mumbai city alone at that point of time.[11] The number has risen exponentially since then and there are now large music schools in all major cities.

The well-established music schools have followed a certain pattern. They are usually run by private or public trusts, and are usually registered as non-profit educational entities. Some even manage to lease plots of land at subsidized rates for long periods of time from the Central or state governments. The school premises built on these plots are non-residential in most cases, but there are situations when the principals and their families may be provided housing facilities on campus. Many of these schools canvass for financial support from private donors or apply for government grants to supplement the income drawn from the tuition fees collected from students. Teachers and accompanying musicians are typically appointed on a contractual basis, and a portion of the tuition fees is paid to the teachers as salaries with the school retaining the balance.

Often, senior students are appointed as teachers. Examinations are held on a regular basis and certificates are provided by a central institution to which the music school may be affiliated.

Most well-established music schools seem to share similar objectives. The objectives include promotion and propagation of Hindustani music through music education provided on a 'systematic' and 'scientific' basis and through periodic concerts. The objectives and the scope of activities of these schools have grown significantly from those that were seen after Paluskar's initiative in this direction. This is expectedly so, considering the passage of time and changes in the society which have required a reappraisal of objectives that had motivated earlier educational ventures. Thus, the Pracheen Kala Kendra, based in Chandigarh, runs courses in music and dance, and also includes research in fine arts as one of its many objectives.[12] There are also examples of a few schools listing documentation and archiving as part of their objectives.[13] The Saptak School of Music in Ahmedabad believes in training students in the guru–shishya format to become performers and listeners.[14] Kolkata-based school Shruti Nandan, a brainchild of the well-known vocalist Ajoy Chakrabarty from the Patiala gharana, focuses on recognizing and honing musical talent in young children.[15]

Even in institutions that have not seen changes in their statement of objectives, an alternate action plan to meet the objectives is discernible.[16] Some music schools rent out sections of their premises as banquet and wedding halls or rent out space to regular schools, apparently because the tuition fees or donations collected fall short of the resources required. This has caused consternation in certain sections since the plots of land had been acquired at subsidized rates from the government.[17]

But setting aside the professed objectives of such schools, we need to take cognizance of the outcome of their work and its overall impact on Hindustani music.

Institutionalization has drawn criticism from some quarters since the early days. Musicologist N.R. Marulkar opined in 1955 that contemporary music education had become like a market-place, where music teachers were preoccupied with publicizing their work and their institutions, and were keen on finding more avenues of income, rather than being involved in actual educational activity. He believed that their motives made them lose sight of their development as artistes and their commitment to making students aware of the seriousness of the art. He further pointed out that many individuals declared themselves music teachers with only a few years of training and hid their inadequacies by falling back on textual material related to music. He believed their lack of practice adversely affected the quality of their students.[18]

Many would tend to believe that Marulkar's assessment applies equally well to the current situation. The primary objective or mission of music schools was not to create performers, but to expose the general public to musical knowledge and equip them to become educated listeners.[19] To an extent, this has happened in the past and probably continues today as well, if we were to go by anecdotal experiences of performers meeting listeners who tell them that they sing or play musical instruments, and that they have received certificates from music schools. But in the absence of any audience survey, it would be difficult to estimate the number of listeners who may have undergone music training at some point of time and if it was this training that prompted them to attend concerts or listen to recorded music on a regular basis, and if their training had improved their understanding of the musical nuances.

The general impression among musicians and connoisseurs about students from music schools is that they are neither trained to be good listeners to appreciate musical nuances nor are they self-motivated. There is no survey that could help us arrive at a conclusion about their musical knowledge and their level of performance. But if we were to go by the syllabi of the music schools, they do not really meet the objective of creating good listeners. There are very few elements in the syllabi that clearly set aside a roadmap for exposing students to multiple forms of Hindustani music, for training them to appreciate nuances and for encouraging them to analyse musical renditions.

Many of the larger music schools boast of audio-video archives and libraries. But whether these resources are easily accessible and are used in a regular and graded manner for training students to become informed listeners are questions that only music schools and their students would be able to answer. The qualitative differences that we observe today in the ability of audiences to understand and appreciate musical nuances indicate that the majority of music lovers are not informed listeners, an issue that music schools could address through their activities.

Some music schools host concerts throughout the year. This is similar to the periodic programmes that were held by Paluskar's GM and B.R. Deodhar's School of Indian Music in Mumbai.[20] Held in the school premises or even in auditoria outside, these concerts may include performances by some of the senior students and faculty members, and they also feature other musicians. The reasons for holding such concerts could be many. They may be held to encourage students and staff to perform, and to inform those within the school and outside about the school's year-long activities and its position as an important teaching institution. Such concerts may also be held to expose students to performances by senior musicians and to guide them to critically appreciate their music. If the second objective is indeed so, students should also be motivated to attend concerts held outside their music school. Regrettably, this does not happen often and the students' listening experience is limited only to those concerts held by their own music school.

Syllabi for a music school addressing the theoretical and practical aspects is decided according to the affiliation that the institution has with a central examining body. In the absence of an affiliation, the school may choose to independently draw up its own syllabus, although the general trend is to follow an existing model. Students are evaluated for theory and practice, but the proportional weightage given to each may differ between institutions. The overall emphasis seems to be on including numerous compositions, raags and taals on the practical side, a feat that is difficult to accomplish even by those training in the guru–shishya parampara. In addition, an equally large number of subjects dealing with music theory are included, with the result that students from music schools are found severely wanting in both aspects. The attention of the schools and the students seems to be on the completion of coursework in the requisite time and on appearing for successive exams with the sole intention of securing certificates. The focus does not seem to be on gaining in-depth knowledge of the art or on internalizing its theoretical and practical aspects; a goal that would definitely be desirable for those wanting to qualify as teachers or performers, who can function in a more meaningful manner.

Music Curriculum of Schools

Besides schools expressly involved in music education, regular schools also include music as a subject in their curriculum or as an extra-curricular activity. Efforts in this direction had begun in the nineteenth century. In Calcutta, Sourindra Mohan Tagore was actively involved in incorporating music in the school curriculum.[21] In Bombay, the Students' Literary and Scientific Society, formed by the professors and students of Elphinstone College in 1848 to spread awareness about education, tried to include music in the academic curriculum of schools established by the society.[22] Isolated examples such as these continued in the early part of the twentieth century, but they did not yield tangible results in terms of universal acceptance of music as a subject to be included as part of academic instruction.

It was only in the years immediately post Independence that music education found government recognition and attempts were made to shape a standardized teaching methodology at the school level. A brief overview of one such case pertaining to the erstwhile Bombay Province will give the readers an idea of the manner in which this subject was approached at that time.

The Education and Industries Department of the government of Bombay appointed a Music Education Committee (MEC), according to a resolution dated 24 March 1948, to survey the field of music education in the Bombay Province.[23] Acknowledging that music did not find a definite place in the syllabus for primary and secondary schools, except in the case of girls' schools, the resolution stated that the government wished to promote the study and appreciation of music in educational institutions and that it was keen to formulate the curriculum for schools in the Bombay Province. The non-official members of the MEC appointed by the government included individuals who were closely associated with Hindustani music, and, as expected, their observations and recommendations were influenced by their training, background and experience in this system of music. Sub-committees were formed to examine subjects like music notation, music courses and syllabus, as well as qualifications and pay scales of music teachers. Interviews were conducted with music teachers in many cities of the region and a questionnaire was sent to primary and secondary schools, training colleges, district and municipal school boards, women's schools and colleges, and to music scholars, institutions and musicians belonging to the several parts of the Bombay Province.

Even though institutionalized music education had been consolidated by then, the committee declared in no uncertain terms that its survey proved that music education in the Bombay Province was unsatisfactory and inadequate.[24] The MEC, therefore, urged the government to:

... give serious consideration to the question of according to music its proper place in the scheme of education in all its stages, prescribing uniform courses and methods of instruction in all Government and Grant-in-Aid Institutions and helping to remedy the present chaotic state of music education in the Province, and to spread the taste for good music among the public.[25]

The MEC also made recommendations regarding music courses after examining those followed by government schools, private schools and institutions, and the matriculation syllabi of the Patna and Andhra universities. The recommendations stated that music should be a compulsory subject from the primary school level up to the first three years of secondary school in order to sensitize students to become discerning listeners, rather than training them to become professional musicians. After the third year of secondary school, music should be a voluntary subject, since special aptitude would be required for pursuit at higher levels of education.[26] The MEC said that technical terms and explanations should be introduced in higher classes, and folk songs and songs in the mother tongue should be taught at the primary level. It also recommended that music should be a compulsory subject in the Primary Teachers' Training College for men and women, and that the government should start special schools for advanced training in music at major centres in the Province. Music teachers should have Sangeet Visharad certificates from established institutions like the Gandharva Mahavidyalaya, besides certificates from Teachers' Training Colleges. The Sangeet Visharad certificates should be made mandatory for those who wished to teach in the special schools set up by the government. A music notation system recommended by the MEC after studying eighteen existing systems should be adopted in schools after the primary level.

The MEC also laid down specifications for administration, class management, teachers' qualifications, salaries, and recommended that museums and libraries pertaining to music should be started. They should conduct periodic lectures on the theory and practice of music. It suggested that a general course for the arts should be introduced as a compulsory subject in the final year of school and that music appreciation should be a part of this course. Graduate and post-graduate degree courses in music were recommended at the university level in the Province.

The MEC severely criticized the harmonium and film music for their supposed corrupting influence. It recommended that the harmonium be used to provide a drone and not to accompany or guide the music.[27] The use of gramophone records was encouraged for evaluating students' ability to critically appreciate music and to provide examples of good music to them.

This brief overview of the MEC's assessment of the extant situation in the field of music education and its recommendations to chart a path for the future shows clearly that the members' perspective centred on art music. Some of the MEC members were erstwhile students of GM and were actively conducting classes according to its syllabus. This seems to have guided their recommendation that graduating from GM should be a basic qualification for job opportunities as music teachers in schools.

There is no evidence of the extent to which the MEC's recommendations were accepted and acted upon in the school curriculum. According to a report from 1958, few students opted for music at the secondary school certificate (SSC) level in the Bombay Province. One reason was that barring Nagpur and SNDT (Mumbai) universities, no other university in the Province had music as a subject in their curriculum. This made it difficult for students who had opted for the subject at the SSC level to get admission to colleges. The syllabus was also very unwieldy for students, who had to cope with other academic subjects too. All examinees had to appear for a vocal examination, even if they were not endowed with good voices. Hence, out of over one lakh students appearing at the SSC level, only a hundred would opt for music. The situation seems to have improved marginally over the next few years. More students are believed to have opted for music at the SSC level after March 1959, when changes were introduced in the music syllabus. The new rules allowed those not endowed with a good voice to play the violin, dilruba or sitar for the examinations.[28]

This description of efforts to introduce music education as a part of schools' curriculum in Bombay Province soon after Independence shows a well-intentioned but limited vision. This was probably experienced elsewhere in northern India too, considering the lack of general musical awareness that has been seen among students since decades. While many people have often spoken in favour of including music training at the school level, their focus has been on art music and there is no cohesive action–plan in place. Education Commission reports from 1948–49 and 1964–66 spoke of the necessity of incorporating training in music and other arts in schools so as to enhance the creative abilities of children and provide a good channel for self-expression. This was also considered to be a good method for building national consciousness, and moral and spiritual character among students. But these reports did not say that music and the arts should be considered as subjects on par with others in the academic curriculum, and that the students' performance in these subjects should be evaluated in the same manner.[29]

It was only in 2005 that the National Curriculum Framework (NCF) candidly admitted that the education system had routinely discouraged arts' education and had merely regarded the arts as useful hobbies or leisure activities. NCF acknowledged that engagement with the arts in schools was peripheral and was mostly for public display on specific days to enhance the image of schools. Taking into account that the general awareness of the arts was at a seriously low level not only among students but also among guardians, teachers and policy makers, NCF recommended that arts education should be made a compulsory subject until Class X in order to acquaint students with the country's artistic and cultural diversity. Students could choose to specialize in particular areas at the secondary and higher secondary levels if they so desired. The NCF mentioned that hierarchies between different artistic streams should not be allowed. It also stressed on the need for resource material on arts education and for special teachers' training programmes in order to effectively execute these recommendations.[30]

Despite this, the reality is that no real headway seems to have been made in introducing music as a subject in schools across the country and in putting together a music curriculum which reflects the approach of NCF. To this day, only the Central Board of Secondary Education (CBSE) offers music as a subject at the secondary school (classes IX and X) and senior school (classes XI and XII) levels. The choice of music is either the Hindustani or Carnatic systems, thus focusing on art music as was the case previously. The curriculum for Hindustani vocal and instrumental music would appear formidable even to performers and scholars.[31] The National Council of Educational Research and Training (NCERT) has uploaded a series of tracks on its YouTube channel, which provide theoretical information regarding raags, supplemented with short practical demonstrations of compositions in those raags. Schools can utilize these resources, but they are limited and much more needs to be done if the present curriculum offered by the CBSE is to yield tangible results.[32]

Some schools, other than those affiliated to CBSE, also employ music teachers. Since these schools do not follow a structured syllabus, whether for art music or otherwise, it is left to the teachers to decide on the course of action. In many cases, the emphasis is on teaching songs in one or multiple languages, many of which may speak of nation building or are of a religious nature. In schools that have musical instruments, students wanting to learn to play them are taught accordingly. Since music is not treated at par with other academic subjects in these schools, the session is more of a hobby class than a course that follows a curriculum and involves evaluation by way of theoretical and practical examinations. Often, schools that do not offer music as a regular subject requisition the services of their music teachers to teach other subjects as well.

Music education has a similar status in most private and public schools. The amenities, coursework and quality of teachers may differ, but the tendency is to treat music more as an extra-curricular activity than a subject at par with others in the curriculum. The recent spate of newly opened private schools has produced fresh avenues for potential music teachers. The competition between these schools to offer the maximum number of activities during school hours has led to the inclusion of music as an extra-curricular activities. This has helped to create reasonably well-paid posts for music teachers, though these are mostly contractual jobs.

The overall impact of music education at the school level on the Hindustani music system has not been measured. It does not seem to have made a vital impact except for creating job opportunities for music teachers. To those lamenting the decline in the quality of this music and its listeners, it seems logical and imperative to introduce its training in schools. They believe this would serve the cause of traditional Indian culture and prevent further damage from the perceived onslaught of Western culture.

But there are several crucial questions that need to be asked. Can or should Hindustani music, or any other system of art music for that matter, be taught at every academic level in schools? Should it be a compulsory subject from the first year of school until the final year? Would it not be impractical and hasty to assume that school children of all age groups will and should identify with Hindustani or any other system of art music? Would such a step not be far removed from the musical reality that surrounds children outside their school premises? Should Hindustani music or art music of any kind not be an option, available only at a later stage to those desirous of pursuing it after they have been exposed to sound and music in general? Film songs, Hindi or otherwise, are the main sources of musical influence in daily life today, given their pervasiveness on virtually every format of broadcast. If this musical reality were to be kept in sight while drawing up music syllabi for schools, would this result in merely teaching film songs in schools?

These and other related issues need to be discussed in order to arrive at an alternative which would be best suited for Indian schools. A simple survey, as the one provided in this book, could be undertaken in schools to understand the situation at the ground level.[33]

Music at University Level

In his address at the All India Music Conference held at Baroda in 1916, Bhatkhande confidently stated that his endeavours to 'revive' Hindustani music and to put in place a system of instruction for mass learning had met with success. He hoped that this would lead to the introduction of music in the curriculum of universities.[34] In 1925, Bhatkhande reiterated his hope in a letter to well-known barrister M.R. Jayakar, a member of the Bombay University Reform Committee. Jayakar succeeded in getting Bhatkhande's graded course incorporated in the report of the University Committee.[35] The Indian Women's University (now Shreemati Nathibai Damodar Thackersey Women's University) in Mumbai offered music as a discipline at the degree level, and Manjulabai Mehta of Baroda, one of the twelve women who were awarded their graduation degrees in art in 1926, had opted for music.[36] The Patna University Senate also introduced music as a subject in the 1930s.[37]

A long time has elapsed since then and music is now taught at the undergraduate and postgraduate levels both in colleges and departments of music affiliated to universities, as well as in universities which specially focus on the arts.[38] I have discussed here, albeit briefly, a few prominent institutions among those imparting training in Hindustani music.

The Faculty of Performing Arts at the Maharaja Sayajirao University of Baroda in Gujarat is one of the oldest university departments which impart training in Hindustani vocal and instrumental music. It even has a separate department for tabla. The faculty has evolved from the School of Music and the educational activities conducted by the Sangeet Shala founded in 1884 by Sayajirao Gaekwad III, the ruler of Baroda. In 1949, the year that the university was established, the School of Music transformed into the College of Indian Music, Dance and Dramatics, which was a part of the Faculty of Fine Arts at the university. Its current nomenclature has been in existence since 1986. Courses are offered from the undergraduate to the doctoral levels, and students from other countries also enrol here. The stated goal of the faculty is 'to train students to develop their creative and intuitive abilities whereby attaining a systemic understanding of the art and science of performing arts and its aesthetic applications.'[39]

The official website of the faculty states that students are encouraged to undertake research projects. Teachers participate in seminars and workshops, and write research papers. Lectures, workshops, seminars and demonstrations are also conducted by visiting teachers and performers. Many students and teachers have received state and national scholarships.[40]

The Faculty of Performing Arts at the Banaras Hindu University was originally established as the School of Music and Fine Arts in 1949, which became the College of Music and Fine Arts in 1950, with renowned vocalist Omkarnath Thakur (1897–1967), a disciple of V.D. Paluskar, as its founder-principal. In 1966, the college was divided into three separate departments, that is, vocal music, instrumental music and musicology. The Department of Musicology, the first of its kind in the country, was headed by eminent musicologist Prem Lata Sharma. A dance section was introduced in 1973 and a separate dance department was set up in 2007. The Faculty of Performing Arts also provides training in Carnatic music.[41]

The faculty has a large student population, including those from overseas. It caters to multiple levels of academic instruction, from a preliminary diploma to a doctoral degree. Many kinds of courses are offered and several forms of music are taught as part of the curriculum. Workshops, seminars and concerts are held through the year. New courses have been introduced to provide vocational guidance in disciplines like applied music, multimedia, sound recording and music management. The thrust of the faculty is on 'value-based training' of traditional music, 'focusing on creative abilities and excellence in performance along with research in Musicology and innovative learning'. New methods of teaching are incorporated by faculty members.[42] Some students have received national scholarships, as well as junior and senior research fellowships offered by the culture ministry.[43]

The Indira Kala Sangeet Vishwavidyalaya (IKSV) situated in Khairagarh, Chhattisgarh, was established in 1956. It prides itself as being Asia's 'first University which is fully dedicated to various forms of Music, Dance, Fine Arts and Theatre' and has twenty-three affiliated colleges.[44] Its mission statement reads as follows:

• To provide infrastructure, education, training and research oriented opportunities to encourage creativity, restoration and innovation in all forms of Arts

- To liberate intellectual potential [which] lies within the arts disciples to reach and explore new dimensions of knowledge and true spirits of arts
- To develop a pedagogic system inspired by creative thinking in pursuit of excellence for the development of the open minds; in line with our motto 'May All Live in Tune'
- To act as a catalyst in research activities in all forms of Music and Arts leading to the betterment of the society
- To preserve and restore all forms of Music and Arts in their true spirits for their true spectators[45]

Lucknow's Marris College of Music was established in 1926 by Bhatkhande and was named after Sir William Marris, the governor of the erstwhile United Provinces of British India. In 1966, it was renamed as Bhatkhande College of Music and in 2000, it was recognized as a 'deemed university'. The institution counts some celebrated names among its alumni and its website mentions the names of many former students who have continued to pursue music education and give performances.[46] Presently called Bhatkhande Music Institute Deemed University, the institution has more than 1500 students. Although the official website does not provide a mission statement, the message from Vice-Chancellor Shruti Sadolikar Katkar, a senior vocalist of the Jaipur-Atrauli gharana, provides some indication of the institution's larger objectives. Aside from the ideals of teaching students 'to appreciate the beauty and the effort that makes art divine' and 'to create artistes' who will become good human beings and responsible citizens, Katkar also mentions some tangible objectives. These include equipping students conceptually and practically for potential career prospects in the 'music industry' through workshops and giving students opportunities to organize concerts and perform.[47]

These institutions have been included here only to provide the reader with an idea of their vision and objectives. This is by no means a comprehensive listing of universities involved in Hindustani music education. But based on this information, we can make some observations relevant to music education at the university level.

For one, the high ideals held up by each of the institutions in their mission statements are praiseworthy and yet do not seem to successfully address the reality that affects prospective students. Given the disparate approach to music education at the school level, there seems to be a lack of connection between the music that is taught at the university level and the limited musical exposure that students may have received in the pre-university period. In other words, students who have cleared their higher secondary school level have little or no musical abilities to tackle the university syllabus. This is significantly different from their experience with other subjects. Thus, only a few who are reasonably musically literate based on the training they undergo through private instruction or in music schools manage to gain admission as students in music departments of universities. Diplomas and degrees awarded by music schools come in handy here to prove the student's musical qualifications. Personal interviews and tests for performance capabilities may be included in the process of selecting applicants.

University syllabi often closely resemble what is followed by music schools. This is not surprising since the university faculty and those responsible for drawing up the syllabus are often products of these music schools. Thus, apart from adding some topics like new technology and its impact on music, there is little effort made to revisit the original vision and evaluate its practicality and relevance in present times. The syllabi for music in most universities also lack an inclusive and integrated approach. They are geared to train students primarily in forms of art music, with limited information provided about other categories of music.

Many students who complete their postgraduate, MPhil or PhD studies in music become teachers in music schools and universities. Very few are involved in research thereafter. Not surprisingly, music, research has been a largely neglected area in Hindustani music, except for research done by students during their studies. Doctoral dissertations are often published as books, but they do not have readership outside the community of students and teachers connected with Central and state universities.

Thus, music lovers generally do not have access to the latest work being done by Indian scholars. One reason is also that a large part of the research and research papers appear in Hindi and regional languages. They are published by smaller publishers who may not have access to the wider distribution network available to publications in English. Undoubtedly, greater access could invite critical inputs from all sections, especially since the quality of music research in India does not frequently meet the exacting standards of conceptual framework and research methodology. This is also because the students' objective in publishing is often prompted only by requirements laid down by universities or institutions which employ them as teachers.

There are several questions that arise regarding the original vision which guided the establishment of music departments and special arts and music universities. Did music education at the university level set out to train professionals? Were these potential professionals to be trained as performers or scholars or teachers? Were these objectives reflected in the manner that the syllabi were designed? A survey of university syllabi undertaken a few years ago suggested that the objectives for training imparted at this level were diverse, often struggling between preparing students as performers on the one hand and as teachers or scholars on the other.[48]

But a comprehensive survey spanning universities across the country would help us examine the qualitative and quantitative outcomes of the music education that they impart, understand the career trajectories of students as performers, researchers and teachers, and estimate their contribution to developing a discerning audience. We would also need to understand the current situation in the context of the general state of university education in our country.[49]

Institutionalized Guru–Shishya Parampara

Since the early days of institutionalized music education, there have been attempts to integrate aspects of the guru–shishya pedagogic format into music education. Paluskar's GM had a residential facility for students from financially poor backgrounds, who had to sign a three or six year bond in return. Although Paluskar's training in the Gwalior gharana was passed on to his immediate disciples, GM did not follow a teaching pattern that propagated a particular gharana.

Several years later, Music Centre at the University of Bombay, set up under the directorship of Ashok Da. Ranade, reputed scholar and musician, saw an experiment in combining features of the gharana system and the institutionalized format. The centre's teaching faculty had representation from the major gharanas of Hindustani vocal music and students were placed under the tutelage of specific teachers, who taught them the stylistic features of their chosen gharana.[50]

The ITC-SRA mentioned in the previous chapter prides itself in being the first institution of its kind which gives guru–shishya parampara an institutional basis by bringing together on campus gurus and their chosen disciples for prolonged training. The institution looks after the lodging and boarding facilities of the gurus and disciples, and they receive salaries and stipends respectively. Gurus and disciples are featured in concerts and music festivals held under the banner of ITC-SRA in Kolkata and in other parts of the country. The institution has also sponsored concert tours overseas in the past. The institution houses an audio-visual archive and publishes books on music. The ITC-SRA concerts have also featured artistes from outside the institution, thus drawing a wider listenership for their programmes.[51]

Connoisseurs who have been concerned about the future of Hindustani music often speak in favour of the replication of the ITC-SRA model in other parts of the country either with ITC support or with the backing of other corporate patrons. That has yet to happen, but a similar project is operational in Hubballi, Karnataka. Established in the memory of Gangubai Hangal, renowned Kirana gharana vocalist, the Dr Gangubai Hangal Gurukul provides training along the guru–shishya pedagogic lines to disciples who reside with their gurus on campus.[52]

The Hubballi project does not seem to have as yet created a large number of successful performers. In fact, in 2016, Gangubai Hangal's family had raised objections to the manner in which the gurukul was run and the discrimination faced by four prospective students from Karnataka. The institution refuted these claims.[53] But ITC-SRA has undoubtedly nurtured talent over several years. Some scholars from here have become established performers. Prominent among these are Ajoy Chakrabarty and Rashid Khan. The infrastructural support that ITC-SRA provides to its students is an aspect that several hundred students training to become professional musicians in other parts of the country miss out on. It is possible that this support system could lead to a sense of complacency or a lopsided view of aesthetic standards among the students, since they are primarily living in a cloistered environment on the campus, but this is not an insurmountable problem even if it were to happen. It can be addressed if the institution, the gurus and the disciples are all unprejudiced and respectful of artistic pursuits elsewhere too. Indeed, complacency or musical biases can exist in non-institutional surroundings too.

I have referred to surrogate advertising in the section on corporate patronage. The subject would come up for discussion in the context of ITC-SRA too, since the institution is supported by a company involved in the manufacture of tobacco products, among others. Some may argue against patronage from companies associated with harmful products such as tobacco, alcohol and aerated drinks, even if it is at the cost of Hindustani music losing out on vital support. It remains to be seen if this will ever meet with strong opposition from musicians and other stakeholders, although this does not seem to be the case in the foreseeable future.

On a wider plane, institutionalized music education has met with criticism since the early days for a variety of reasons. Some have felt that despite the increase in such activity, it has not yielded good teachers and performers. Others have held that institutions are breeding grounds for furthering narrow and personal interests, or that they look down upon traditional pedagogy and consider only their methodology as scientific and systematic. At the same time, there are those who feel that institutions have created a huge listenership for music that is curious and critical.[54] The guru–shishya and institutionalized forms of music training continue to have their votaries, but both methods now face new challenges posed by the internet and digital technology as we will see in the next chapter.

5

Tangible Resources and Creating Awareness

Though the Hindustani music tradition has essentially been an oral one, texts have played an important role as sources of reference for successive generations. Written by scholars and performers based in different parts of the country, these commentaries, memoirs, critiques and collections of compositions go back several centuries and are available in multiple languages such as Sanskrit, Persian, Urdu, Hindi, Marathi, Bengali and Gujarati. Some are historical documents that authenticate earlier trends or are source material for past repertoire. Compilations of vocal compositions that were published in the nineteenth century or similar collections of notated vocal and instrumental compositions made available in the twentieth century are examples of this. There are other publications that provide descriptions and analyses of the life and work of musicians of those times. They help in understanding previous performance practices, theoretical frameworks and cultural contexts, all of which equip successive generations in extending the boundaries of the tradition. In most cases, scholars produced these publications, but performers also participated in this activity from time to time.[1]

With the arrival of the print medium, there was a proliferation and wider distribution of publications related to Hindustani music. The institutionalization of music education created a need for textbooks which could serve the needs of a multitude of students in schools and universities. These textbooks were written primarily by those who had studied or were teaching in these institutions.

Documentation and Research

In addition to the documentation and research conducted by students and teachers at universities, several other Indian institutions and scholars have also been involved in this activity outside the university framework. There have been many cases of grass-roots level documentation, which have proved beneficial for further research. In more recent years, newer formats based on audio-video and digital technologies have been used for the documentation process. But there are certain shortcomings that cannot be ignored. Documentation efforts have at times been duplicated either due to limited knowledge about available source material or because it has not been published widely. In some cases, documentation has been a mere clinical compilation of information and statistics, rather than a process guided by specific and well thought-out objectives.

Original research places an entirely different set of demands on those wishing to engage in it. It requires defining the area of inquiry clearly and needs critical thinking, both ingredients often found lacking in research conducted by many Indian scholars and institutions.

Few Indian scholars and musicians writing in English have been successful in reaching out to a wider audience.[2] Much of the work from India is available only in Hindi or regional Indian languages. It acquires a wider readership primarily when it is used as a resource by non-Indian scholars and is cited by them. Often Indian scholarship on Hindustani music has also remained focused on musicology, and a discipline like ethnomusicology has been largely neglected. The path-breaking work done by Ashok Da. Ranade, stands apart in this context. He was a prolific author not just in Marathi but also in English, which made his publications accessible to an international audience.[3]

The scholastic output of non-Indian scholars is primarily published in English by prominent publishers who have a domestic and an international reach. As a result, their work is easily available to specialists in the field as well as to general readers. They also frequently publish in online international journals and are equally proactive in making their work available on multiple websites.

Non-Indian ethnomusicologists have contributed immensely in developing a layered understanding of the cultural context in which the theory and practice of Hindustani music has evolved over the past several centuries. The greater opportunities of pursuing interdisciplinary studies overseas, as compared to those available in India on an institutional basis, has led several scholars to examine many aspects of this music beyond musicology. Interdisciplinary research has brought together music and areas like anthropology, cultural studies and history. This has expanded our understanding of the present nature of this system of music and its future possibilities. But it must be noted that those trained in other disciplines, both outside India and here, are often not educated in the subtleties of the performing tradition, due to which preconceived theoretical constructs creep into their writing.

Non-Indian scholars need to frequently publish research papers to comply with university stipulations. Probably more funds for research are available to them and the amounts may be far greater than those available to Indian scholars. If more funds are available here, it would facilitate field trips and access to source material, and significantly reduce the pressure on the scholars. But the quality of scholarship should not be limited by funding. The rigour of research methodology, the development of critical faculties and the ease with language are issues that require training and application, which can be achieved without funding.

While funding for independent Indian scholars is available to a limited extent from some government and non-government sources, most of the research output from India is not available for open public access. Newer ways of publishing such work in the original language as well as through translations would definitely prove beneficial. An important exception in this is the India Foundation for the Arts, located in Bengaluru, a body that 'supports practice, research and education in the arts in India' and encourages the publication of research funded by it through academic papers, monographs and films.[4]

It is a sad comment that to this day there are no academic journals devoted to Hindustani music, partially or entirely, which match international standards. The *Sangeet Kala Vihar* mentioned earlier continues to be published as a monthly magazine, but its scope, style and articles do not qualify it as an academic journal. Sangeet Karyalaya, originally set up in 1932 as Garg and Co. in Hathras, Uttar Pradesh, is a publishing house dedicated to books on music and dance. It has also been bringing out a monthly magazine called *Sangeet* since 1935.[5] This too does not come up to the standards expected of academic journals. The *Journal of the Indian Musicological Society* has been published as a quarterly from 1971, and contains informative, analytical articles and papers specially written for the journal or presented in seminars organized under the aegis of the society. The journal was accessible to subscribers or available in libraries. After discussions on the relevance of the journal in current times, it has been decided to continue its publication after modifying it. There has also been some debate on whether the journal should continue as a print publication or as an e-journal or even in both formats.[6]

Archives

The question of accessibility brings us to the role of archives as repositories of material in audio, video, text, photographic and other formats. These archival collections could contain live concert and field recordings, personal memorabilia and commercial publications, as well as other sources. The two defining features of an archive, preservation and transmission, were earlier performed by the gurus in the Indian oral tradition well before the institutional form of the archive was established. But there was one notable difference. While the gurus were repositories of knowledge, their actions were not objective. The acquisition of knowledge and its transfer were both based on the choices they made. They decided on the kind of knowledge they wished to acquire and whether or not to impart it to a particular individual or a group of people. The institutional archives, on the other hand, are a source of impersonal, objective and systematized storage of tangible resources, which represent knowledge from the past and present to be preserved and provided to posterity. It is important to appreciate similarities and dissimilarities between living and institutional repositories in order to understand parameters that guide current archival policies. The two are closely interlinked and can influence each other in a positive manner.

Earlier chapters have discussed the scope and efficacy of archives which are run by autonomous bodies established by the Union government several decades ago. Other than these, there are several archives spread across India housing material related to Hindustani music. Some of them are run by cultural organizations set up by state governments, while others are run by private and public organizations.

One of the most prominent archives is the Archives and Research Centre for Ethnomusicology (ARCE) situated in Gurugram, Haryana, which is a repository of audio, video and textual sources voluntarily deposited by scholars from all over the world. ARCE's collection of numerous kinds of music also includes material on Hindustani music.[7] Many online archives hosted in India and abroad feature Hindustani music recordings. The Archive of Indian Music, set up in collaboration with the Manipal Centre for Philosophy and Humanities, Manipal University, is one such online archive which focuses on early commercial recordings. The British Library, under its Endangered Archives Programme, has digitized and made accessible 78 rpm discs and old record label catalogues, some of which pertain to Hindustani music.[8] Some universities outside India have rich archives of audio, video and text sources related to Hindustani music. The University of Washington in Seattle, USA, and the School of Oriental and African Studies in London, UK, are noteworthy examples of such archives.[9]

There are also several private collectors who have, over time, procured audio and video material which were originally recorded on varied formats. But their collections are not open to the public. The Dr Ashok Da. Ranade Archives in Pune is one of the rare cases of a private collection being converted into an archive for public use.[10] But private collections aside, at least public archives should facilitate easy access and distribution, as that is the reason why they came into existence in the first place. Grants are given to them by government and non-government organizations on the express understanding that their collections be made accessible to the public at large. The reality is far from this and it is therefore important to examine existing archival policy.

Primarily, archival collections pertain to audio and video recordings of commercially published or live concert recordings. Critical questions need to be asked regarding the manner in which the live recordings were acquired and the agreements that may have been reached between the performers and the archives about sharing them. For example, what was the agreement between the original rights holders and the collectors or archives regarding the housing and circulation of their work? Were requisite permissions taken from all the rights holders, whether soloists or accompanists, before recording, acquiring or publishing the work? Was the work acquired as a result of a commercial transaction between the collectors or archives and the original rights holders, and was this arrangement also meant for the public broadcast of the work?

I must hasten to add that these questions are neither to dissuade archives from publicizing their collections, nor to treat commercial transactions with disdain. Commercial transactions would actually benefit the archives, as well as the original rights holders. But the unfortunate truth is that most collectors and archives do not have the necessary permissions in place either for recording, acquisition or distribution. What may have been ignorance earlier has now become a complete travesty of the law. Both public and private institutions are culprits in this regard. Many of them have recognized the commercial value of their collections and have entered into contracts with record labels and other entities for the sale of work in their archives, in flagrant violation of the law that requires the permission of the rights holders for any commercial or non-commercial transmission of their work. The situation has worsened with the spread of the internet, since it provides several online options for publishing. Thus, the material housed in archives is traded without the consent of its creators. The creators, if at all they are taken into consideration, are the last in the reckoning of these transactions.[11]

Undoubtedly, public archives and private collectors possess source material which could help us piece together the history of Hindustani music dating back to the early twentieth century. They give a range of reasons to explain their acts of circulating their material without proper permissions from the original rights holders. They claim ignorance of the law or that they need to be compensated financially for the years of work they put in to carefully acquire and house these rich resources, and for their future upkeep. They also adopt a pious and self-righteous stance by proclaiming that they are promoting heritage, which needs to be shared with the present and future generations, and not locked away or kept secret. They blame the musicians for being possessive about their knowledge and for their unwillingness to share their recordings.[12] Quite clearly, none of these justifications are legally tenable, as the law does not condone the illegal recording, acquisition or distribution of audio-video material. Interestingly, most archives in India do not have their catalogues displayed on their websites, probably because a large part of their collections has been recorded or acquired illegally.

Eminent ethnomusicologist Anthony Seeger has delineated the ways in which archives can lay down parameters towards formulating a good archival policy and initiatives that can be undertaken in following ethical practice in this area. He says that archives 'should argue for ethical as well as legal and practical approaches to the materials in their possession'.[13] He goes on to say:

Archives should provide rights information and rights transfer forms to researchers before they start their work and should pay careful attention to ethical issues when materials are deposited. Archives should also mobilize to help artists and members of communities that are being recorded understand how to protect their rights; at the same time, archives should educate members of communities about the uses of archives and show how properly written agreements can both protect the community members and permit the archive to do its work.[14]

In addition, Seeger points out that archives need to review their acquisitions policies, that they need to ascertain that rights have been transferred as per law and that they need to have proper agreements for acquisitions in place before entering into new ones for using the material.[15]

Most musicians do not question the obvious violation of the law and unethical approach adopted by public archives, particularly those run by concert organizers, probably due to the fear that this would cause a problem between them and the institutions, and cost them future concert opportunities. As a result, private collectors and public archives have been circulating unhindered, entire collections or parts of it, on online platforms or through record labels.

Studio and live concert recordings are also uploaded on online social media platforms on a non-commercial basis by passionate private collectors. Fellow music lovers often commend them for their efforts at collating and sharing the material. However, music can be shared only with the prior permission from the rights holders. The proprietorial role adopted by collectors and archives is illegal, whether or not their professed purpose of distributing material is in the larger interests of preserving and propagating traditional knowledge.

Educational Programmes

Other efforts to spread information about Hindustani music that have also been in operation for several decades broadly qualify as educational programmes. Some of these are aimed at specific groups, while others are more in the nature of community outreach programmes. These programmes essentially feature musicians conducting lecture-demonstrations, workshops and masterclasses, and also participating in seminars. In some events the musicians share their experiences and explanations with listeners through guided listening sessions, which focus on recorded music of one or more maestros. All such programmes are held with support from public or private organizations. In many cases an entry fee is charged and a portion of the total revenue is offered as honorarium to the musicians.

While lecture-demonstrations, workshops and masterclasses may be directed towards students of music, often there is little difference between the way workshops and masterclasses are conducted. Workshops and masterclasses usually end up being mass teaching sessions, irrespective of the diverse musical capabilities of the participants, although sometimes the qualifications or requirements from the participants are specified clearly.

Workshops and masterclasses have posed a challenge to the traditional guru–shishya teaching format. The lecture-demonstration was a one-way communication with the musician explaining and the audience only listening without having a hands-on learning experience. Attendance to such a session was considered acceptable under the guru–shishya parampara, even if it was conducted by another guru. But workshops and masterclasses were looked at with suspicion by the gurus as they believed that their disciples should learn only from them and no one else. Due to this problem, participants are sometimes asked to submit written permissions from their gurus before they can register for workshops and masterclasses. Sometimes disciples are not really concerned about procuring permissions from their gurus and displeasing them. Alternatively, disciples attend these sessions as observers and not participants. Gurus may accept this as a compromise believing that their disciples will not actually learn from other musicians and disciples are glad that they have a chance to witness other musicians in teaching sessions.

Society for the Promotion of Classical Music and Culture Amongst Youth

The idea of lecture-demonstrations received an impetus through the activities of the Society for the Promotion of Indian Classical

Music and Culture Amongst Youth (SPIC MACAY), one of the key organizations involved in the promotion of Hindustani music and other arts among students in schools, colleges and other educational institutions. Founded in 1977 by Kiran Seth, Professor-Emeritus IIT-Delhi, the organization describes itself as 'a non-profit, voluntary, non-political and participatory student movement registered under the Societies Registration Act, 1860' and donations to it are tax exempted under Section 80 (G) of the Income Tax Act, 1961.[16]

To begin with, the organization adopted the lecture-demonstration format for meeting its objective 'to present Indian classical art forms in a comprehensive manner in front of today's youth'. The organization believes that its programmes gave the youth 'an understanding of the basics of the classical art forms', and have 'done away with the misconception that classical arts are difficult to understand'.[17]

Over the last several years, the organization has abandoned the lecture-demonstration format, but it continues to arrange concerts in schools and colleges in India and, to a limited extent, overseas, as a means to achieve its declared goal of enriching 'the quality of formal education by increasing awareness about different aspects of Indian heritage and inspiring the young mind to imbibe the values embedded in it'.[18] These concerts are held in classrooms, school or college auditoria, or hostels, depending upon the local arrangements. For the organization, these concerts held 'in an ambience conducive for touching the highest heights, both by the artistes and the rasikas' give artistes 'a chance to undertake an inward journey and reach depths of performance (taking us along too)'.[19]

With a central executive body in New Delhi, the organization receives support from corporates, individuals, charitable trusts and also from the Union government through the Ministry of Culture, Ministry of Youth Affairs and Sports, and Ministry of Human Resource Development. The organization is also supported by Rikskonsertene, Norway, and Goethe Institute, Germany. This international backing has enabled cultural exchange between India and these countries. More than 300 concerts featuring Indian artistes have been held in Scandinavia and Germany, and more than 200 concerts featuring international artistes have been held in India.[20]

The organization's official website states that in 2012–2013, it had held more than 7500 programmes across more than 1500 institutions spread over 800 towns in India and over 50 cities overseas. The website says that these programmes impacted more than 3 million students and that they were organized by thousands of volunteers, including students, teachers, housewives, retired people and professionals. Among the many ideals highlighted repeatedly is that of voluntary participation and that 'SPIC MACAY celebrates Nishkaam Seva—the spirit of volunteerism—of giving selflessly without expectation, a value that is intrinsic to our culture and important to nurture in today's world.'[21] This spirit is also mentioned in a series of short essays contained in the booklet *Chintan*, which was published with support from the Oil and Natural Gas Corporation (ONGC), a public sector company, to mark the thirtieth anniversary of the organization.[22]

In its long journey since its inception, the organization has established local chapters and sub-chapters across the length and breadth of the country. These chapters and sub-chapters have their own office-bearers. The Delhi-based Central State Facilitators links the Centre with local chapters.[23] This chain of chapters has ensured that the organization has a mechanism to host concerts across the country provided the finances are in place. The finances needed for their concerts are not as high as those required for many professional concerts. This is because performers are paid low honoraria, and travel and accommodation costs are kept to the bare minimum, although more popular and better-known artistes are provided five-star accommodation. A greater number of concerts and the growing web of chapters and sub-chapters denotes an ever-increasing footprint of the organization. Consequently, a single group of musicians is asked to perform more than one concert on the same day. These crowded performance schedules cause physical and mental strain on performers, but many of them perhaps treat the concerts as a way of reaching out to newer audiences. Some probably even agree to perform more than one concert in a single day in order to earn a larger total honorarium. For the organization, the greater number of concerts featuring the same performers in a limited period obviously brings down costs, which would otherwise have been incurred if they were to be presented over an extended period of time or were to be hosted repeatedly.

From an organization that once held lecture-demonstrations in educational institutions, SPIC MACAY can now vie with event management companies, but with the balance tilted heavily in its favour. While the regular event management companies operate in all types of concert venues and for different kinds of clientele, factoring in the professional fees of performers, vendors and others, the organization benefits from not having to deal with much of this. According to the website, educational institutions wishing to host concerts under its banner can do so 'by coordinating with the local chapter of SPIC MACAY. SPIC MACAY usually expects the institution to contribute for the part expenses incurred towards the organisation of the program. This would depend upon various factors. Govt. schools may be exempted from any charges depending upon the fund availability status of SPIC MACAY local chapter.'[24]

The organization lists several activities that are directly linked to Hindustani music. Among these are the lecture-demonstrations and performances held in educational institutions, in annual conventions and other cultural festivals, and programmes specially designed to encourage close interaction between gurus and young students. Major concerts are also held in public areas like parks, but these are organized by the SPIC MACAY Foundation, about which the official website has no information other than the names of its coordinators.[25] Additionally, the organization also liaises with musicians for concerts which are held under the Incredible India programme conducted by the Ministry of Tourism.[26] Some of the video recordings of concerts presented by the organization have been uploaded on the internet for non-commercial public viewing.[27]

In 2013, the organization launched, in partnership with Doordarshan, a television reality show called *Naad Bhed—the Mystery of Sound*, which aimed at 'promoting and popularising Indian classical music and rewarding the best young practitioners of classical music'.[28] Pointing out the difference in the approach of other shows that 'made stars out of middle-class Indians who can sing, dance, emote or laugh in front of the camera, all in the name of TRPs', the organization announced that being 'in the business of preserving and promoting Indian cultural heritage for 36 years' it was 'not looking at finding new "singing stars" '.[29] This, according to the organization, was its way of bringing 'respect for the rich Indian heritage of classical music'.[30] It believed, 'Those who participate or watch the show may or may not become converts to the cause but if a parent were to say with pride that their child participated in this reality show, just as he or she is doing now for other genres, then the show will have achieved its purpose.'[31]

Elimination rounds were held at Doordarshan Kendras in several cities, and the semi-finals and finals were telecast on the DD Bharati channel. Well-known Hindustani and Carnatic musicians were judges in these shows, and even Kiran Seth, though not a practising musician, shared space with these luminaries. Cash awards were announced for winners in different categories, as these were seen as an 'added incentive' to the 'prestige' which the competition offered.[32]

For an organization that celebrated virtues like faith and patience, and pointed out the ephemeral quality of popular music, the decision to undertake a reality show that was conventionally the chosen format for popular music must certainly have been a considered choice.[33] The organization's belief in patience is best represented in these words:

> If you go up too quickly, chances are that you will come down equally fast. This does not imply that one must reduce one's efforts. Only the focus should be on the process. Each step must be worked at very hard and the litmus test is that a sense of satisfaction must be obtained all along.[34]

A reality show, irrespective of which form of music it showcases, is about instant recognition and financial benefits. The selection process may be arduous and long, but the nature of the show blurs these jagged edges. While the reality show conducted by the organization did not have the glamour associated with shows featured on private channels, backed by huge budgets financed by corporate houses, since it was a competition it would seem contrary to the organization's original belief of avoiding competitiveness in the arts.

The organization has received patronage from the corporate sector as well, but its biggest support comes from musicians and other performers of arts, who have always readily agreed to provide their time and expertise, notwithstanding the low honoraria they are offered. The organization acknowledges this:

> Our movement has been lucky enough to get never ending support of our eminent artistes, the Masters, who are sustaining Indian Classical Music, Culture Heritage as the foundation on which the entire country's 5000 years old Heritage is surviving. Such legendary artistes consider performing for SPIC MACAY as their way of giving back to the Society and the Country are[sic]. Some such names are, Ustad Nasir Aminuddin Dagar and Ustad Zia Fariduddin Dagar, Prof. T.N. Krishnan, Pandit Birju Maharaj, Vid. Malavika Sarukkai, Smt. Sonal Mansingh, Ustad Asad Ali Khan,

Ustad Munnawar Ali Khan, Ustad Zia Mohiuddin Dagar, Ustad Bismilla Khan, Pt. Bhimsen Joshi to name a few.[35]

While there is no doubt that the role of eminent performers has been vital and that the above list is only indicative, we do not find mention of the significant role played by the hundreds of musicians who form part of the accompanying ensembles with the more prominent and better-known soloists. This lacuna is perhaps a reflection of the reality that is often seen in the differences in travel and hospitality arrangements for the better-known performers and those for their accompanists. If the stage can be shared by all, it seems out of place to have an inequitable arrangement for basic requirements. This inequality exists in arrangements made by most organizations, government or non-government, and they have become widely accepted norms. Even musicians are accustomed to these differences and rarely protest in favour of a more equitable system.

The organization does not enter into formal contracts with all performers.[36] Such contracts would bring a sense of professionalism to its activities, as they would define the rights and responsibilities of the organization, all soloists and accompanying musicians. The philosophy of the organization as portrayed in the booklet *Chintan* mentioned earlier is that the organization considers it is vital to create a conducive ambience at a concert. It states:

A clean environment, audience seated in the baithak style with footwear neatly arranged outside, no cellular phones permitted inside the hall, no movement and conversation during performances, no [fl]ash photography and no clapping during a performance would go a long way in creating the ambience conducive for touching the highest heights, both by the artists and the rasiks.[37]

These are essential for creating a good concert environment, but it is also important to have a professional approach to the rights of the performing artistes. Strangely, the need for such professionalism does not find any mention amidst all the ideals that are written about copiously.

That SPIC MACAY has made an impact on the government at many points of time is obvious from not only its success in receiving financial support from many ministries and public sector companies, but also from the fact that Kiran Seth, a strong votary of selfless involvement, has been a member of several government bodies and was awarded the Padma Shri for his contribution to the arts in 2009.[38]

The experience derived from years of working on the SPIC MACAY circuit has benefitted many volunteers. Though many of them did not possess any musical knowledge to begin with, or may not even have acquired this along the way, or may not have attended a single concert held outside the organization's fold, they have drawn upon their experience in the organization and have become successful event managers in their own right. The relations they established with musicians during their years in the organization are put to use and they are invited to perform for many other events.

6

New Formats for Dissemination

In the early years of the twentieth century, recording technology enabled the mechanical reproduction of Hindustani music and drastically changed the process of sharing music. It could now be distanced or removed from its creators, and could reach audiences across the country long after it had been performed, a fact that was unimaginable in the times when music was performed only in live concerts. While the advantages of technology were self-evident, the challenges before musicians were large. Performance practice had to suit the new format and musicians had to tailor their repertoire, technique and presentation.

From acoustic recordings to electrical ones, from shellac and vinyl discs to cassettes and compact disks, and then on to file sharing on the internet, the journey of commercially recorded Hindustani music has been long and eventful, significant phases of which have been documented by scholars.[1] On an aesthetic level, this journey has not only seen the disembodiment of music from its original source, but has also altered our perception of the very sound of music. With digital recording technology taking precedence over its analogue predecessor, musicians and listeners are now accustomed to a clean and almost sterile sound. In many ways, this has also impacted the way in which musicians wish to present their music in live concerts, as access to the latest digital sound amplification equipment has enabled them to radically transform their sound in live concerts.[2]

The rising power of the internet and digital technology has provided a huge range of options for distributing music and information related to it to a wider audience across the world. This chapter looks closely at the ways in which record labels, musicians, concert organizers, event managers, young entrepreneurs and audiences have benefitted from this rapidly changing technological world.

Distribution of Recordings

Older formats of music distribution such as cassettes, compact disks, video compact disks and digital versatile discs have given way to audio and video files, which can be made available commercially or non-commercially on the internet. Record labels have modified their operational strategies to match the technology. As a first step, they downsized their recording activities to focus only on film and non-film popular music. Art music sections were closed or they mainly rereleased old recordings.[3] These record labels also began selling old recordings through their websites and on online retail stores.[4] Many physical stores selling records have closed down in major cities for lack of buyers. Some individuals and smaller labels have tried to sell their products at concert venues and have met with some success at larger music festivals. This has been seen at concert venues overseas too, when local organizers have sold recordings which feature the performers they are presenting. In the past, musicians carried their CDs or cassettes overseas and earned from sales at the venues.

Obviously, there were no import duties paid for these sales, with the result that customs officials in many countries became more vigilant when it came to such merchandise being carried without proper paperwork. But irrespective of the method adopted to sell recordings at concert venues in India and abroad, the fact is that sales have dropped significantly due to easy online access to music.

The internet has empowered many independent labels like Underscore Records, Meera Music and Sonic Octaves to publish new recordings and sell them as physical copies or digital downloads through their websites or through other websites.[5] In many such cases, musicians are paid royalties calculated as a percentage of the revenues, although there are cases when labels retain the copyrights on the sound recordings and pay a lump sum fee to the musicians. The sales now are not as large as in the pre-internet days, as recordings are easily available on social media platforms free of cost. Many music lovers often do not hesitate to upload recordings to share them with the larger community of Hindustani music listeners. They do not realize that this reduces sales, and thus, adversely affecting the income of the musicians.

In keeping with changing times, Underscore Records and Sonic Octaves have also sought to create and sell merchandise specifically related to Hindustani music, such as posters, mousepads, T-shirts and key-chains.[6] Underscore Records also includes a print section which has books on the different forms of music and dance in India.[7]

The internet has also given rise to aggregators who negotiate contracts with record labels to access their catalogue for mobile ringtones and caller tunes, or for the sale of recordings through multiple online stores. Hindustani music is not as extensively used for mobile ringtones and caller tunes as film music. In my experience as a director of Underscore Records, aggregators seldom propose a transparent manner of maintaining a log of sales. They prefer making paltry lump sum payments irrespective of the number of downloads. Other aggregators making complete recordings available through multiple online stores pay the producers a part of the total revenue on a periodic basis. In such cases, it defeats the original purpose if aggregators make entire tracks available free of cost on social media platforms like YouTube. This does not help record labels and musicians financially, but aggregators probably view this as an investment to bring more publicity to the music in geographical regions that are not key areas for their sales.[8]

Some musicians who can afford it, get a personal website customized to their specifications. The website allows music lovers to purchase tracks directly from them, thus eliminating any other distribution agency.[9] The customers make payment through credit or debit cards or payment wallets. Sometimes cash-on-delivery option is also given. The card payments entail entering into an agreement with a credit card gateway, which is a difficult exercise for individual musicians. At the present moment, there is no available data to indicate the efficacy of these individual efforts.

In most other cases, musicians distribute their work digitally through established record labels, websites and online stores. Like the unpredictability, the lack of transparency and lack of accountability in the case of sales of CDs through record labels, the digital option available through these stores also has similar constraints in what should be a seamless and transparent arrangement. On the other hand, commercial portals like CDBaby and Amazon can be used to sell recordings directly to the customers without the involvement of a third party. This process is more transparent, as these portals have an easy interface and provide royalty statements and sales figures 24x7. These platforms can be customized to suit particular requirements of Hindustani music, and also other genres and categories of music. The need to engage with them arises since existing platforms are usually designed to sell film or non-film popular music, with the result that they do not address the specific needs of other genres. A typical Hindustani music recording could last for as long as forty-five minutes. Obviously, the pricing for such long tracks needs to be different from song tracks which usually last between three to six minutes. Platforms that adapt to the characteristics of this music go a long way in increasing revenues for musicians. Clarity about legal requirements concerning intellectual property rights (IPRs) and easy access to inventory and sales figures at any time also go a long way in establishing complete transparency, promoting fair business practices and professionalism for everyone involved.

Most Hindustani musicians have yet to realize the potential of distributing their music through such common digital distribution platforms in order to avoid the trouble and financial constraints of setting up their own channels. This is either because they are not aware of these options or are not confident enough to personally handle the modalities.

Facilitating Musicians

Musicians find the internet to be an empowering tool for their careers. Many of them use Facebook, Twitter or WhatsApp to inform music lovers about forthcoming performances and domestic or international concert tours or to obtain performance opportunities. Segments of concerts or photographs from the events are also shared on these platforms. Instagram is also used to post photos, media-sharing sites like YouTube have become an integral part of a young musician's professional life, as it is here that recordings of live concerts are often uploaded for sharing them non-commercially with listeners all over the world. Even concert organizers and event managers use net-based resources to publicize forthcoming concerts, and to post reviews or reports.

An attempt to acquaint musicians and instrument-makers with different web-based applications that could further their online communication abilities and their professional networking opportunities was made in 2009 by Underscore Records Pvt. Ltd.[10] But on the whole, musicians do not seem to have been inspired to use online resources like blogs or even Facebook, Twitter or WhatsApp, to regularly articulate, in some detail, their experiences or opinions about musical or extra-musical matters. They use these resources to largely focus on self-praise or self-projection, rather than reach out to the wider community of Hindustani music lovers and musicians to exchange ideas and information. These resources have also not been used to help musicians come together for a common cause, that is, to understand and analyse the professional challenges they all face in various degrees, and to build a sense of fraternity to strengthen the Hindustani music ecosystem.

Interestingly, some musicians even upload short riyaaz or practice sessions to highlight the manner in which they are working on specific repertoire. This seems to have changed the complexion of riyaaz. From what was once a solitary journey that was inward-looking and dwelt on refining technique, strengthening stamina and internalizing repertoire, these musicians seem to position riyaaz on par with performance, something to be shared with listeners.

The guru–shishya parampara continues to be regarded as the preferred and time-tested choice for training students of Hindustani music who wish to pursue it as a profession. The guru continues to play a vital role in the life of a disciple. Rituals and symbols associated with this traditional form of teaching continue to be followed to this day. Guru-Purnima is observed with much enthusiasm in the month of Ashadh according to the Hindu calendar as a day to celebrate and honour the guru and the role they play in their disciples' lives. Over time, this has acquired festive proportions with performances organized to showcase the capabilities of the shishyas and to publicly acknowledge the guru. Social media has been used to inform music lovers of these celebrations and also to share recordings of recitals held during the day. These webcasts take place even if the celebrations are conducted at the homes of the gurus. Thus, this symbol of guru–shishya relationship is being exhibited more widely than ever before with the help of the internet.

Soundcloud is also used for sharing audio music files and for online teaching, though not in real time. Skype has been popular with those who wish to conduct online teaching sessions, and some musicians or music schools earn tuition fees on a regular basis through such sessions for students in India and overseas. For training students based in other countries, teachers have to decide upon mutually convenient timings, factoring in the time difference between India and the student's country.

Teachers also modify their pedagogic methods to meet the challenges of the new technology. As an example, microphones built into computers and digitally transmitted video images may not clearly represent the student's tonal quality or technique. The delay in transmitting sound, though only as small as approximately three seconds, does not allow the teacher and student to sing or play instruments in unison, as would be the case if both were in the same room. The teacher and student have to compromise and adjust their actions at times, if the internet connection is slow and the audio-video quality is indifferent. Nonetheless, the existence of computer software that allows such long distance teaching is a boon for many.

With growing open-source platforms that can be customized, soon musicians, irrespective of their language of communication, will take to them in a big way. Meanwhile, some musicians also depend upon other music-related sites that carry information about several musicians. Such sites or specific applications that cater to more than one musician are cheaper than maintaining individual websites.[11]

There are also a few applications that are specifically directed to service professional needs of musicians. They help musicians upload their biodata, photos, concert calendar and similar information required to facilitate professional engagements. Some sections of these applications are free, but there are also in-app services which need payment or are based on a revenue sharing system between the service provider and the user of the application.[12]

On the musical front, numerous applications are now available which provide software specifically designed to facilitate the music-making process. For example, there are several applications available for electronic tanpura and electronic tabla, both of which are used in practice and teaching sessions. Both free and paid versions are available, with the paid ones offering extra facilities. The electronic tanpura is also used often in concerts, either as a replacement or a supplement to acoustic tanpuras.[13] The development of such software is not surprising, as it is the next step from the electronic tanpura and electronic tabla machines.[14] The accessibility and mobility afforded by the software-run instruments are far greater than that of acoustic instruments or their earlier electronic incarnations.

Any change in technology is bound to adversely affect certain sections of society. But change is inevitable and conditions need to be created to harness the opportunities afforded by new technology, while not breaking away completely from what was existing until then. The use of applications through smartphones, tablets or computers has been criticized for being counter-productive for Hindustani music, as it is felt that performers and students may give up the original acoustic instruments altogether. As a result, they may not be able to cope with the situation when they have to use these and not the electronic versions. It is feared that the fine art of tuning the tanpura and even playing it in an aesthetic manner could become a thing of the past. Similarly, students may depend entirely on the theka, or the string of syllables that represents the rhythmic cycle as played on the electronic tabla, instead of being able to negotiate the subtleties that emerge when the instrument is actually played. There is definitely an element of truth in this argument. Probably the teachers can train students to first handle an acoustic tanpura and also practice with a tabla player. This can be supplemented with the applications available on different electronic devices. The use of electronic tanpuras is in some ways a threat to the livelihood of tanpura-makers, who have been handcrafting this instrument for generations.[15] The role of the teacher in establishing the importance of using an acoustic tanpura, and in not replacing it completely with an electronic one, would help in ensuring that tanpura makers are not rendered obsolete in the face of changing technology.

Platform for Sharing Information

The space allotted to concert reviews and pre-concert publicity in newspapers and magazines has shrunk in the past two decades or so. Such material now appears on websites featuring culture or arts. In cases where concert information or reviews do appear in print, they acquire a sort of permanence, since the print versions get archived on the digital platform. Some connoisseurs have blogs about their concert experiences, reviews of live concerts or recordings and information about music and musicians.[16] There are also a few instances of academic discussions which are evidently popular among musicians and music lovers.[17] An example of a well-known music critic's work being documented and digitized for online access posthumously is the website dedicated to the writings of Mohan Nadkarni. Such cases, however, are not very common.[18]

Underscore Records had earlier started Sangeet Kosh, a website planned as an Indian music Wikipedia. One part of the website was planned as a directory containing contact details of musicians and all other individuals and agencies connected with music activity. Although this project has not made much headway after the initial stage due to lack of funds, it is mentioned here as it includes information on Hindustani music and its performers, besides many other music systems and genres.[19]

Music lovers have used online resources extensively to interact with their favourite musicians or to inform one another about concerts. Inappropriately, some members of the audience make audio and video recordings of live concerts, without taking permissions from the performers. They upload excerpts or even entire concert recordings on YouTube for free public viewing. While in most cases these persons have no mal-intent, these are certainly bootlegged recordings, and are illegal and unethical. Often the quality of such recordings is quite poor, with the result that the original purpose of sharing good memories of a concert, is defeated. Concert organizers also often record performances without taking permissions from the musicians. They too upload these recordings to attract public attention towards themselves and their activities, rather than to promote the musicians and their music. Since there are many such tracks on the internet, other musicians also upload live concert recordings, which are of an indifferent quality. The emphasis is more on being seen and heard, and not so much on recording quality. In the long run, this trend is not good for Hindustani music as it provides an average representation of the live version. For the musicians, this is unprofitable for two reasons. First, because it does not represent their music in the best manner, and second, because easy access to music on a non-commercial basis does not motivate listeners to purchase recordings.

Another group of people who record live concerts are the audiophiles, who swear by specific recording equipment. Many of them are not musically literate, but are passionate collectors of well-recorded music. Some of them start as curious collectors, but gradually build their recording skills with experience. Usually they do not procure permissions from all members of the ensemble. Their recordings often do not have the correct sound and tonal balance between all the members of the performing group. They may or may not choose to upload these recordings on the internet, but their collections often find the way to other collections and archives. Once this happens, there is no telling when the material will be uploaded on the internet.

The internet and all that it offers can be harnessed in a larger and better manner to create awareness about Hindustani music, increase audiences and promote networking possibilities. For example, resources that will enable all stakeholders to understand legal and commercial issues regarding music can be made available online. Similarly, music appreciation programmes can be undertaken through podcasts and special multimedia features. Steps in this direction have been sporadic and concerted efforts are required to be made over a long period for a noticeable and meaningful impact.[20]

7

Hindustani Music Overseas

No discussion on the present state of Hindustani music would be complete without considering the audience it has gained across the continents in the twentieth century, through government or privately sponsored performances and educational programmes. For musicians, concert tours abroad seem to add the gloss necessary for their careers to be regarded successful in the public eye. Musicians craving for performance opportunities overseas often accept terms that may not be completely satisfactory. Far from the image that overseas tours conjure up, most musicians do not necessarily return with a sizeable sum of money. It matters little whether these tours feature public concerts or those held in private residences, more popularly known as 'house concerts'. Such tours find mention in musicians' biodata, whether the concerts are formal or informal.

Performing abroad is not a new phenomenon. Musicians have always been itinerant, as their profession has required them to travel far and wide to perform for new audiences. There are

numerous documented cases of Hindustani musicians performing
overseas even as early as the nineteenth century. Rudra veena player
Musharraf Khan (d.1909), a court musician at Alwar, performed in
London in 1886.[1] A few years later, sarod player Karamatullah Khan,
(c.1848/1851–1933) and his younger brother, Asadullah Khan
alias Kaukab Khan (1858–1915), performed in Paris in 1902.[2] Sitar
player Yusuf Ali Khan (1887–1962) of Lucknow was sent to London
along with his brother, tabla player Gurbat Ali, to perform during
the Coronation Festival Exhibition in 1910.[3] Rudra veena player
and vocalist Inayat Khan (1882–1927), more popularly known as
Sufi or Hazrat Inayat Khan, grandson and disciple of Maula Baksh of
Baroda, toured all over Europe and USA between 1910 and 1926.[4]
Sarod player Allauddin Khan (1862–1972) travelled with Uday
Shankar's dance troupe across Europe.[5] Vocalist Omkarnath Thakur
visited Italy as a participant of the International Music Conference
in Florence held in 1933.[6] Scholar-musician B.R. Deodhar travelled
to Europe in 1933 to attend the World Music Conference in
Florence. He also visited Austria and Prague.[7] Rudra veena player
Shamshuddin Khan and vocalist Jagannathbuwa Purohit (1904–
1968) were two other musicians to have performed overseas in the
pre-Independence period.[8] Vocalist Keshavbuwa Ingle travelled to
East Africa in 1938.[9] An organization called the Asian Music Circle
was also set up in the UK in 1946 to promote Indian and Asian arts
and culture. It featured performances by eminent musicians like
Ravi Shankar, Ali Akbar Khan (1922–2009), Vilayat Khan (1928–
2004), Alla Rakha and Chatur Lal (1925–1965).[10]

Except for a few cases, there is inadequate information about
the nature of performances that featured musicians who journeyed
outside India in the nineteenth and early twentieth centuries. The
colonial government did not support Indian musicians for their
concert trips and it was only in the 1950s that government support
to such tours was given.

Indian Council for Cultural Relations

Established in 1950 by Maulana Abul Kalam Azad, India's first education minister after Independence, the Indian Council for Cultural Relations (ICCR) lists the following objectives in its Memorandum of Association:

To participate in the formulation and implementation of policies and programmes relating to India's external cultural relations;
to foster and strengthen cultural relations and mutual understanding between India and other countries;
to promote cultural exchange with other countries and peoples;
to establish and develop relations with national and international Organization [sic] in the field of culture;
to take such measures as may be required to further these objectives.[11]

The ICCR is an autonomous body under the Ministry of External Affairs.[12] As a major step towards creating international understanding through culture, the ICCR has sent several cultural troupes to various parts of the world, showcasing diverse styles of music and dance, among other arts from India. Other than tours of individual performers, it has also organized special Festivals of India in many countries.[13] Some cultural centres set up by the ICCR across the world employ music teachers for a fixed period of time.[14] The work envisaged by the ICCR is therefore of great significance to the propagation of music and for providing opportunities to performers.

To be able to perform in concerts supported by the ICCR or to seek financial or similar aid for concerts from the ICCR, musicians need to be empanelled with the council. A committee consisting of performers and scholars from different arts scrutinize the applications. Three categories of artistes have been created, namely, proficient, established and outstanding, and candidates are placed in one of these categories depending on the committee's assessment of their merit.[15] The committee's decision with regard to an applicant's empanelment is final. The absence of any mention of parameters for listing candidates under one or the other category shows a lack of transparency, and leads to suspicion and discontentment among candidates.[16]

The list of empanelled artistes and scholars available on the official website has not been updated after 28 February 2017. Some of them have already passed away, and yet their names were included. Many were past their performing prime, or had not been heard in live concerts across the country. Evidently, there was a huge gap between what the list indicated and the actual ground reality. Perhaps, it is unwieldy for the central office of the ICCR to keep track of such information from all over the country, but its regional offices should be able to update the list every year or so.[17]

Apart from featuring Indian performers in concerts held outside the country, the ICCR also provides scholarships to international students desiring to learn Indian music and dance. Institutions and gurus permitted to teach such scholars under this scheme have been listed on the ICCR website. From a total of fifty-three institutions and gurus for music and dance, only ten are for Hindustani music. The parameters for choosing these institutions and gurus have not been provided either.[18]

The ICCR executes cultural projects on behalf of the external affairs ministry, culture ministry, Lok Sabha and Ministry of Overseas Indian Affairs, which comes under the external affairs ministry. It also helps non-governmental organizations in Delhi–National Capital Region by providing empanelled performers or financial support for cultural activities held in the region. A monthly programme called *Horizon Series*, featuring two performances of Indian artistes, is held at the ICCR's Azad Bhavan auditorium in

New Delhi. The ICCR also organizes monthly programmes as a part of the *Horizon Series* in each of its regional offices across the country. There are no details regarding the financial emoluments provided to performers featured in such concerts.[19]

Despite its avowed mission to encourage cultural relations between India and other countries, we seldom come across an active effort on the part of the ICCR to support intercultural dialogue involving Hindustani and non-Indian musicians in workshops and performances. It is a pity that such dialogues have to wait until sponsorship comes from non-Indian sources or from organizations in India which are mainly concerned with specific events, rather than developing a long-term action plan in this regard.

Given the situation that musicians find themselves in vis-à-vis the ICCR, it is not surprising that many of them have come to regard it as a bureaucratic set up which lacks transparency in its empanelment process and in its choice of empanelled performers for concerts. The fees and allowances that are provided to performers are far below what their expectations are or what they would otherwise be paid. While the unhappiness is not voiced openly, it is quite clear when matters are discussed privately. Noted musicians are often not keen to perform under the ICCR banner unless the occasion brings them a lot of publicity, or they are coaxed to do so by top officials or those at the ministerial level. The lack of interest is proof enough of their disenchantment with the situation.[20]

But in cases where musicians do travel as members of delegations sent out by the ICCR, it would not be out of place to expect them to be able to articulate and inform foreign audiences about their music and to likewise be apprised of the music and musicians of the countries they would be visiting. We would imagine that this would be a necessary first step towards inculcating a sense of understanding and appreciation between cultures. However, a concert tour organized and sponsored by the ICCR is regarded by musicians as yet another performance opportunity and not as a means to fulfil a larger vision. The absence of any initiative on the part of the ICCR to encourage musicians to adopt a more proactive role in establishing meaningful dialogue across cultures can only mean that the desire of the organization is limited to completing a set of events each year, which include organizing and supporting foreign concert tours. Clearly, this is far from the objectives that the organization set out to achieve in the first place.

Ravi Shankar, Ali Akbar Khan, Alla Rakha

While the initiatives of the ICCR gave a stamp of formality to concert tours, it was probably the tours undertaken by maestros Ravi Shankar and Ali Akbar Khan that ushered in a new era of Hindustani music concerts in the West and, in many ways, set the stage for subsequent tours undertaken by other performers. The first LP or long-playing record of this music titled *Music of India: Morning and Evening Ragas* featuring sarod player Ali Akbar Khan was released by the New York-based Angel Records.[21] While in the USA in 1955, Khan had three concerts and was the first performer of Indian art music to appear on American television. Renowned violinist Yehudi Menuhin (1916–1999) played a significant role at each of these performances.[22]

The 1960s saw the youth in the West rebel against the establishment. Many sought sources of solace, peace, novelty and more. India was seen as an exotic charm and Hindustani music was one of the key areas that attracted considerable interest. There were enormous challenges faced by Indian musicians playing for largely uninitiated audiences during this period. As ethnomusicologist Gerry Farrell says:

When Indian musicians first started to perform in the West in larger numbers in the 1960s, they were perplexed by the attitude of their new audiences, mainly the young, who slouched around smoking, stoned drunk, or generally drifting in semi-consciousness to the music.[23]

At that time, Ravi Shankar described such situations quite graphically:

> I have been facing a surprising problem with some of my concert audiences since about 1965, especially in England. I found many young people who were 'high'; sitting in the front rows of the hall, they were altogether in another world. Often, too, they sat there in front of me carrying on indecently with their girl friends or boy friends, and many of them even lit cigarettes (if that, in fact, was what they were) whenever they pleased. Their conduct disgusted me, for too many people in this dazed stupor send out bad vibrations that are extremely upsetting.[24]

It was amid these circumstances that Hindustani music was established in the West. In 1966, Ravi Shankar collaborated with Yehudi Menuhin at the Bath Festival in England and recorded an album with him titled *West Meets East*.[25] The following year, the two maestros, accompanied by tabla wizard Alla Rakha, performed at the United Nations General Assembly in New York to celebrate Human Rights Day on 10 December 1967. The performance was filmed and broadcast worldwide, and Ravi Shankar and Alla Rakha became the earliest artistes of Hindustani music to be watched by a global audience.[26] Ravi Shankar's Kinnara School and Ali Akbar Khan's Ali Akbar College of Music, set up in the USA in the 1960s, also encouraged non-Indians to learn Hindustani music.[27]

Soon, Western jazz and rock musicians began taking a keen interest in Indian music, spreading it among newer audiences. Ravi Shankar's collaborations with George Harrison, a member of the The Beatles, in the live *Concert for Bangladesh*, and the album and film with the same name, took Hindustani music to an extraordinarily large Western audience. With *the Concert for Bangladesh* reaching gold record status and receiving the Grammy Award for Album of the Year in 1972, Ravi Shankar, Ali Akbar Khan and Alla Rakha gained an unprecedented exposure to Western audiences.[28]

Ravi Shankar's *Festival of India* concerts and album of 1968 was followed in 1974 by a sequel called *Ravi Shankar's Music Festival of India*. This was a collaborative venture with George Harrison. Both concert tours and recordings included top-notch musicians from India, many of who later toured the West extensively and become acclaimed performers there.[29]

Thus, the West's association with Indian music was inspired by many circumstances. As succinctly put by ethnomusicologist Daniel M. Neuman:

> The cultural motivations for the Western engagement with Indian music were complex and can only be adumbrated here: a source of new sounds for musicians, a celebration of the mystical and discovery of ecstasy by seekers, a search for the exotic by the alienated, and, viewed more generally, a symbol complex conveying seeming certainty in the culture blur of the 1960s.[30]

Neuman also enumerates the features that made Indian art music more accessible in North America, like the improvisatory nature of the music which allowed it to be adapted to varied conditions and its virtuosic aspect, particularly in the case of drumming. He mentions that the small size of the musical ensembles made them more mobile and less expensive to tour, and that performances could even be held in an informal home setting.[31]

Hindustani Music for the Indian Diaspora and at Foreign Universities

House concerts became particularly popular with the Indian diaspora. Organizations dedicated to presenting Hindustani concerts were founded in the USA, Canada, the UK, the UAE and other countries, all of which had a significant presence of Indians consisting of middle-class professionals like doctors, professors and engineers. Many of these organizations worked on a subscription model, much like the music circles in India. Some of the music circles in other countries continue to exist to this day. The Indian Classical Music Circle of Austin was founded in 1975 and revived in 1991.[32] Basant Bahar was started in the San Francisco Bay Area in the early 1980s.[33] Indian Classical Music Circle of Dallas–Fort Worth was started in 1983.[34] A rare example of an organization set up by musicians to promote music concerts was seen in the case of The Music Circle, established in Los Angeles in 1973 by sitar maestro Ravi Shankar and his disciple Harihar Rao (1927-2013).[35] Outside the USA, The Raga Mala Society of Calgary was founded in Canada in 1975.[36] In the UK, the Asian Music Circuit began its activities in 1989.[37]

Concomitantly, there was a growing interest in Hindustani music among non-Indians, who were either studying this music styke, involved in music research or were interested in Indian culture. This was a period when ethnomusicology courses called 'Introduction to World Music' or 'World Music' were offered by music and anthropology departments in foreign universities.[38] This resulted in the inclusion of Hindustani music in some of these courses and musicians from India were invited by these universities to conduct lecture-demonstrations, workshops and masterclasses. In some cases, musicians would be invited as artistes-in-residence, which would require their presence on the university campus for longer periods of time, from a few months to an entire academic year.[39]

A major initiative undertaken by the University of Pittsburgh needs to be mentioned here. Starting in 1985–86 as the main sponsor for the Indian art music segment of the Festival of India in the United States, the University of Pittsburgh went on to enter into a bilateral exchange programme with the ICCR, which involved annual visits of four groups of Indian musicians to the USA for performances, lectures and workshops on Indian art music. According to the terms of this arrangement:

> The international travel expenses usually were borne by ICCR and a consortium of American universities/colleges and other similar organizations interested in Indian classical music provided funds for health insurance, domestic travel, living expenses and honoraria payments of visiting musicians on a mutually agreed basis. The University also agreed to provide assistance in all matters related to the US Immigration and the Federal income tax regulations.[40]

Under this programme more than 1700 performances and 300 workshops were held in over 80 universities, colleges, schools and other organizations. Over US$1.80 million were raised in the USA and Canada for these activities.

The success of this initiative led to the establishment of the Center for the Performing Arts of India (CPAI) in 1992 as a component of the University Center for International Studies.[41] The center did not have a physical facility and paid staff. Balwant N. Dixit, Professor of pharmacology, was the director of the center and his wife, Vidya Dixit, assisted him in all activities undertaken by it. It was later closed after several years of successful planning and execution of many concert tours. In the words of Balwant N. Dixit:

> After my retirement in 2013–14 I decided to close the center since the University was not much interested in continuing it. Nationally, it also became clear to us that interest in Indian classical music in the USA has declined significantly. I was concerned about the quality of organization if it was transferred to some other entity.[42]

Over the decades, Hindustani music concert tours have primarily been organized in the USA, Canada, the UK, Germany, Netherlands, Italy and France, and to a lesser extent in Australia,

New Zealand, Japan and a few other countries. On some occasions, the ICCR has provided travel grants to musicians traveling to these countries, and has funded tours that took place as part of Festivals of India. Concert tours to East European and SAARC countries have also been undertaken under the aegis of the ICCR.

Sometimes, organizations for Hindustani music in the USA and elsewhere have access to grants from their governments. Hindustani music in the UK received a significant impetus when the UK government made grants through the Arts Council to organizations set up to project multicultural activities. The extent of funding in the UK is possibly due to the existence of a larger Indian diaspora there, even though individuals working in organizations have informally complained of severe cutbacks in the past few years. The diaspora in the UK has been living there for a significantly longer period of time, thus perhaps helping increase its influence on the government. It would be relevant to compare the extent of funding that Hindustani music receives overseas to what it receives in India. The processes involved in inviting grant applications, sanctioning them and assessing their impact at the end of the grant period could also be compared to the lacunae that may exist in the Indian context.

The number of universities abroad offering courses in Indian music has reduced. Few overseas institutions offer courses expressly dedicated to Hindustani music performance. Noteworthy among these are the California-based CalArts and the Department of Ethnomusicology at the University of California, Los Angeles.[43] The Rotterdam Conservatory of Music at Codarts in Netherlands offers courses in Hindustani music.[44] Codarts Research, the research wing of Codarts, has published educational material related to Hindustani music.[45] I have mentioned earlier the University of Washington in Seattle, USA, and the School of Oriental and African Studies, London, UK, also have archived material relating to Hindustani music.[46]

Contractual Terms for Overseas Tours

As a part of their schedule overseas, musicians are involved in multiple activities. Depending upon the type of invitation extended by the organizers, they perform, conduct lecture-demonstrations, workshops and/or masterclasses, appear for interviews on local radio and television programmes, and even record for record labels if such offers come their way. In some cases, they are even invited to participate in intercultural musical collaborations. Many musicians seek opportunities abroad once they gain a foothold in a particular country.

In the past the arrangements between musicians and host organizations were primarily informal in nature, except in the case of universities, but today contracts are often drawn up in the form of a legally binding agreement. This has become necessary due to stricter immigration laws, which have ensured, among other things, that musicians do not travel for professional engagements on incorrect visas. Some countries need special performer's or entertainment visas, whereas others do not have a separate visa for performers, provided they leave the country within a stipulated period of time. The existence of strong musicians' unions in some countries requires their prior permission. Hence, details related to schedule, travel, fees, hospitality, publicity, permissions for recording concerts, visa requirements, union permissions and such matters find mention in contracts.

Contractual arrangements have streamlined the processes. They have impacted the equation between the main performers and accompanying musicians in a favourable manner. Earlier, the accompanists were at the mercy of the main performer for all arrangements during the tour, as the professional agreement was between the main performer and the host organization. The understanding between the main performer and accompanying musicians was of no concern to the host. Matters have now improved and, in many cases, separate contracts are drawn up between the accompanists and the host. Dixit says that the CPAI signed separate contracts with the main and accompanying musicians of each ensemble to prevent any problems between them, and to ensure compliance with legal requirements as prescribed by immigration and taxation authorities for touring musicians performing in the USA and Canada.[47]

The empowerment of accompanists has also resulted in instances of some of them acting as tour managers and entering into agreements with host organizations for liaising with multiple main performers. Organizations choose this method to capitalize on the relations that these accompanists may enjoy with many soloists. The importance of the accompanists is also seen in the case of those who have temporarily or permanently migrated overseas and have established their base there. The network they build with host organizations as a result of their presence in that country is put to good use when inviting main performers, as they may act as tour managers or provide accompaniment, or play both roles. This reduces the costs involved in bringing accompanists from India and also gives concert opportunities to musicians who have migrated there.

There is no doubt that overseas concert tours have brought a degree of professionalism to the manner in which musicians negotiate their professional engagements abroad. Organizations outside India have also tried to add production values to their concerts. Sandeep Virdee, artistic director of the Darbar Festival, UK, has referred to the production values that his organization has sought to put in place:

> Nowadays, with the consumerism we began to focus on production values. . . . So we concentrated in terms of how does the stage look like, how does the lighting work, what microphone technology are we using, what sound engineers are we using, etc. All these things

matter hugely to the next generation. If we are saying that we want to do something for the next generation, we have to think about what they are used to, and deliver that quality for them.[48]

But such initiatives often stop short of establishing complete professionalism in overseas concert tours. For example, organizers try to minimize costs by reducing performers' fees, insisting on the inclusion of local accompanists rather than flying in musicians of the main performer's choice from India, making hospitality arrangements with Indian families rather than in hotels and compromising on production quality, audio equipment and personnel to handle the equipment. Some organizations, breaching the terms of contracts that they sign with musicians or in the absence of permissions, publish recordings of live concerts on multiple platforms. There may not be any commercial purpose for such actions, but the reality remains that it is done without prior permission from the performers as required by law.

There are many organizations that stand out as exceptions to all this. Often compromises or contraventions mentioned here are made when organizers face a shortage of funds and lack professional help to plan and execute concert tours. Much of the work in arranging concerts is often done by volunteers to offset the mounting costs. But organizers cannot justiy their unprofessional actions by crediting themselves for having taken the initiative of propagating Hindustani music in the West in the first place. Neither organizers nor musicians can claim the sole credit for this.

Of course, musicians have also exhibited a lack of professionalism on many occasions. From not travelling on proper visas to carrying their commercial recordings to other countries without proper import licences, to transgressing contractual terms by performing for other organizers or at house concerts without prior permission from the original host, to placing unreasonable demands on their hosts, musicians too have been responsible for situations that are far from pleasant.

Presenting Hindustani music overseas has been a joint effort of the organizers and musicians, often with aims that are more immediate and personal, and not as idealistic as portrayed otherwise by both sides. Organizers of Indian descent, some of whose families have lived overseas for generations, may be driven by nostalgia or a desire to rediscover their Indian roots, or to even assert their cultural identity in a foreign land. On the other hand, musicians undertake concert tours overseas expressly to further their careers and not necessarily to selflessly spread Hindustani music.

Concert tours overseas have definitely helped to attract more listeners. Musicians who have migrated overseas conduct regular classes for teaching Hindustani music. In some cases, the classes are called schools of music, which may lead a person to imagine a full-fledged building which houses the school premises. Often, the teaching takes place at the musician's or student's home, or in a rented space which is not necessarily run only as a music school. The website for the Pandit Jasraj Institute of Music for Research, Artistry and Appreciation—the Mewati Gurukul (PJIM) provides details about eight locations for its music classes in the USA.[49]

Hindustani music through scholarship and performance has left an indelible mark in many parts of the world. After the concert tours mentioned earlier, iconic tabla player Zakir Hussain, santoor maestro Shivkumar Sharma and bansuri virtuoso Hariprasad Chaurasia have been prominent performers on the international circuit. The popularity of this music in many parts of the world, particularly in Europe and the USA, is reflected in the presence of record companies based outside India which have published recordings of this music during the past few decades. Many of these have been live concert recordings, which were recorded during concert tours overseas. These record labels are owned primarily by expatriate Indians. Significant among them have been Chhanda Dhara from Germany, Navras Records from the UK and Neelam Audio & Video Inc. from the USA.[50] Nimbus Records from the UK also published Hindustani music extensively.[51] In 1991, Zakir Hussain also established a record label in the USA called Moment! Records.[52] There have also been several foreign record labels like India Archive Music and Makar devoted only to Indian art music and run by non-Indians.[53]

Hindustani music has benefitted greatly from its contact with non-Indian audiences, particularly those in the West. Non-Indians have also contributed through their scholarship. Many have become performers of this music in their own right, and often perform in music circles and festivals in India. Musicologist Joep Bor goes as far as to state that Indian music has stayed alive because it has fed on the West and vice versa, and that this mutually beneficial association will keep the music alive in future as well.[54]

Conclusion

For some readers, the facts presented in this book may paint a gloomy picture of the Hindustani music ecosystem, and the changes that have occurred over time may appear as a worrisome departure from the rich and fascinating past. Well-meaning musicians and administrators have spoken and written about the need to 'save' Hindustani music from decay and extinction. But our past experiences prove that this genre has not only managed to survive in the face of challenges, but has also thrived at several points in time. It is understandable for those who have spent decades listening to Hindustani music to be nostalgic, but we must recognize that this could be an impediment to even the smallest of changes, leave alone radical ones, which may be required for a healthier climate to prevail. For example, it is pointless to continue with obsolete sound systems or to refuse to renovate concert venues only because reputed artistes of yesteryears performed in the same circumstances several decades ago. It is important to change mind-sets in order to take a leap forward. Therefore, any thoughts of 'rescuing Hindustani music from the throes of death' are best abandoned at the earliest, as they obfuscate the real issues and do not inspire any confidence, particularly among the present generation.

Conversely, others may feel that musicians, scholars and students have shown great resilience in the face of an inevitable reality, but that their strength and resolve will finally help lead them to a happy future.

Perhaps each of these differing perspectives about the Hindustani music environment holds some elements of truth. It is impossible to provide a clear roadmap for moving towards a sustainable future, but I hope to indicate some areas in which tangible efforts can be made.

Enlightened patronage

First and foremost, those concerned about the future of Hindustani music should consider the interests of its performers. Often, non-musicians speak vociferously about promoting and propagating art music without considering the trying financial circumstances that musicians have to face. Regrettably, some musicians who head institutions also hold the same opinions without so much as a care for their colleagues. It must be understood that musicians too live in the real world, not an idyllic one, face uncertainties of every kind and, despite this, choose to pursue their profession. Hereditary musicians, the original custodians of this music, have managed to survive due to their adaptive strategies, but they have had to accept that first-generation-musicians are active in the field and that they have to share limited performance opportunities with them.

Notwithstanding the accolades and awards that have been showered on individual musicians in India and overseas, including national civilian awards like the Padma Shri, the Padma Bhushan, the Padma Vibhushan and even the Bharat Ratna, the general lot of

musicians face an uphill task in negotiating an unpredictable career.[1]
Even world-renowned sitar player Ravi Shankar, the one Indian
musician who has been considered the epitome of success, spoke of
the difficult times that musicians were going through: 'A few people
like myself who are the top superstars have fewer problems, we can
manage—if not at home, then abroad. But most of the classical
musicians here have not made it to that superstar level. They are
struggling.'[2]

Shankar felt that young performers could not survive on art
music concerts alone and had to embrace other forms of music:

> We have reached a dangerous crossroad, and the danger is the
> survival of our classical music. . . . We also have wonderful
> sponsorships from cigarette or liquor companies for music festivals
> and all that. But the serious young musicians have to start playing
> jazz or pop to earn more money.[3]

From the evidence provided in this book, it is clear that the present
situation has arisen due to the absence of active and enlightened
patronage to Hindustani music from the state, corporate entities
and civil society in general. It would be a truism to say that a creative
community equipped with a wealth of talent and imagination
is an essential prerequisite for the arts to flourish in any society,
but it is as important to have an audience that provides adequate
and sustained financial support to the arts and its practitioners.
This is not to suggest that the quality of art or its existence can be
measured by the extent of financial support it receives, as artistic
activity has been pursued even in the absence of monetary backing
and in the most trying circumstances. But the general experience is
that patronage has played a crucial role in supporting culture and
tradition. Whether it is to enhance the personal prestige of patrons
and help them acquire social and political legitimacy in society,
or to gain public recognition through media announcements, it is

obvious that specific interests have motivated patronage since time immemorial. Patronage, as pointed out by historian Romila Thapar, 'becomes the legitimizer of the patron and, in addition, to a possible role of authority, may take on other social roles.'[4] Indeed, if this were not true, silent and anonymous philanthropy would have been the order of the day.

Thus, the future of the arts can appear promising only if society chooses to celebrate creative efforts from the past and respects present artistic work and its creators. Society also needs to encourage innovation, not merely as a novelty, but as a vital element for keeping traditions alive and relevant. Layers and subtexts that lie hidden behind artistic activity also need to be dispassionately examined.

Periodic review

Disappointingly, support for Hindustani music has come in spurts, often to boost the public image of individuals, the state or corporate patrons. There is a general lack of imagination in developing a long-term perspective for this music and to advance policies which could strengthen its status in society. Non-governmental organizations such as music clubs and music circles have worked since the nineteenth century towards promoting and propagating Hindustani music by providing musicians with performance and teaching opportunities. Institutions set up by the government and many ministries at the Union and state levels have also initiated policies which have benefitted this system of music and its performers. Patronage from the corporate sector in several forms has been useful too.

But it appears that these agencies have seldom attempted understanding the perspective that had prompted them to support this music in the first place. Often, this support was closely influenced by the politics of cultural nationalism from the nineteenth century and is not in consonance with the present. There are very few instances of agencies reviewing their original vision, policies and specific activities in order to evaluate if they continue to be relevant, if they require any alteration or if they need to be completely forsaken in a drastically changed environment. In the rare instances that such reviews have been undertaken, the style of functioning has been altered superficially while retaining the basic objectives. In such cases, it is also unclear if the comments and suggestions made have been acted upon. For example, there is no clear indication from annual reports of music-related individual institutions working under the Ministry of Culture whether specific measures have been taken to address issues raised by the HPC. The HPC held that the quality of clerical staff in the ministry 'is not attuned to look at their work in the ministry as anything but files and papers, with no creative ideals and little artistic or aesthetic sensitivity'.[5] It was probably for this reason that the HPC recommended that every two years all staff at the ministry should undergo a week-long orientation course designed by experts, which would provide an introduction to arts and aesthetics, cultural ethos and administration related to cultural activities and also to global cultural trends. Similarly, it recommended that new entrants to the ministry should be provided a brief regarding cultural theory and arts appreciation.[6] While other ministries were supported by experts, the HPC stated, 'The Ministry of Culture has none of these. It instead behaves as if it knows best for its institutions... We need expertise today in the Ministry.'[7] The HPC recommended that young people, who were passionate about the arts, should be engaged on contractual basis to improve the management of cultural institutions under the ministry spread across the country.[8]

Curiously, the HPC recommended that the government should set up Indian Institutes of Art and Culture with 'an academic stream for the management of art and culture, including art administration, and the management of cultural institutions' and with representation of 'all major art forms in one campus', when it actually found the ministry wanting in its administration of existing institutions.[9] We would imagine that new institutions would only increase the workload of the ministry, thus adversely affecting the outcome. That apart, a detailed account of actions taken on the basis of these and other such recommendations would prove beneficial to arriving at a better understanding of institutional working. This is also imperative since these institutions are funded by the public exchequer and are, therefore, answerable to the public at large.

The Ministry of Culture also needs to re-examine its grant-making policies as well as those of institutions falling under its purview. Transparency and accountability on its part as well as on the part of the grantee need to be firmly embedded in the process. The grant amounts also need to be reviewed, as paltry sums cannot really benefit the grantee over long periods.

Dialogue with musicians

Major policy decisions taken by governments with regard to the economy, education and such other matters, also need to factor in their impact on arts practitioners and their fields of work. The most recent events of demonetization and the introduction of Goods and Services Tax (GST) have adversely impacted several concert organizers, musicians and instrument makers. For one, many of the smaller transactions in the world of Hindustani music took place in cash, but the lack of cash for months after demonetization reduced the amount of work that would otherwise have been available to performers and instrument-makers in normal circumstances. This is not to say that the experience was different from what had been witnessed by most other sections of Indian society during these days. It is only to point out that yet another section also suffered the consequences of demonetization. In the case of the new GST legislation, the list of exemptions includes concerts that have ticket rates under ₹500 each and indigenous handcrafted instruments.[10] Performers earning less than ₹1,50,000 in a single concert are exempt from GST, but there seems to be some debate among musicians and tax experts whether this rule applies only if the total annual income is not more than ₹20,00,000 or if it holds good irrespective of the total annual income. Some experts believe that if the total annual income is more than this amount, the fees for every concert attract an 18 per cent GST.[11] This is in addition to the tax that may be levied on the total income. Understandably, performers expect organizers to pay the additional GST component. This deters organizers from inviting performers falling in the GST category, much as they would like to avail of their popularity. Organizers believe that the absence of more popular performers hampers the sale of tickets and reduces the possibility of procuring sponsorships. With the number of programmes reducing as a result of these tax implications, this may unfavourably affect younger performers, who could also have been featured, had the programmes taken place. For the majority of performers, not only do their concerts not yield high fees but on the rare occasion that they can earn more than ₹1,50,000 in a single concert an 18 per cent GST is levied on the amount. We may argue that the GST component does not affect a majority of performers, as their total earnings in a single year are well within the taxable limit. But would it not have been more reasonable and simpler to tax the total income at a higher rate or to levy a GST rate that is more manageable in a market which is always short of funds? Most performers also supplement their concert income with teaching assignments, recording sessions, and other music-related activities. In fact, income from concerts almost always falls short of what would be required by most musicians. Income from these additional activities would fall within the purview of GST, since they are not related to live performance. If the government wishes to bring all services within the tax net, it seems logical to expect more flexibility on this count. Only a detailed survey will help us reach conclusions in this context, but the significant point here is that representatives from the stakeholders need to be constantly consulted or engaged by policy makers in order to avoid widespread panic and frustration. Typically, consultations related to the performing arts in such contexts involve representatives from the film industry. I have yet to come across representatives from the traditional performing arts who participated in these discussions.

In the context of CSR, the government could encourage companies in clearer terms to support Hindustani music or for that matter traditional music of all kinds. Likewise, the government could ensure that its mandate extends not only to supporting not-for-profit organizations, but also initially to new organizations or companies that may be set up to work in this area. Naturally, policies would need to be framed for the latter to be undertaken within reasonable limits. Additionally, the government through its relevant agencies at the centre and state levels could prepare detailed periodic surveys that would provide information regarding those involved in the practice of Hindustani music. This information would be significant for planning and executing future projects.

Ideally, transparency, accountability and professionalism should be made non-negotiable given the mutual distrust that exists among all the stakeholders. This should be particularly so in case of institutions which fall within the purview of the union or state governments, directly or indirectly. Old contracts need to be reviewed and should be replaced by new ones which serve the interests of all parties concerned. Likewise, permissions for recording live concerts and for the public sharing of recorded material need to be taken from musicians by government and non-government agencies.[12] Such measures would go a long way in creating a space for dialogue between the stakeholders and for encouraging each group to go beyond mere platitudes regarding the state of Hindustani music. They would ensure that everyone listens to subtle nuances in the conversations that ensue. Obviously, this means that musicians would need to be an integral part of this dialogue and their voices would need to be heard through representatives and not through nominees appointed by institutions. An example is the absence of any transparency with regard to the collections housed in the NCAA repository, discussed earlier in the book.

I have come across some private collectors who believe that the legal advice they have received with regard to their collections of concert recordings informs them that they do not require permissions from the performers to commercially release these recordings because the copyright period has expired. However, in most of these cases, I have observed that their stand on such issues is driven entirely by commercial gain and does not actually respect the law of the land.

Need for professionalism

In the case of public broadcasters, there is no doubt that AIR and DD possess a treasure trove of archival recordings holding great potential for future distribution. Organized commercial distribution of these recordings on multiple formats, particularly digital platforms, is the crying need of the hour. But it is equally important that present-day musicians are also provided attention without reducing the immense significance that these old recordings have. AIR and DD need to revisit their earlier programming patterns for Hindustani music and revamp them in consultation with performers, so as to increase audiences without diluting the musical content. I am not for a moment suggesting that all officials or artistes employed at AIR and DD lack the motivation or expertise to examine and revise current programming periodically, but their hands are perhaps tied by the bureaucratic set-up and by policy decisions from higher-ups that they have to execute unfailingly.

On their part, musicians would need to move away from their current obsession of securing awards instituted by the union or

state governments or by autonomous bodies and would instead
have to consider themselves as part of a larger fraternity.[13] It is
common to hear stories about one or the other musician indulging
in nepotism and corruption to secure awards for themselves, their
kin or disciples. Regrettably, they appear less watchful of policy
decisions, which impact the present and future of Hindustani
music. To mention just one experience that reflects the apathy, I
had prepared a questionnaire and circulated it among a hundred
musicians in the age group of twenty-five to thirty-five.[14] The idea
was to conduct a survey that would ascertain the challenges faced by
young musicians in their pursuit of Hindustani music performance
and teaching as a viable profession. Despite repeated requests from
the team collecting the data, there was abysmal response from those
approached. Musicians have been commenting and sharing posts
about politicians and political parties since the general elections
of 2014, but they do not voice their opinions publicly on matters
that directly concern their field. Perhaps this is due to fear of
repercussions that may come from those heading the government
or non-government institutions or to prevent any antagonism that
would lead to a loss of concert opportunities or accolades that they
may otherwise receive. Not only are there no attempts towards
negotiating with the government, I have yet to come across a
collective effort to plan and provide welfare measures for musicians
past their performing prime, to design ways of rehabilitating
musicians who have suffered physical injuries or psychological
setbacks while pursuing professional assignments or to negotiate
special insurance policies for handcrafted instruments.[15] Clearly,
a positive collective effort on the part of musicians in place of
an opportunistic one would go a long way in adding weight to
discussions among stakeholders.

Some musicians have made attempts at professionalizing their
work by engaging managers, associating with artiste management
companies and hiring publicists who may also handle their social

media accounts. But more could be done to empower musicians to further financial gains through the commercial distribution of their music through multiple online stores. It is obvious that the mobility of music made possible by online streaming options or sales of digital downloads has attracted many big players like Apple Music, Amazon Music and Google Music to the giant Indian music market.[16] Currently, these avenues are populated with Hindustani music produced and distributed by large record labels. A similar situation exists with Hindustani music available on online streaming channels like Spotify, Gaana and Jiosaavn.[17] While music produced and distributed by individual musicians does not seem to be available on these platforms, there is the instance of Twaang where this has been attempted.[18] Whether all these options will impact Hindustani music and musicians in a major way is yet to be seen, but they need to be explored by the companies and musicians. Even sales through individually owned websites can attract more interest now with easy access to multiple payment options made available by payment gateways like Instamojo.[19]

Collaboration and Coordination

It is not often that public and private organizations or even the agencies working under different ministries collaborate in the field of performing arts. An important collaborative venture among many agencies was seen in the form of the Swarna Mahotsav, a festival of art music and dance, held from 16 August to 21 October 1997, to mark the fiftieth anniversary of Independence. Several leading Hindustani musicians were featured during this festival. The inaugural concert held on 15 August 1997 included a Hindustani music recital by shehnai maestro Bismillah Khan and a Carnatic recital by eminent vocalist M. Balamurali Krishna (1938–2016). Approximately 150 soloists with about 1,000 accompanists from numerous parts of India were featured in major cities. Zonal

Cultural Centres; Kalakshetra Foundation, Chennai; Tamil Nadu Eyal Isai Nataka Manram, Chennai; Indian Museum, Kolkata; and National Centre for the Performing Arts, Mumbai collaborated with Sangeet Natak Akademi for this festival.[20] More such joint efforts need to be seen frequently, as they will help in pooling of resources. A less ambitious and more tangible step in this direction could be taken in a single city or town where multiple organizations could come together with government and private support at least once every year to organize a festival of music, a seminar or similar activities. This would, hopefully, reduce the proprietorial and competitive environment that exists among some organizations and which does not help the cause of music in any way. It would also be immensely profitable if all major institutions, particularly those being run on government funds, were to inform the public well in advance through all online and offline formats about their calendar of events, including the names of performers who would be featured in all concerts. Currently, most performers are engaged very late in the day, as the bureaucratic set-up seems to delay such matters. But advance notice about programmes would ensure that music lovers could plan their itinerary accordingly. This would be particularly useful for visitors from overseas or from other parts of the country.

Listeners' Perspective

There have been and will always be critics of current trends in performance. Some journalists have pointed either to a bright or a bleak future.[21] From a typical music circle programme that caters to an audience of 100–300 to large concerts that are backed by corporate entities, the increase in the market size of Hindustani music concerts has created a platform for event managers and artist managers, and has given rise to a heightened commercialization of the performances. This has impacted music in multiple ways, leading many senior musicians and aficionados to compare prevailing levels of performances with what existed earlier. It is natural to make such comparisons, as the foundation of traditional music is its association with the past and its ability to build upon this inheritance. But there is often a tendency to consider orthodoxy as tradition by deifying or ossifying old concepts. Genealogy is confused with tradition without realizing that belonging to a lineage does not necessarily indicate a close association with tradition, for it is the music and talent that has to speak for itself. Surely, a tradition cannot remain invariable if it has to stay alive. There is enough evidence to show that synthesis and syncretism have been at work over centuries to create what we now regard as the Hindustani cultural tradition.[22] These processes have been reflected in its musical tradition despite the continuance of the raag-taal paradigm. It would, therefore, be unrealistic to expect the music to possess only its original flavour, whatever it may have been. Critical comments based on logical reasons and not influenced by a sense of nostalgia are also vital for a healthy musical climate to emerge.

The uninitiated in the audience are not represented in debates about the quality of music experienced today. Their numbers at concerts change depending upon the performers. Many among them may not also be overly bothered about the performers' level of scholarship. Perhaps this is why their opinions do not matter to musicians and scholars, but it would be presumptuous to believe that their lack of initiation in the subject leads them to crave for gimmicks and dilution. It would be in the interest of creating a healthy listening climate that encourages musical analysis, to have a frank dialogue among all concerned. This would even yield answers to other issues, which may appear mundane but are genuine and impact the music in the long run. For example, the limited time available for open-air concerts in the evenings has been a concern after the law has stipulated that such concerts can continue only until 10 p.m.[23] Those living in cities often do not want to commute long distances for concerts or to even set aside time for concerts on a weekday. These factors have negatively impacted the music, by reducing the duration of each performance and restricting the choice or raags to those prescribed until the winding-up time. This has led to the shrinking of concert repertoire.[24] Reminiscing about the concerts in her heyday, Gangubai Hangal bemoaned the constraints on time in concerts held now:

> The conventional baithak used to be a lengthy affair involving the minimum of 4 to 5 singing hours. A single artist at a conference used to get one whole evening reserved for him. Sometimes one had to make a number of appearances at a single music conference. At present four artists render their musical skills within five hours. How is an artist likely to find true self-expression in these so-called music events?[25]

One way of starting a fruitful dialogue to address these issues could be by conducting surveys among audiences regarding performances. These surveys could include questions about the venue, sound system, publicity and other related issues. Apparently, some institutions have been conducting such surveys. Representing the Shanmukhananda Sangeet Sabha, a premier performing art institution in Mumbai, Amarnath Sury said about the Sabha's surveys:

> Once in at least two or three years we have an audience response through a questionnaire for three or four months, to take a feedback and try to see whether we are on track on which the majority of members want the institution to go. Based more or less on the membership survey we schedule our programmes in different categories like music, drama, instrumental, vocal or Hindustani etc. I am constrained to say that this will depend upon the composition of your membership actually.[26]

A greater frequency and reach of such surveys and a better access to the data collected thus would help in reviewing the current situation and in developing viable alternatives. The accuracy of the data collected in such surveys will always be questioned, but this is possibly one way of bringing about a healthy conversation between all concerned sections.

There are some enthusiasts who say that the numbers in the audience are dwindling with each passing day or that fewer young listeners are seen today. Such opinions are, of course, not based on any detailed study of the past and present and do not really help to arrive at any understanding of the situation. These people's love for the music often gets the better of them, leading them to even believe popular music is at fault for driving away potential Hindustani music listeners. But the same section of aficionados who are woeful about declining numbers in the audience believe strongly that this music comes into its own only in chamber concerts meant for a few listeners.

Innovative Educational Programmes

These inherently contradictory positions aside, for Hindustani music to prosper and receive popular support, it would be perhaps be appropriate to develop innovative educational programmes. It is encouraging that new schools of music that are necessarily focusing only on Hindustani music, have also chosen to include this system of music in their coursework. Two instances that come to mind in this regard are the True School of Music, Mumbai, and the Global Music Institute, Greater Noida.[27] But with regard to Hindustani music education in general, the traditional guru–shishya method of teaching and the institutional format are conducted by different entities in an isolated fashion. While parallel streams of music education may appear to be rich resources for strengthening the music ecosystem, the lack of an integrated approach leaves many gaps to be filled. Interestingly, the Shankar Mahadevan Academy seems to have brought elements of the two systems together by making available compositions created by Agra gharana exponent Khadim Hussain Khan (1907–1993) through his disciple Lalith Rao. The teaching and commercial model followed in this case is quite unique. Courses are designed as per compositions which can either be learnt in a self-study format by listening to audio recordings of Rao's disciples or by learning online from them. No payment is required for self-study, but for online training the fee is determined for each course. Put simply, each composition is taught within a stipulated timeframe for a certain fee.[28] This is a significant departure from regular tuitions that have been conducted until now either in the physical presence of the guru or through online sessions, neither of which followed a strict pattern of teaching compositions in a specific timeframe.

Music education in academic institutions needs to enhance critical listening capabilities among students, instead of imposing upon them a straitjacketed syllabus and coursework often recommended by senior musicians and aficionados. It is obvious that all children cannot be adept as performers and a majority of them, as a result, become demotivated if the curriculum lays greater stress on performing ability. Exposing schoolchildren to the sounds and music from India and overseas in the initial stages instead of focusing on one or the other system of art music would enrich their aural and musical experience and help to develop their critical and analytical faculties. An inclusive curriculum representing the country's musical diversity at the primary and middle school levels could help children decide whether to opt for specialized training in one or the other form or system of music at the secondary and higher secondary levels. The vision and objectives of such educational programmes cannot be arrived at without detailed consultations and in the absence of data regarding the present exposure of students to separate kinds of music, their musical preferences and allied matters. Such a mammoth project can only be undertaken at an institutional level backed by union and state governments.

The music curriculum of the schools would need to have a link with the curriculum offered by universities so as to equip students with a firm grounding in the basics and to ensure a smooth entry into higher levels of instruction.[29] At the university level, it would be difficult to imagine that every student will be equally competent in theory and practice. So, a syllabus and coursework that prepares a balanced and integrated foundation that can launch the student into one of these two areas at the postgraduate level is required. This would be imperative considering that students training in universities rarely take them to a performance career, and those who choose to, do so as a result of the training they receive in the guru–shishya parampara and not because of their university education.

Attention also needs to be provided to exceptionally gifted children, who may not be as inclined to pursuing regular academic education as compared to their interest in music. Curriculum could be developed to encourage such children to primarily continue their musical studies while also undergoing specially structured courses in other academic subjects.

These steps call for a complete revamp of the music education system. I wonder if those who have been designing syllabus and coursework can even begin to fathom the issues involved. With no disrespect to them, it is obvious that most of them have been trained in the established institutionalised format and hence are guided by this framework.

A new approach calls for introspection and brainstorming on the part of all involved, including registering the views of students with regard to their musical proclivities. As regards musical exposure at a macro level, the SPIC-MACAY model seems to have become less effective, as my experience has been that despite hundreds of chapters running across the country in schools and colleges, there are few students and faculty members who become active listeners or learners outside the boundaries of the organization. On the other hand, increasingly, social media platforms are being used to educate music lovers. A major initiative in this direction has been taken by Anuja Kamat, a young singer who has been uploading short educational videos to her YouTube channel. These videos have drawn huge interest from various quarters.[30]

Research and documentation in the numerous aspects of Hindustani music also needs more support from public and private institutions. Much of this material may be in regional languages, requiring translation into English in order to be available to a wider readership. Research scholars in India need to produce material that can stand the test of international standards. Perhaps sustained exchange programmes with universities and scholars from other parts of the world could yield favourable results.

Vocalists and instrumentalists have recorded their repertoire for documentation projects undertaken by various archives. But there have been rare instances of musicians taking such an initiative. Noteworthy among the latter are vocalists Neela Bhagwat and Indudhar Nirody. Bhagwat, a Gwalior gharana vocalist, has compiled all compositions that she learnt from her gurus and has shared these as publicly accessible documents and on DVDs.[31] Nirody has recorded on audio format all compositions included in Bhatkhande's six-volume *Hindustani Sangeet Paddhati: Kramik Pustak Malika*.[32] But more needs to be done to ensure that collaborations between practitioners, scholars and institutions take place on a continuing basis using modern technology, so as to document knowledge handed down to future generations through an essentially oral tradition.

Reaching International Audiences

In the international sphere, the presence of Hindustani music has definitely grown in the decades after the 1950s. The twenty-first century has seen a surge of web-based applications which circumvent the problems associated with ensuring the presence of all participants in a single physical space and instead allow relatively unhindered musical collaborations across continents. Today, performances and teaching sessions are taking place over far-flung geographical regions with the help of these applications. Live concerts in India and overseas can now be viewed due to streaming or recorded webcasts. Darbar Festival, UK, and corporate sponsor Hindustan Computers Limited (HCL) are sharing concerts presented by them through their web-based applications.[33]

It remains to be seen whether the present circumstances surrounding Hindustani music and its inclusion in collaborations augur well artistically and financially in the long run for the music and its practitioners, or if they need to be re-examined keeping in view the challenges thrown up by globalization. For the moment, despite efforts to raise its stature to the globally dominant Western streams of music-making, Hindustani music continues to be one of the many non-Western systems bunched together in the world music category of physical and online record shops and probably in the imagination of a majority of music lovers overseas.

Way Forward

It would be illogical for anyone to believe that there has been no development whatsoever in the field of Hindustani music since Independence. There are innumerable instances of significant changes that have taken place through the past seven decades or so. However, we need to evolve a broader perspective for a sustainable future. States have seen and will probably continue to see some semblance of support to the arts including Hindustani music, but it is a long-term vision at the Centre that is required for sustained development across geographical regions. The new environment in the twenty-first century has challenged earlier notions of patronage and commerce. Performance and pedagogy have assumed new meanings in terms of musical dissemination. These factors in turn have impacted the music-making process by challenging our understanding of tradition and experimentation. The role of the state as represented by policy makers, administrators and government institutions vis-à-vis Hindustani music calls for a detailed discussion along with a review of patronage from corporate entities, non-government bodies and the general public. Above all, the deeper impact of these extra-musical factors on performance practice and the compulsions faced by musicians in the process need to be considered in order for this musical tradition to flourish in the future.

Appendix – 1

THE AIR CONTRACT

1. The Artist shall not solicit, remove or accept any fee or other valuable consideration from any person other than All India Radio for or in recognition of the Artist singing, performing or having sung or performed or promising to sing or perform any particular items, song as musical work or for refraining from singing or performing any particular item, song or musical work during this engagement. Moreover, that Artists shall not in the performance of this engagement broadcast any remark which in the opinion of All India Radio representative will draw undue attention to any particular items, song or musical work. Should any such remark be made, save with the consent of All India Radio representative and except in the exact form approved by him. This contract shall be considered as terminated forthwith and the Artist's action shall be considered a definite breach of the terms and conditions herein laid down. A Statement that any particular item, song or musical work is being performed, 'by special request' or a similar announcement to the same general effect shall be

deemed to be calculated to draw undue attention to the item, song or musical work concerned.

2. The Artist shall rehearse and perform to the best of his skill and ability and carry out all reasonable instructions given to him by the representative of All India Radio.

3. The Artist shall not broadcast any advertisement or matter of an advertising nature whatsoever without first obtaining the permission of the Station Director.

4. The Artist shall warrant that at the time of signing this Agreement he is not under any engagement (or otherwise barred by any contract) precluding him from fulfilling this Agreement and that he has not concealed any change of professional name or description.

5. All India Radio shall have the absolute right of rejection of all or any part of the entertainment submitted by the Artist and shall not be called upon to give any reasons for any such rejection. Should the Station Director reject all or any part of such entertainment the Artist shall with all despatch submit other matter or material in place of that rejected for the approval of All India Radio.

6. All India Radio shall not be liable to the Artist or to the legal personal representative of the Artist for any loss, damage or injury to the Artist's person or property during or in connection with this engagement unless caused by the negligence of All India Radio or its own officers or servants and recoverable on that ground under the law applicable in India.

7. The Artist shall at all times keep All India Radio fully indemnified in respect of the consequences following upon any breach of the aforesaid warranties and undertakings and in respect of all actions, proceedings, claims, demands, and expenses whatsoever which may be made or brought against or suffered or incurred by All India Radio in consequences of any breach of any such warranties or undertakings or on the ground that any such work as aforesaid is an infringement of any right of any other persons or is libellous [sic] or slandrous [sic] or controversial obscene or indecent.

8. All India Radio shall be entitled without further payment to make a mechanical reproduction of any rehearsal or of the performance, broadcast, and to use it for purpose not involving public performance, and to broadcast extracts therefrom in documentary or, historical programmes and in trailer programme.

9. All India Radio shall be entitled upon payment of the additional fee shown over-leaf to broadcast a mechanical reproduction of the performance of [sic] extracts thereform [sic]. The additional fee will not be paid if a mechanical reproduction is broadcast is [sic] lieu of the broadcast performance.

10. In this contract, broadcast means the radiation of the item from one or more transmitters of any Broadcasting Organisation.

11. In the event of the Artist alleging incapability [sic] to perform by reason of illness or physical incapacity, the certificate of a qualified medical practioner [sic] proving the fact of such incapacity shall forthwith be sent to All India Radio by the Artist Stating [sic] the nature of the illness and that in consequence thereof the Artiste in unable to perform. All India Radio shall in such event not be liable to pay any fee or remuneration to the Artist except for performances actually given by him hereunder.

12. Should the Artist for any reason (except illness or physical incapacity certified as hereinbefore produced or such other unavoidable cause may be proved to the satisfaction of the Station Director) fail to appear and perform as stipulated in this agreement, he shall pay to All India Radio as and from liquidated damages a sum equal to the sum which the Artist would have received for such appearance and performance in addition to the cost of All India Radio of providing a deputy and any other costs, damages and expenses incurred by All India Radio by reason of default of the Artist but nothing in this clause shall affect the right of All India Radio to apply an injection [sic] of restrain [sic] the Artist from performing in breach of this contract or the right of All India Radio to determine this agreement under clause (13) below.

13. Where this Agreement relates to a troupe of two or more performers working under the control or management of the Artist, the Arties shall, at the time the contract is signed, furnish All India Radio in writing with such names of the performers as the Station Director may require and shall not substitute a performer for a person so names without the written consent of the Station Director. The Artist shall further secure the written consent of the other member or members of the troup [sic] to the terms of this Agreement. The Artist agrees to pay each member of the troupe the proportion of any fee payable to the Artist to which the member is entitled.

14. All India Radio reserve [sic] the right without assigning any reason whatsoever to determine the contract. In such an event, the Artists shall not have or make any claim against All India Radio except for the fee (which shall be determined by All India Radio) proportionate to the work actully [sic] done by the Artist under the contract.

15. Any notice under this Agreement maybe served upon the Artist by posting the same to his last known address or to the agent through whom this contract is made.

16. In the event of the Artist being a Government servant, the broadcast of this programme and the payment to him of the fee shall be subject to his obtaining the sanction of the Head of his Office or Department to his [sic] effect and this sanction should be in the hands of the Station Director 10 days before the date of the broadcast.

17. All India Radio shall have the right to forbit [sic] the appearance of an Artist before the microphone and to reject his performance, if in the opinion of the Station Director, the Artist is not sober enough or in a fit enough state of health to perform according to the standard expeced [sic] of him. In such cases the Artist will not be entitled to the fees agreed upon or any portion thereof or to any compensation whatsoever.

Appendix – 2

QUESTIONNAIRE FOR SCHOOLCHILDREN

Name: _____

Age: _____

School: _____

Class: _____

Do you learn music at your school? Yes/No

If yes, what kind of music do you learn? Describe briefly eg Vocal/ Instrumental; Classical/Non Classical etc.

Do you also learn music after school? Yes/No

What kind of music? Describe in detail:

Name five of your favourite songs or pieces of music:

1._____

2. _____

3. _____

4. _____

5. _____

2

Have you read any books on music? If so, tell us about them:

Do you play any games related to music? If so, tell us about them.

Do you attend music concerts? If so, tell us about the last three concerts you heard:

1._____

2. _____

3. _____

Do you have a music collection: Yes/No

If yes, tell us about your collection:

CDs: How many approximately?

Cassettes: How many approximately?

LPs/Gramaphone [sic] Records/Vinyl: How many approximately?

MP3: How many approximately?

What kind of music do you collect:

Film music

Folk music:

Classical music:

Indipop:

Devotional music:

Other (specify):

Do you have an email ID?: Yes/No

If yes, would you like to have an internet forum to discuss music?
Yes/No

- Please take permission from your parents before you say yes to
  the above question.

If you have any special comments or suggestions, please put them
down for us below:

Appendix – 3

SURVEY OF YOUNG PROFESSIONAL HINDUSTANI CLASSICAL MUSICIANS AGED BETWEEN 25–35 IN 2017

Name:

Age: Gender:

Vocal/Instrumental (Please specify instrument/Please specify genre in case of vocal –dhrupad, khayal, thumri, multiple, etc.):

1. At what age did you begin learning music?
2. What or who prompted you to begin learning music?
3. Did you choose vocal or instrumental music when you started learning? Did you choose a genre or form of music that is different from the one you now pursue? How did you make these choices?
4. Did you start learning at home, from a guru or in a music class or was there any other form of training to begin with (online classes, etc.)?
5. Did you change to another music class or another guru later? Why?

6. If you learnt in a music class and from a guru, what were the differences you noticed in the teaching methodology, your expectations, your music teacher or guru's expectations, the outcome in both cases or one of the two if you chose only one form of teaching?
7. At what age did you decide to make a career in music?
8. What was your understanding about making a career in music when you made this decision?
9. What kind of demands did you feel would be placed on you as a professional musician?
10. How long have you been pursuing a career in music?
11. Where do you normally perform? (venues, cities, countries)
12. How often do you perform in a month/year?
13. What would be your average annual income from your live concerts?
14. Do you also record your music for commercial release? Please mention the labels.
15. How often do you record your music for commercial release?
16. What is your average annual income from commercial releases? Around 2 Lacs
17. Do you receive royalties or lump-sum payment for commercial releases?
18. Do you perform on AIR? What is your grade? How often and where?
19. Do you perform on DD? How often and where?
20. Do you find it possible to lead a financially stable life as a professional Hindustani musician?
21. Do you participate in any musical performances and recordings other than conventional Hindustani performances? Where? Why?
22. What is your average income from musical performances and recordings other than conventional Hindustani performances?
23. Do you feel that your personal experience was different from what you had expected from a musical career? If so, how?
24. Do you have any expectations as a professional musician?
25. Do you feel the field of music places more demands on you as a professional musician than what you had expected? What is the difference in demands?

26. Are you convinced and satisfied as a professional musician? How?

27. Are you unconvinced and dissatisfied as a professional musician? How?

28. Do you teach? If so, where and when?

29. What is your average annual income from teaching?

30. Do you possess any qualification in Music like B.A, M.A etc? If so, where have you procured this qualification from?

31. If you have qualifications mentioned in q.30, do they affect your career in any way? Please describe.

32. Apart from your profession as a musician, do you also pursue any other professional career or any business or are you employed elsewhere? Please describe.

33. How does an additional employment or business activity impact your career as a musician?

34. Do you have a platform where you can raise issues related to your career?

35. How difficult or easy is it to establish yourself as a performer in the field of Hindustani music?

36. Do you have any expectations from various sections of society (include government and non-government) with respect to your status as a professional musician?

37. Please add any other information that you would like to.

Date: Signature: _____

Place:

Bibliography

ENGLISH

Primary Sources

Bhatkhande, V.N., *A Short Historical Survey of the Music of Upper India* (Bombay: B.S. Sukthankar, 1934).

Chaubey, S.K., *Indian Music Today* (Allahabad: Kitab Mahal, 1945), p. 136.

The Times of India, 24 February 1952.

Chintan: Reflections on SPIC MACAY and Its Core Values (Delhi: SPIC MACAY Communications, 2007).

Cousins, Margaret E., *The Music of Orient and Occident: Essays Towards Mutual Understanding*, (Madras: B.G. Paul and Co., 1935).

Fielden, Lionel, *Report on the Progress of Broadcasting in India: Up to the 31st March 1939*, (Delhi: Manager of Publications, 1940).

Hazrat Inayat Khan, *The Divine Symphony or Vadan*, Sufi Movement, 2nd ed. (Geneva: E.E. Kluwer, 1931).

Hazrat Inayat Khan, *Notes form the Unstruck Music from: The Gayan* 4th revised ed. (Holland: N.V. Publishing Co., 1936).

Hazrat Inayat Khan, *Nirtan or The Dance of the Soul*, 2nd ed. (Holland: N.V. Publishing Co., 1938).

173

Government of India Act, 1935, available at http://www.legislation.gov.uk/ukpga/1935/2/pdfs/ukpga_19350002_en.pdf accessed on 6 April 2019.

Jayakar, M.R., *The Story of My Life, Vol. II, 1922-1925* (Mumbai: Asia Publishing House, 1959).

Joshi, Balwant, Dr Dilip Inamdar, Prof. Charudatta Bhagwat, Dr S.S. Gore (eds.), *World of Gandharvas,* (New Bombay: Sound Library Project of Akhil Bharatiya Gandharva Mahavidyalaya Mandal, 1993).

Report of the Committee for Music Education, 1948-49, Government of Bombay, (Bombay: Education & Industries Department, 1949).

Report of the Students' Literary and Scientific Society, and of the Vernacular Branch Societies, together with the Reports of the Girls' Schools for the Session of 1862-63 (Bombay, 1863).

Report of the Students' Literary and Scientific Society for the Session of 1871-72 (Bombay, 1874).

Sahasrabuddhe, Balwant Triumback, *Hindu Music and the Gayan Samaj* (Madras: The Madras Jubilee Gayan Samaj, 1887).

Shankar, Ravi, *My Music, My Life,* Sixth Reprint (New Delhi: Vikas Publishing House Pvt. Ltd., 1978).

Tagore, Raja Sir Sourindro Mohun, 'Universal History of Music: Compiled from Diverse Sources Together with Various Original Notes on Hindu Music' in *The Chowkhambha Sanskrit Studies,* Vol. XXXI, 2nd ed. (Varanasi: The Chowkhambha Sanskrit Series Office, 1963).

Tagore, Surendra Mohan, *Public Opinion and Official Communications about the Bengal Music School and Its President* (Calcutta: Panchanun Mookherjee, 1876).

Secondary Sources

Attali Jacques, 'Noise: The Political Economy of Music', English translation Brian Massumi in *Theory and History of Literature,* Volume 16, Tenth Printing (Minneapolis: University of Minnesota Press, 2009).

Awasthy, G.C., *Broadcasting in India,* (Mumbai: Allied Publishers Private Limited, 1965).

Baruah, U.L., *This Is All India Radio—A Handbook of Radio Broadcasting in India* (New Delhi: Publications Division, Ministry of Information and Broadcasting, Government of India, 1983).

Blanning, Tim, *The Triumph of Music: Composers, Musicians and Their Audiences, 1700 to the Present* (London: Penguin Books, 2008).

Bor, Joep, and Bruguierre, Philippe, *Masters of Raga, Meister Des Raga, Les Maitres Du Raga* (Berlin: Haus der Kulturen der Welt, 1995).

Chandra, Pankaj, *Building Universities that Matter: Where are Indian Institutions Going Wrong?*, Reprinted (Hyderabad: Orient Blackswan Private Limited, 2018).

Deshpande, Vamanrao, *Between Two Tanpuras*, trans. Ram Deshmukh and B.R. Dhekney from Marathi original *Aalaapini*, with the addition of a piece on Bhimsen Joshi (Mumbai: Popular Prakashan, 1989).

Deshpande, Vamanrao H., *Indian Musical Traditions: An Aesthetic Study of the Gharanas in Hindustani Music*, 2nd revised & enlarged ed. (Bombay: Popular Prakashan, 1987.

Farrell, Gerry, *Indian Music and the West* (Oxford: Clarendon Press, 1997).

Gopal, S., and Iyengar, Uma (eds.), *The Essential Writings of Jawaharlal Nehru*, Volume I, (New Delhi: Oxford University Press 2003).

Kinnear, Michael S., *A Discography of Hindustani and Carnatic Music* (Westport: Greenwood Press, 1985).

Kinnear, Michael S., *Sangeet Ratna—The Jewel of Music: A Bio-Discography of Khan Sahib Abdul Karim Khan* (Victoria, Australia: Michael Kinnear, 2003).

Kinnear, Michael S., *The Gramophone Company's First Indian Recordings, 1899– 1908* (Mumbai: Popular Prakashan, 1994).

Kinnear, Michael S., *The 78 r.p.m. Record Labels of India*, 2nd ed. (Victoria: Bajakhana–Michael Kinnear, 2016).

Kumar, Ravindra, chief ed., *The Selected Works of Maulana Abul Kalam Azad: Vol. III—1947–48*, (New Delhi: Atlantic Publishers & Distributors, 1991).

Lavezzoli, Peter, *Bhairavi: The Global Impact of Indian Music* (Noida: HarperCollins Publishers India, 2009).

Lelyveld, David, 'Upon the Subdominant: Administering Music on All-India Radio' in *Consuming Modernity: Public Culture in a South Asian World*, ed. Carol A. Breckenridge (Minneapolis: University of Minnesota Press, 1995), pp. 55–60.

Manuel, Peter, *Cassette Culture: Popular Music and Technology in North India* (Chicago: The University of Chicago Press, 1993).

Misra, Susheela, *Great Masters of Hindustani Music* (New Delhi: Hem Publishers Pvt. Ltd., 1981).

Misra, Susheela, *Music Profiles*, (n.p., 1955).

Mukherji, Kumar Prasad, *The Lost World of Hindustani Music* (New Delhi: Penguin Books, 2006).

Nayan, Ritnika, *Indie 101: The Ultimate Guide to the Independent Music Industry in India* (New Delhi: Music Gets Me High, 2017).

Neuman, Daniel M., *Studying India's Musicians: Four Decades of Selected Articles* (New Delhi: Manohar Publishers & Distributors, 2015).

Neuman, Daniel, *The Life of Music in North India: The Organisation of an Artistic Tradition* (New Delhi: Manohar Publications, 1980).

Passman, Donald S., *All You Need to Know about the Music Business*, UK ed. (London: Penguin Books, 2002).

Post, Jennifer C., (ed.), *Ethnomusicology: A Contemporary Reader* (New York: Routledge Taylor & Francis Group, 2006), p. 2.

Pradhan, Aneesh, *Hindustani Music in Colonial Bombay*, (Gurgaon: Three Essays Collective, 2014).

Ranade, Ashok, 'Gandharvas and Musical Changes – Attempt at Cultural Perspectives' in *World of Gandharvas*, eds. Balawant Joshi, Dr Dilip Inamdar, Prof. Charudatta Bhagwat, Dr S.S. Gore (New Bombay: Sound Library Project of Akhil Bharatiya Gandharva Mahavidyalaya Mandal, 1993).

Ranade, Ashok D., *Maharashtra: Art Music*, Maharashtra Information Centre, Government of Maharashtra (New Delhi, 1989).

Ranade, Ashok Da., *Perspectives on Music: Ideas and Theories* (New Delhi: Promilla & Co. with Bibliophile South Asia, 2008).

Ratanjankar, S.N., *Pandit Bhatkhande* (New Delhi: National Book Trust, India, 1967).

Role of Media in Promotion of Music in India, (Mumbai: ITC-SRA Western Region, January 2012).

Roy, Ashok, *Music Makers: Living Legends of Indian Classical Music* (New Delhi: Rupa & Co., 2004).

Schipper, Huib, 'Hindustani Music: Resilience and Flexibility in Recontextualizing and Ancient Tradition', eds. Huib Schipper, Catherine Grants, *Sustainable Futures for Music Cultures: An Ecological Perspective*, (New York: Oxford University Press, 2016).

Seeger Anthony, 'Intellectual Property and Audiovisual Archives and Collections' in *Folk Heritage Collections in Crisis* (Washington DC: Council on Library and Information Resources, May 2001). Also available at http://www.clir.org/pubs/reports/pub96/rights.html) accessed on 15 February 2019.

Thapar, Romila, *Cultural Transaction and Early India: Tradition and Patronage*, 4th impression (New Delhi: Oxford University Press, 2001).

Trivedi, Madhu, *The Emergence of the Hindustani Tradition: Music, Dance and Drama in North India, 13th to 19th Centuries* (Gurgaon: Three Essays Collective, 2012).

Vatsyayan, Kapila, 'Cultural Development: A Profile' in Narain, Iqbal (ed.), *A Centenary History of the Indian National Congress*, Volume Four, 1947–1964, (New Delhi: All India Congress Committee (I) and Vikas Publishing House Private Limited, 1990).

Wade, Bonnie C., *Thinking Musically: Experiencing Music, Expressing Culture*, (New York: Oxford University Press, 2004).

HINDI

Primary Sources

Bhatkhande, V.N., *Hindustaanee Sangeet Paddhati: Kramik Pustak Maalikaa, Chauthi Pustak*, Hindi translation, ed. Prof. Harishchandra Shrivastav, 4th ed. (Allahabad: Sangeet Sadan Prakashan, 2005).

Bhatkhande, V.N., *Hindustaanee Sangeet Paddhati: Kramik Pustak Maalikaa, Chhati Pustak*, Hindi translation, ed. Prof. Harishchandra Shrivastav (Allahabad: Sangeet Sadan Prakashan).

Vilayat Hussain Khan, *Sangeetagyon ke Sansmaran*, (Hindi) (New Delhi: Sangeet Natak Akademi, 1959).

Secondary Sources

Deodhar, B.R., 'Sangeet-Sevak Shriman Damodardas Khanna, Calcutta' in *Sangeet Kala Vihar, Varsha 8, Ank 3* (Gandharva Mahavidyalaya Mandal, 1955).

Garg, Laxminarayan, *Hamaare Sangeet Ratna*, Pratham Bhaag, (Hindi) (Hathras: Sangit Karyalaya, 1957).

Ranade, G.H., 'Sangeet ke Aadhunik Bheeshmaachaarya' in *Bhatkhande Smriti Granth* (Khairagarh, MP: Indira Kala Sangeet Vishwavidyalaya, 1966).

MARATHI

Primary Sources

Deodhar, B.R., 'School of Indian Music' in *Deodhar's School of Indian Music, Golden Jubilee Souvenir* (Mumbai, 1975).

'Lokhitwadi', Gopal Hari Deshmukh, 'Sangeetshastra' in *Lokhitwadikrit Nibandhsangraha: Gopal Hari Deshmukh* (Marathi), ed. Anant Kakba Priyolkar (Mumbai: Popular Prakashan, 1996).

Secondary Sources

Deodhar, B.R., *Gaayanaachaarya P. Vishnu Digambar* (Mumbai: Akhil Bharatiya Gandharva Mahavidyalaya Mandal, 1971).

Deodhar, B.R., *Thor Sangeetkaar* (Mumbai: Akhil Bharatiya Gandharva Mahavidyalaya Mandal, 1973).

Kapileshwari, Balkrishnabuwa, *Shrutidarshan* (Pune: Continental Prakashan, 1963).

GUJARATI

Primary Sources

Kapadia, Pestanjee Firozeshah, *Gayan Uttejak Mandali: Tenee Ponee Sadinee Tawaareekhno Ahewaal* (Mumbai: Mrs Freni M. Cama, 1946).

DISSERTATIONS

Bhattacharyya, Anirban, 'From Salon to Sammelan: Changes in the Contexts of Performances in Calcutta (1875–1950)' (Unpublished MMus dissertation, School of Oriental and African Studies, London, 2011).

Cherian, Anita Elizabeth, 'Fashioning a National Theatre: Institutions and Cultural Policy in Post-Independence India' (Unpublished doctoral dissertation, New York University, New York, 2005).

McNeil, Adrian, 'The Dynamics of Social and Musical Status in Hindustani Music: Sarodiyas, Seniyas and the Margi-Desi Paradigm' (PhD diss., Department of Music, Monash University, Melbourne, 1992).

Mishra, Vrinda Uday, 'Decolonising the Raj: Bombay under Provincial Autonomy, 1937–1939' (PhD diss., Faculty of Arts, Monash University, Melbourne, 2003).

Mukherjee, Bimal, 'Jaipur Binkar/Sitar Gharana' in *Seminar on Sitar* (Sangeet Research Academy, 1990).

Rosse, Michael David, 'The Movement for the Revitalization of "Hindu" Music in Northern India, 1860–1930: The Role of Associations and Institutions' (PhD diss., University of Pennsylvania, Philadelphia, 1995).

PERIODICALS

'Saregama India’s largest aggregator of digital music', available at http:// www.livemint.com/Consumer/aaoA9lQQYq1PadcNJEpBEJ/Saregama-India8217s-largest-aggregator-of-digital-music.html accessed on 15 February 2019.

Tiwari, Soumya Vajpayee, 'Furore over Sangeet Natak Akademi awards', available at https://www.mid-day.com/articles/furore-over-sangeet-natak-akademi-awards/19557153 accessed on 16 February 2019.

Mukherjee, Arindam, 'Heir Gloom', available at http://www.outlookindia.com/article/heir-gloom/232619, accessed on 16 February 2019.

'AIR Audition Tests at Bombay: 400 Artistes on List' in *The Times of India*, 26 September 1952, p. 1, www.proquest.com as on July 12, 2015.

'A.I.R.'s Tests: Mandal's Views Misunderstood' in *The Times of India*, 12 June 1953, p. 3; www.proquest.com accessed on 19 May 2016.

'Agitation Will Benefit All Artistes: Mandal Gives Assurance' in *The Times of India*, 28 May 1953, p. 3; www.proquest.com accessed on 12 July 2015.

Annual Report, Balance Sheet and Income & Expenditure of A.B.G.M.V. Mandal and Sangeet Kala Vihar for the Year 2016-2017 (Mumbai: Akhil Bharatiya Gandharva Mahavidyalaya Mandal, 2019).

'Audition Test Controversy: A.I.R. Blamed' in *The Times of India*, 27 June 1953, p. 11; www.proquest.com accessed on 12 July 2015.

'Audition Test Issue: Offer to Hear Artistes' Views' in *The Times of India*, 16 May 1953, p. 11; www.proquest.com accessed on 12 July 2017.

'Audition Tests' in *The Times of India*, 15 May 1953, p. 6; www.proquest.com accessed on 12 July 2017.

'Bombay Artistes Resent A.I.R. Audition System: Decision To Boycott Programmes' in *The Times of India*, 14 May 1953, pp. 1, 3; www.proquest.com accessed on 12 July 2015.

'"Campaign Of Vilification Must Stop"—Reply to Radio Artistes' in *The Times of India*, 3 June 1953, p. 3; www.proquest.com accessed on 19 May 2016.

Dadar Matunga Cultural Centre Golden Jubilee Souvenir, Mumbai, 2003.

Nair, Shobha, 'He blends music and business', available at http://www.dnaindia.com/lifestyle/grandeur-he-blends-music-and-business-1049333 accessed on 15 February 2019.

Easwaran, Jyoti, 'Pandit Shivkumar Sharma Is an Extraordinary Musician', available at http://gulfnews.com/life-style/music/pandit-shivkumar-sharma-is-an-extraordinary-musician-1.716997 accessed on 15 February, 2019.

Venkatraman, Latha, 'Indian Music Group continues to enchant Mumbai students', available at http://www.thehindubusinessline.com/todays-paper/tp-others/tp-variety/indian-music-group-continues-to-enchant-mumbai-students/article2166283.ece accessed on 15 February 2019.

'Fusion has existed in India for a thousand years: Tabla maestro Zakir Hussain' available at http://indianexpress.com/article/lifestyle/art-and-culture/fusion-has-existed-in-india-for-a-thousand-years-tabla-maestro-zakir-hussain/ accessed on 14 February 2019.

Sircar, Jawhar, 'The Covert Control Raj: Prasar Bharti and its shortcomings', available at http://indiatoday.intoday.in/story/prasar-bharti-information-and-broadcasting-ministry/1/359913.html accessed on 14 February 2019.

Das Gupta, Surajeet and Mitra, Sounak, 'Prasar Bharati: Can Sircar turn it around?' at http://www.business-standard.com/article/companies/prasar-bharati-can-sircar-turn-it-around-112102400078_1.html accessed on 14 February 2019.

'Prasar Bharati CEO bats for youth-savvy content', available at http://www.business-standard.com/article/news-ians/prasar-bharati-ceo-bats-for-youth-savvy-content-115090800919_1.html accessed on 14 February 2019.

Jaisinghani, Bella, and Jain, Bhavikar, 'Private school, wedding halls on plots given to artistes in Mumbai despite rules saying land can't be sub-let or used for business', available at http://timesofindia.indiatimes.com/city/mumbai/Private-school-wedding-halls-on-plots-given-to-artistes-in-Mumbai-despite-rules-saying-land-cant-be-sub-let-or-used-for-business/articleshow/50881934.cms accessed on 15 February 2019. https://timesofindia.indiatimes.com/india/Now-Big-B-can-insure-his-voice/articleshow/1560517.cms accessed on 29 March 2019.

Report of a panel discussion titled 'Changing in Organizational Aspects: Cultural Institutions/Organizations' held under the aegis of the Sangeet Research Academy in January 2010, Mumbai, contained in *Journal of the Indian Musicological Society*, Volume 41, 2011-2012 (Mumbai: Indian Musicological Society, 2012).

Journal of the Sangeet Natak Akademi-20, Sangeet Natak Akademi, (New Delhi: April–June 1971).

Kinnear, Michael S., 'The First Indian Disc Record Manufacturers', in *The Record News: The Journal of the Society of Indian Record Collectors*, Vol. 5 (Mumbai: January 1992).

Kinnear, Michael S., 'Reading Indian Record Labels: "RAMAGRAPH" – The History of the RAM-A-PHONE and RAMA-GRAPH disc records' in *The Record News: The Journal of the Society of Indian Record Collectors*, Vol. 20, (Mumbai: October 1995).

Marulkar, N.R., 'Aajche Shikshan-Satra Aani Tyaachi Saangataa' in *Sangeet Kala Vihar, Varsha 8, Ank 3*, ed. B.R. Deodhar (Miraj: Gandharva Mahavidyalaya Mandal, March 1955).

McNeil, Adrian, 'Generational Friction: An Ethnographic Perspective on *Guru Seva* Within a Lineage of Tabla Players in Kolkata' in *MUSICultures, Vol. 44 No.1*, (Edmonton: Canadian Society for Traditional Music, 2017).

Miner, Allyn, 'The Sitar: An Overview of Change', in 'The World of Music, le monde de la musique, die welt der musik India', *Journal of the International Institute for Comparative Music Studies and Documentation*, Vol. XXXII, No. 2 (1990), (Berlin).

Mudgal, Shubha, 'Monetary Ambiguity' at https://www.livemint.com/Leisure/ D4AWZl5oY4RrH2ztfyp5HJ/Monetary-ambiguity.html accessed on 14 February 2019.

'Music as Compulsory Subject in Schools: Dr. Keskar's Suggestion' in *The Times of India*, 6 November, 1957, p. 3; www.proquest.com accessed on 21 March 2017.

Mutatkar, Sumati, 'Music and the Radio (Looking Back and Beyond)' in the *Akashwani Sangeet Sammelan 1998 Brochure* (New Delhi: Prasar Bharati Broadcasting Corporation of India, Ministry of Information & Broadcasting, Government of India, 1998).

Neuman, Daniel M., 'Indian Music and the English Language Fifty Years Later' in *Proceedings: International Seminar on 'Creating & Teaching Music Patterns'* (Kolkata: Department of Instrumental Music, Rabindra Bharati University, 2013).

Parikh, Pandit Arvind, and Ranade, Ashok Damodar, 'Diversity and Media Explosion: A Dialogue of the Indian Scenario' in *Music Performance*, Volume 2, Issue 3 (United Kingdom: Harwood Academic Publishers, 2000). https://books.google.co.in/books?id =ir2KQ8duankC&pg=PA26&lpg=PA26&dq=music+forum+ arvind+parikh&source=bl&ots=VW_laOgb3n&sig=nJYU2T4t YlZ-p9tqgGHeKMdBaBM&hl=en&sa=X&ved=0ahUKEwiNr MvovZ3UAhXENo8KHVZQCao4ChDoAQgsMAI#v=one page&q=music%20forum%20arvind%20parikh&f=false accessed on 15 February 2019.

Pinkerton, Alasdair, 'Radio and the Raj: Broadcasting in British India (1920–1940)' in *Journal of the Royal Asiatic Society*, Series 3, 18, 2 (United Kingdom, 2008).

Pradhan, Aneesh, 'Perspectives on Performance Practice: Hindustani Music in Nineteenth and Twentieth Century Bombay (Mumbai)' in *South Asia: Journal of South Asian Studies*, Vol. XXVII, No. 3 (Carfax Publishing, Taylor and Francis Group, December 2004).

Pradhan, Aneesh, with additional inputs from Mudgal, Shubha, 'Institutionalized Music Education in North India: Some Observations', in *Sangeet Natak*, Vol XLIII, Number 2 (New Delhi: Sangeet Natak Akademi, 2009).

Rajaram, Poorva, 'Why the Centre Should Not Hold' in *Tehelka Magazine*, Vol. 8, Issue 19, 14 May 2011 http://archive.tehelka.com/story_main49. asp?filename=hub140511Why.asp accessed on 22 October 2017.

Ramakrishnan, Anupama, 'Harmonium solo on AIR after four decades' available at http://www.deccanherald.com/content/667361/harmonium-solo-air-four-decades.html accessed on 14 February 2019.

Ramanan, Sumana, 'Upholder of a great tradition' available at https://
mumbaimirror.indiatimes.com/opinion/columnists/sumana-ramanan/
upholder-of-a-great-tradition/articleshow/67239004.cms   accessed   on
March 5, 2019.

Satphale, Anup and Kantawala, Zainab, 'GST relief for music and theatre
performances' at https://timesofindia.indiatimes.com/city/pune/gst-relief-
for-music-and-theatre-performances/articleshow/62652300.cms, accessed
on 24 March 2019.

Shastri, Vittal, 'Hubballi: Hangal family plans stir over Gurukul affairs' at https://
www.deccanchronicle.com/nation/current-affairs/020316/hubballi-
hangal-family-plans-stir-over-gurukul-affairs.html accessed on 21 March,
2019.

'S.S.C. Chaa 1959 March Paasun Amlaat Yenaaraa Sangeetaachaa Navaa
Kaaryakram', in *Sangeet Kala Vihar, Varsha 11, Ank 8*, ed. B.R. Deodhar
(Miraj: Gandharva Mahavidyalaya Mandal, August 1958).

'Struggle Against A.I.R. Will Continue' in *The Times of India*, 24 May 1953, p. 2,
www.proquest.com as on 19 May 2016.

Swarna Samaroh: Festival of Music and Dance (New Delhi: Sangeet Natak
Akademi, 1997).

The 80th Annual Report (2016-2017) (Mumbai: The Suburban Music Circle,
2017).

The Journal of the Society of Indian Record Collectors, Mumbai.

Thussu, Daya Kishan, 'Privatizing the Airwaves: the Impact of Globalization on
Broadcasting in India' in *Media, Culture & Society*, Vol. 21 (London, Thousand
Oaks and New Delhi: Sage Publications, 1999).

WEBSITES

Rajadhyaksha, Ashish, Radhika, P., Tenkayala, Raghavendra, *World CP
International Database of Cultural Policies – Country Profile: India*, available
at http://www.worldcp.org/india.php?aid=1 accessed on 14 February
2019 and https://www.scribd.com/document/240789454/International-
Database-of-Cultural-Policies-Country-Profile-INDIA accessed on 6 April
2019.

https://www.mea.gov.in/Images/pdf1/S7.pdf accessed on 14 February 2019.

http://www.indiaculture.nic.in/history accessed on 14 February 2019.

http://www.indiaculture.nic.in/sites/default/files/budget/Performance_
Budget_Chapter_1.pdf accessed on 14 February 2019.

http://inc.in accessed on 14 February 2019.

http://www.cpim.org accessed on 14 February 2019.

http://www.samajwadiparty.in/index.php accessed on 14 February 2019.

http://rjd.co.in/index.html accessed on 14 February 2019.

http://www.bspindia.org accessed on 14 February 2019.

http://aiadmk.org.in/en/ accessed on 24 March 2019.

http://dmk.in/home accessed on 28 June 2016.

http://ncp.com.nu accessed on 14 February 2019.

https://aamaadmiparty.org accessed on 19 March 2019.

http://aitcofficial.org/the-party/ accessed on 19 March 2019.

http://www.bjp.org/en/core-issues/vision-of-modi accessed on 14 February 2019.

http://shivsena.org/m/art-academy/ accessed on 28 June 2016.

http://pldkalaacademy.org/about.html accessed on 28 June 2016.

http://manase.org/# accessed on 28 June 2016.

http://www.ravishankar.org/reflections accessed on 14 February 2019.

http://prasarbharati.gov.in/default.aspx as on July 8, 2016.

http://allindiaradio.gov.in/Profile/Growth%20and%20Development/Pages/default.aspx accessed on 14 February 2019.

http://prasarbharati.gov.in/PBAct.php accessed on 25 March 2019.

'Prasar CEO Jawhar Sircar hits back: Why can't Ministry send Review results to us?', available at https://indianexpress.com/article/india/india-others/prasar-ceo-hits-back-why-cant-ministry-send-review-results-to-us/ accessed on 21 April 2019.

'Prasar Bharati operating in extreme constriction:Sircar', available at http://bureaucracytoday.com/latestnews.aspx?id=2166 accessed on 14 February 2019.

http://jawharsircar.com/about_Career.html accessed on 14 February 2019.

Sircar, Jawhar, 'Why India can't have its BBC' at http://blogs.timesofindia.indiatimes.com/toi-edit-page/why-india-cant-have-its-bbc/ accessed on 14 February 2019.

'AIR, DD's content quality has come down: Prasar Bharati Chief', available at http://theindianawaaz.com/air-dds-content-quality-has-come-down-prasar-bharati-chief/ accessed on 14 February 2019.

Sircar, Jawhar, 'Smriti Irani is Only the Latest Star in the I&B Ministry's Serial Wars With Prasar Bharati', available at https://thewire.in/229362/smriti-irani-latest-star-ministrys-serial-wars-prasar-bharati/ accessed on 14 February 2019.

Chaturvedi, Swati, 'Exclusive: Angered by Prasar Bharati's Defiance, Smriti Irani Blocks Salary Funds for DD, AIR', available at https://thewire.in/government/angered-prasar-bharatis-defiance-smriti-irani-blocks-salary-funds-dd-air accessed on 6 March, 2019.

Pande, Mrinal, 'A deceit called autonomy', available at http://indianexpress. com/article/opinion/columns/a-deceit-called-autonomy-prasar-bharati-act-5071837/ accessed on 14 February 2019.

http://prasarbharati.gov.in/Mission.php accessed on 25 March 2019.

http://prasarbharati.gov.in/PBAct.php#Fu accessed on 25 March 2019.

http://allindiaradio.gov.in/profile/milestones/pages/default.aspx accessed on 6 March 2019.

http://allindiaradio.gov.in/Profile/Growth%20and%20Development/Pages/ default.aspx accessed on 16 February 2019.

Sircar, Jawhar, 'Remembering Akashvani', available at http://akashvanisamvaad. blogspot.com/2014/05/prasar-bharati-ceo-jawhar-sircars.html accessed on 25 March 2019.

Sircar, Jawhar, '60 Years of an iconic festival: Akashvani Sangeet Sammelan', available at http://jawharsircar.com/assets/pdf/Akashvani_Sangeet_ Sammelan_Jawhar_Sircar.pdf accessed on 14 February 2019.

http://allindiaradio.gov.in/Profile/Mission/Pages/default.aspx accessed on 14 February 2019.

http://prasarbharati.gov.in/Annual_ReportPDF/English_14-15.pdf, p. 17 accessed on 25 March 2019.

http://allindiaradio.gov.in/Profile/Factss%20at%20Glance/Pages/default.aspx accessed on 14 February 2019.

http://allindiaradio.gov.in/Profile/NationalPrograms/Pages/default.aspx accessed on 25 March 2019.

http://allindiaradio.gov.in/Oppurtunities/Music/Pages/Music.aspx accessed on 14 February 2019.

http://prasarbharati.gov.in/Annual_ReportPDF/2015-16-English.pdf, pp. 13, 28, 33, 49-50, accessed on 25 March, 2019.

http://allindiaradio.gov.in/Oppurtunities/Tenders/Documents/New%20 Music%20Gradation%20Policy%20of%20AIR-2014%20(Modified).pdf accessed on 16 February 2019.

https://www.facebook.com/ravindra.katoti.1/posts/10155707810278369 accessed on 14 February 2019.

http://allindiaradio.gov.in/Profile/NationalArtists/Pages/default.aspx accessed on 14 February 2019.

http://pbinfo.air.org.in/feedback/ReceptionReport.aspx accessed on 14 February 2019.

http://allindiaradio.gov.in/Information/RTI/Pages/default.aspx accessed on 14 February 2019.

https://www.facebook.com/AkashvaniAIR/ accessed on 25 March 2019.

https://twitter.com/AkashvaniAIR accessed on 25 March 2019.

http://doordarshan.gov.in/about-doordarshan accessed on 25 March 2019.

https://www.youtube.com/watch?v=hadACBHTcsM accessed on 14 February 2019.

https://www.youtube.com/watch?v=_3nMytTVJ3s accessed on 14 February 2019.

https://www.youtube.com/watch?v=wlkIGgCXqlE accessed on 14 February 2019.

https://www.youtube.com/watch?v=jViVTBioWWc accessed on 14 February 2019.

https://www.youtube.com/watch?v=QZGrOfzSM9Q accessed on 14 February 2019.

http://copyright.gov.in/documents/copyrightrules1957.pdf accessed on 14 February 2019.

https://www.facebook.com/shubha.mudgal/posts/10155910989665820 accessed on 14 February 2019.

https://www.facebook.com/shubha.mudgal/posts/10156052024745820 accessed on 14 February 2019.

http://doordarshan.gov.in/program-highlights?field_sub_sites_tid_1=2325 accessed on 25 March 2019.

https://twitter.com/aneesh/status/717750319531352065 accessed on 14 February 2019.

http://www.prasarbharatiarchives.co.in/doordarshan/music accessed on 14 February 2019.

http://www.mib.gov.in/# accessed on 14 February 2019.

http://filmsdivision.org/about-us.html accessed on 14 February 2019.

http://filmsdivision.org/fd-archieves.html accessed on 14 February 2019.

http://filmsdivision.org/distribution.html accessed on 14 February 2019.

http://rstv.nic.in/about-us accessed on 14 February 2019.

https://www.youtube.com/results?search_query=shakhsiyat accessed on 14 February 2019.

Devdutt, 'Culture Policy: Some Reflections' available at http://www.theatreforum.in/static/upload/docs/National_Cultural_Policy_Reflection.pdf accessed on 25 March, 2019;

Approach Paper on the National Policy on Culture & Observation, Comments, Recommendations Thereon, 1992, Government of India, available at http://www.worldcp.org/india.php?aid=421 accessed on 9 May 2017.

Report of the Working Group on Art and Culture for XII Five-Year Plan (2012-2017), Ministry of Culture, Government of India, New Delhi, January 2012. Available at http://planningcommission.gov.in/aboutus/committee/wrkgrp12/wg_tourist0202.pdf accessed on 22 April 2019.

http://www.indiaculture.nic.in/mission-statement accessed on 14 February 2019.

http://www.indiaculture.nic.in/schemes accessed on 14 February 2019.

http://www.indiaculture.nic.in/sites/default/files/Schemes/Minutes%20 of%2023rd%20meeting.pdf accessed on 14 February, 2019.

National Mission on Cultural Mapping and Roadmap: Mission Document, Ministry of Culture, available at http://www.indiaculture.nic.in/sites/default/files/ CulturalMapping/MissionDocument.pdf, accessed on 14 February 2019.

http://www.sangeetnatak.gov.in/sna/introduction.php accessed on 14 February 2019.

http://sangeetnatak.gov.in/sna/constitution.php accessed on 14 February 2019.

Estimates-Committee—1960-61: Hundred and Thirty-ninth Report (Second-Lok-Sabha) Ministry of Scientific Research and Cultural Affairs, Cultural and International Activities (New Delhi: Lok Sabha Secretariat, 1961). Available at https://eparlib.nic.in/bitstream/123456789/58136/1/ec_02_139_1960. pdf accessed on 22 April 2019.

http://www.sangeetnatak.gov.in/sna/publication.php accessed on 14 February 2019.

http://www.sangeetnatak.gov.in/sna/journal.php accessed on 14 February 2019.

http://sangeetnatak.gov.in/sna/documentation.php as on 14 February 2019.

http://sangeetnatak.gov.in/sna/cds-dvds.php accessed on 14 February 2019.

http://sangeetnatak.gov.in/sna/reports.php accessed on 14 February 2019.

http://www.sangeetnatak.gov.in/sna/interpretation.php accessed on 14 February 2019.

http://ccrtindia.gov.in/aboutus.php accessed on 14 February 2019.

http://ccrtindia.gov.in/statistics.php accessed on 14 February 2019.

http://ezccindia.org/ezcc.html accessed on 14 February 2019.

http://www.nczccindia.in accessed on 14 February 2019.

http://www.nczccindia.in/aboutus.html accessed on 14 February 2019.

http://www.rajeevsethi.com/projects/1986-Apna-Utsav-a.htm accessed on 14 February 2019.

http://www.nczccindia.in accessed on 14 February 2019.

Pandit, Srimoyee, 'Mani Shankar Aiyar Committee on Zonal Cultural Centres formed to Revamp ZCCs submitted Report', available at http://www. jagranjosh.com/current-affairs/mani-shankar-aiyar-committee-on-zonal-cultural-centres-formed-to-revamp-zccs-submitted-report-1302869564-1 accessed on 14 February 2019.

http://ignca.gov.in/about-ignca/organizational-structure/ accessed on 25 March 2019.

http://ignca.gov.in/divisionss/kalanidhi/ accessed on 25 March 2019.

http://ignca.bestbookbuddies.com accessed on 25 March 2019.

http://ignca.gov.in/divisionss/kalanidhi/cultural-archive/sangita-music/ accessed on 25 March 2019.

http://ignca.gov.in/product-category/book/kalamulasastra-series/texts-on-music-dance/ accessed on 25 March 2019.

https://www.youtube.com/watch?v=sLJPlKPwnTs&t=675s accessed on 17 February 2019.

http://ignca.gov.in/divisionss/kaldarsana/bhinn-shadj-innovative-classical-music-series/ accessed on 25 March 2019.

http://ignca.nic.in/PDF_data/vns_ic_Report_Siddhe_Devi_en.pdf accessed on 14 February 2019.

http://ignca.gov.in/wp-content/uploads/2017/04/vnc_ic_Report_Sdevi_04_20174.pdf accessed on 14 February 2019.

http://ignca.gov.in/wp-content/uploads/2017/04/vnc_ic_Report_Sdevi_04_20173.pdf accessed on 14 February 2019.

http://ignca.gov.in/wp-content/uploads/2017/04/vnc_ic_Report_Sdevi_02_2017.pdf accessed on 14 February 2019.

http://ignca.gov.in/wp-content/uploads/2017/04/vnc_ic_Report_Sdevi_04_20171.pdf accessed on 14 February 2019.

http://ignca.gov.in/wp-content/uploads/2017/04/vnc_ic_Report_Sdevi_04_2017.pdf accessed on 14 February 2019.

National Cultural Audiovisual Archives: Project Progress Report, Ministry of Culture, Government of India, (New Delhi: Indira Gandhi National Centre for the Arts, 2017). Available at http://ncaa.gov.in/repository/download/NCAA_Project_Progress_Report_(2014-17).pdf accessed on 14 February 2019.

http://ncaa.gov.in/repository/common/about accessed on 14 February 2019.

http://ignca.nic.in/about.htm#BOARD accessed on 14 February 2019.

http://ignca.nic.in/about.htm#MEMBER accessed on 14 February 2019.

https://twitter.com/search?q=%40aneesh%20%40izuberi&src=typd accessed on 8 April 2019.

http://ncf.nic.in/about-us.html accessed on 22 April 2019.

http://ncf.nic.in/about-us/ncf-role-income.html accessed on 22 April 2019.

http://ncf.nic.in/about-us/annual-reports.html accessed on 22 April 2019.

http://ncf.nic.in/board-of-trustes.html accessed on 22 April 2019.

Report of HPC on the Akademis and other Institutions under the Ministry of Culture, May 2014, available at

http://www.indiaculture.nic.in/sites/default/files/hpc_report/HPC%20REPORT%202014.pdf accessed on 14 February 2019.

http://suburbanmusiccircle.org/suburbancircle/about.html accessed on 14 February 2019.

http://dadarmatungaculturalcentre.org/preamble accessed on 25 March 2019.

http://dadarmatungaculturalcentre.org/facilities accessed on 25 March 2019.

https://weddingz.in/mumbai/dadar-matunga-cultural-centre-dadar-west/ accessed on 25 March 2019.

http://underscorerecords.com/Resources accessed on 15 February 2019.

http://www.harballabh.org/home.php accessed on 25 March 2019.

http://www.doverlanemusicconference.org accessed on 15 February 2019.

http://xaviers.edu/main/index.php/indian-music-group-img accessed on 15 February 2019.

https://www.thekendra.com/ssm-festival.php accessed on 15 February 2019.

http://sawaigandharvabhimsenmahotsav.com accessed on 15 February 2019.

https://www.facebook.com/vishnudigambarjayanti/ accessed on 15 February 2019.

http://www.allarakhafoundation.org/demo/a-homage-to-abbaji-on-his-barsi-3rd-feb-2018/ accessed on 15 February 2019.

The Business of Responsibility: India Corporate Citizenship Report 2011, (Citi, 2011), available at https://www.online.citibank.co.in/portal/india-corporate-citizenship-report.pdf, p. 24, accessed on 15 February 2019.

http://www.itcsra.org/Origin-of-ITC-SRA as on May 30, 2017.

Raut, Sharbani, "India: Surrogate Advertisements In India" at http://www.mondaq.com/india/x/606974/advertising+marketing+branding/CROSS+BORDER+INSOLVENCY+A+NEW+REGIME accessed on 15 March, 2019.

http://www.worldcat.org/title/saptarishi-a-constellation-of-stars/oclc/43977124 accessed on 15 February 2019.

http://ebook.mca.gov.in/Childwindow1.aspx?pageid=17923&type=CA&ChildTitle=Schedules&SearchText= accessed on 15 February 2019.

Handbook on Corporate Social Responsibility in India (Gurgaon: PricewaterhouseCoopers Private Limited, 2013), available at https://www.pwc.in/assets/pdfs/publications/2013/handbook-on-corporate-social-responsibility-in-india.pdf accessed on 15 February 2019.

http://www.ncpamumbai.com/about accessed on 15 February 2019.

https://www.tajmahalteahouse.com/pages/taj-mahal-tea-house-sessions accessed on 19 March 2019.

http://www.saregama.com/static/about_us accessed on 15 February 2019.

http://www.musictoday.in/inside.phtml?genere_id=1 accessed on 15 February 2019.

http://www.timesmusic.com/genre/indian-classical-9-1.html accessed on 15 February 2019.

https://www.discogs.com/artist/1600354-AshaRani-Mathur accessed on 17 March 2019.

https://www.linkedin.com/in/asharani-mathur-2615b610/?ppe=1 accessed on 25 March 2019.

http://sursanjeevan.com/RPSur_PtKatti.html accessed on 15 February 2019.

https://www.indiatoday.in/swarutsav/about_us.jsp accessed on 15 February 2019.

https://www.youtube.com/results?search_query=sadhana+vrindavan+gurukul accessed on 15 February 2017.

https://www.youtube.com/user/InsyncChannel accessed on 15 February 2019.

https://www.youtube.com/watch?v=K-AleMLtWsE accessed on 15 February 2019.

https://www.youtube.com/watch?v=vd2IPYeKZ1c accessed on 15 February 2019.

https://www.youtube.com/watch?v=0AP8cmvuoUM accessed on 15 February 2019.

https://www.youtube.com/watch?v=VddfTbjOIzU accessed on 15 February 2019.

Das Gupta, Surajeet, 'What is WorldSpace radio all about?' at https://www.rediff.com/money/2005/aug/19radio.htm accessed on 19 March 2019.

https://en.wikipedia.org/wiki/1worldspace accessed on 15 February 2019.

https://www.shiksha.com/hospitality-travel/event-management/colleges/colleges-india accessed on 15 February 2019.

http://abgmvm.org/about-us/ accessed on 15 February 2019.

http://abgmvm.org/courses-and-examination/ accessed on 15 February 2019.

http://abgmvm.org/music-teachers-conferences/ accessed on 15 February 2019.

http://abgmvm.org/workshops-seminars/ accessed on 15 February 2019.

http://www.pracheenkalakendra.org/?page_id=91 accessed on 15 February, 2019.

http://www.sangitmahabharati.org accessed on 15 February, 2019.

http://www.saptak.org/saptakDesk/saptakArchives accessed on 15 February 2019.

http://www.saptak.org/saptakDesk/saptakSchool accessed on 15 February 2019.

https://ajoychakrabarty.com/mobile/shrutinandan.php accessed on 15 February 2019.

http://ajivasan.com accessed on 15 February 2019;

http://www.extraprepare.com/mumbai/listing/kangaroo-kids_3838.html accessed on 15 February 2019.

http://www.ajivasanhall.com accessed on 15 February 2019.

The Report of the University Education Commission (December 1948–August 1949), Volume I, First Reprint Edition (Delhi: Ministry of Education, Government of India 1962), available at http://www.educationforallinindia. com/1949%20Report%20of%20the%20University%20Education%20 Commission.pdf accessed on 15 February 2019.

Report of the Education Commission (1964–66) Education and National Development, First Edition (Delhi: Ministry of Education, Government of India, 1966), available at https://archive.org/details/ReportOfTheEducat ionCommission1964-66D.S.KothariReport accessed on 15 February 2019.

National Curriculum Framework 2005 (New Delhi: National Council of Educational Research and Training, 2005), available at http://www.ncert. nic.in/rightside/links/pdf/framework/english/nf2005.pdf accessed on 15 February 2019.

Secondary School Curriculum 2017-18, Volume – I: Main Subjects for Classes IX & X (New Delhi: Central Board of Secondary Education, 2017), pp. 113–126; *Senior School Curriculum 2017-18, Volume – III: Music and Dance for Class XI & XII* (New Delhi: Central Board of Secondary Education, 2017), available at http://49.50.70.100/web_material/Curriculum17/SrSecondary/ Senior%20School%20Curriculum%202017-18%20Volume%20-3.pdf accessed on 6 August 2017.

https://www.youtube.com/results?search_query=NCERT+music accessed on 15 February 2019.

https://targetstudy.com/colleges/ba-hons-music-degree-colleges-in-kolkata. html accessed on 15 February 2019.

http://mu.ac.in/portal/department-of-music/ accessed on 15 February 2019.

http://www.unipune.ac.in/dept/fine_arts/centre_for_performing_arts/cpa_ webfiles/academic.htm accessed on 15 February 2019.

http://www.iksv.ac.in/about accessed on 15 February 2019.

https://www.youtube.com/watch?v=hbFojsXZSGk&t=2s accessed on 15 February 2019.

http://www.msubaroda.ac.in/faculty.php?fac_id=12&action=home accessed on 15 February 2019.

http://www.bhu.ac.in/performing_arts/ accessed on 15 February 2019.

http://www.bhu.ac.in/performing_arts/vocal_music/index.php accessed on 15 February 2019.

http://www.bhu.ac.in/performing_arts/instrumental_music/index.php accessed on 15 February 2019.

http://www.bhu.ac.in/performing_arts/vocal_music/index.php accessed on 15 February 2019.

http://www.iksv.ac.in/about accessed on 15 February 2019;
http://www.iksv.ac.in/affiliated-colleges accessed on 15 February 2019.
http://www.iksv.ac.in/vission-mission accessed on 15 February 2019.
http://bhatkhandemusic.edu.in/history/ accessed on 15 February 2019.
http://bhatkhandemusic.edu.in/message-from-vc/ accessed on 15 February 2019.
https://w.soundcloud.com/player/?url=https%3A//api.soundcloud.com/tracks/282848791&auto_play=true&hide_related=true&show_comments=false&show_user=true&show_reposts=false&visual=true&sharing=false&download=false&liking=false&%22 accessed on 15 February 2019.
http://www.itcsra.org/Aims-and-Objectives accessed on 15 February 2019.
http://www.itcsra.org/Facilities-and-Library accessed on 15 February 2019.
http://www.itcsra.org/Full-Term-Scholarship accessed on 15 February 2019.
http://www.itcsra.org/ITC-SRA-Publication accessed on 15 February 2019.
http://www.gangubaihangalgurukul.gov.in/aboutus.htm accessed on 12 August 2017.
http://www.gangubaihangalgurukul.gov.in/vision.htm accessed on 12 August 2017.
http://ashokdaranade.org/wordpress/index.php/about-adr/publications/ accessed on 15 February 2019.
http://www.indiaifa.org/india-foundation-arts.html accessed on 15 February 2019.
http://www.indiaifa.org/grants-and-projects.html?keys=hindustani+music&tid=All&tid_1=All&date=All accessed on 15 February 2019.
http://www.sangeetkaryalaya.in/page/about-us accessed on 15 February 2019.
https://www.indiastudies.org/ethnomusicology/ accessed on 15 February 2019.
https://www.indiastudies.org/ethnomusicology/collections/ accessed on 15 February 2019.
https://eap.bl.uk/search/site/chandvankar accessed on 15 February 2019.
https://music.washington.edu/ethnomusicology-archives accessed on 15 February 2019.
https://www.soas.ac.uk/courseunits/15PMUH025.html accessed on 15 February 2019.
https://www.facebook.com/pg/Dr.AshokDa.RanadeArchives/about/?ref=page_internal accessed on 15 February 2019.
http://www.aneeshpradhan.com/tender-archives-at-ncpa/ accessed on 15 February 2019.

http://www.spicmacay.com/about accessed on 15 February 2019.

http://www.arvindguptatoys.com/arvindgupta/spicmacay-eng.pdf accessed on 15 February 2019.

http://www.spicmacay.com/chintan accessed on 15 February 2019.

http://spicmacay.com/coordinators accessed on 15 February 2019.

http://spicmacay.com/basic-page/how-organise-spic-macay-events accessed on 15 February 2019.

http://www.spicmacay.com/about/activities accessed on 15 February 2019.

http://www.spicmacay.com/coordinators accessed on 15 February 2019.

http://pib.nic.in/newsite/PrintRelease.aspx?relid=177210 accessed on 15 February 2019.

https://www.youtube.com/user/spicmacay/videos accessed on 15 February 2019.

http://spicmacay.com/naadbhed accessed on 15 February 2019.

http://www.spicmacay.com/about/four-pillars-spic-macay assessed on 15 February 2019.

http://spicmacay.com/our-supporters accessed on 15 February 2019;

http://www.spicmacay.com/about accessed on 15 February 2019.

http://www.rediff.com/money/2007/sep/29spec.htm accessed on 15 February 2019.

http://underscorerecords.com/Catalog accessed on 15 February 2019.

https://www.facebook.com/MeeraMusic/ accessed on 15 February 2019.

http://www.sonicoctaves.com/store/ accessed on 15 February 2019.

http://underscorerecords.com/catalog/listing/Merchandise/1 accessed on 15 February 2019.

http://www.singingsleeves.com accessed on 15 February 2019.

http://underscorerecords.com/catalog/listing/Print/1 accessed on 15 February 2019.

www.UnderscoreRecords.com accessed on 15 February 2019.

http://www.shubhamudgal.com/shop/ accessed on 15 February 2019.

https://www.sudeepaudio.com/profile/article/vocal accessed on 15 February 2019.

http://artclickindia.com/AboutUs.aspx accessed on 15 February 2019.

https://itunes.apple.com/in/app/itablapro-tabla-tanpura-player/id337350026?mt=8 accessed on 13 September 2017;

http://tampura.bzhtec.com/en/Introduction.html accessed on 15 February 2019.

https://www.radel.in accessed on 15 February 2019.

http://www.soundlabs.in/dumas-chukame-1137.html accessed on 15 February 2019.

https://musicmumbai.wordpress.com accessed on 15 February 2019.

http://debatesangeet.blogspot.in accessed on 15 February 2019.

http://www.parrikar.org accessed on 15 February 2019

http://swaratala.blogspot.in accessed on 15 February 2019.

https://www.swarganga.org accessed on 15 February 2019.

http://www.mohannadkarni.org accessed on 15 February 2019.

http://sangeetkosh.net accessed on 15 February 2019.

http://underscorerecords.com/Resources accessed on 15 February 2019;

http://underscorerecords.com/Podcast accessed on 15 February 2019.

http://www.sufimovement.org accessed on 15 February 2019.

Kumar, Anu, 'How an Indian man and his English wife introduced George Harrison to Ravi Shankar to create history', available at https://scroll.in/magazine/881709/how-an-indian-man-and-his-english-wife-introduced-george-harrison-to-ravi-shankar-to-create-history accessed on 15 February 2019.

http://iccr.gov.in/content/constitution accessed on 15 February 2019.

http://iccr.gov.in accessed on 15 February 2019.

https://www.indiabudget.gov.in/ub2018-19/eb/sbe28.pdf accessed on accessed on 23 March 2019.

http://iccr.gov.in/content/outgoing-troupes accessed on 15 February 2019.

http://iccr.gov.in/content/list-centres accessed on 15 February 2019.

http://iccr.gov.in/content/empanelment-artists accessed on 22 February 2017.

http://iccr.gov.in/sites/default/files/empanelmentguidelines.pdf accessed on 15 February 2019.

http://iccr.gov.in/sites/default/files/RLIST2017.pdf accessed on 24 March 2019.

http://iccr.gov.in/content/dancemusic-institutions accessed on 15 February 2019.

http://iccr.gov.in/content/incoming-troupes accessed on 15 February 2019.

http://webtv.un.org/watch/ravi-shankar-and-yehudi-menuhin-human-rights-day-concert-10-december-1967/2033645153001 accessed on 15 February 2019.

https://www.britannica.com/biography/Ravi-Shankar accessed on 15 February 2019;

https://aacm.org/ali-akbar-khan/ accessed on 25 March 2019.

https://en.wikipedia.org/wiki/Ravi_Shankar%27s_Festival_from_India accessed on 15 February 2019.

https://en.wikipedia.org/wiki/Ravi_Shankar%27s_Music_Festival_from_India accessed on 15 February 2019.

https://www.icmca.org/about/mission-vision/ accessed on 15 February 2019.

http://www.basantbahar.org/about/history accessed on 15 February 2019.

http://www.icmcdfw.org/about.aspx accessed on 15 February 2019.

https://www.musiccircle.org/our-founders accessed on 6 August 2018.

http://www.ragamala.ca/about-us/ accessed on 25 March 2019.

http://www.amc.org.uk/about_us.html accessed on 25 March 2019.

http://www.india-arts.pitt.edu/over.html accessed on 25 March 2019.

https://music.calarts.edu/programs/north-indian-music accessed on 15 February 2019.

https://music.calarts.edu/programs/world-percussion accessed on 15 February 2019.

https://www.ethnomusic.ucla.edu/music-of-india-ensemble accessed on 15 February 2019.

https://www.codarts.nl/worldmusic/ accessed on 15 February 2019.

https://www.womex.com/virtual/codarts_research accessed on 26 September 2017.

Dixit, Balwant N., 'Globalization and Indian Classical Music: The North American Scene' at http://www.india-arts.pitt.edu/globalization.html accessed on 15 February 2019.

http://www.pjim.org/Locations.html accessed on 15 February 2019.

https://www.discogs.com/label/95098-Chhanda-Dhara accessed on 15 February 2019.

https://www.facebook.com/pg/neelamaudiovideo/about/?ref=page_internal accessed on 15 February 2019.

https://www.wyastone.co.uk/catalogsearch/result/?q=india accessed on 15 February 2019.

http://www.momentrecords.com/#section-about accessed on 15 February 2019.

https://www.discogs.com/label/155986-India-Archive-Music accessed on 15 February 2019.

https://www.discogs.com/label/504229-Makar accessed on 15 February 2019.

https://www.youtube.com/watch?v=KksTVgmSQ1s accessed on 15 February 2019.

http://dashboard-padmaawards.gov.in/?Field=Art accessed on 25 March 2019.

'GST Rate & HSN Code for Musical Instruments - Chapter 92', available at https://cleartax.in/s/musical-instruments-gst-rate-hsn-code accessed on 24 March 2019.

'Schedule of GST Rates', available at https://cbec-gst.gov.in/pdf/Schedule%20 of%20GST%20rates%20for%20services.pdf accessed on 22 April 2019.

Mahure, Pritam, *GST in India*, 7th ed. (n.p., 2018), available at https://drive. google.com/file/d/13baoX7goPWRrqtr_JI2aA_asWE7ObRfD/view accessed on 16 February 2019.

Kusnur, Narendra, 'Need to promote younger Hindustani classical music talent', available at https://narenmusicnotes.wordpress.com/2013/09/05/need-to-promote-younger-hindustani-music-talent/, accessed on 16 February 2019.

http://cpcb.nic.in/noise-pollution/ accessed on 16 February 2019.

https://www.youtube.com/watch?v=7QLtSXPz-Vg accessed on 16 February 2019.

https://www.youtube.com/watch?v=ZAckVRVStfA accessed on 16 February 2019.

https://www.youtube.com/watch?v=Jac2ENe93Sw accessed on 16 February 2019.

https://www.youtube.com/watch?v=puP8KUHKy2w accessed on 16 February 2019.

https://www.youtube.com/watch?v=7QLtSXPz-Vg&t=2s accessed on 29 March 2019.

https://www.youtube.com/watch?v=ZAckVRVStfA&t=24s accessed on 29 March 2019.

https://www.youtube.com/watch?v=Jac2ENe93Sw&t=40s accessed on 29 March 2019.

https://www.youtube.com/watch?v=puP8KUHKy2w&t=19s accessed on 29 March 2019.

https://www.youtube.com/watch?v=QLFZj7IwNR0 accessed on 29 March 2019.

https://www.youtube.com/watch?v=iY2Z_giTMb0 accessed on 29 March 2019.

https://www.youtube.com/watch?v=Mtk6ZN70ktU accessed on 29 March 2019.

http://www.georgeharrison.com/dark-horse-records-announces-ravi-shankar-george-harrison-box-set-release/ accessed on 30 March 2019

http://www.khabar.com/magazine/features/every_concert_teaches_me_something_different accessed on 30 March 2019

http://sangeetnatak.gov.in/sna/journal-sangna.php accesses on 31 March 2019; http://sangeetnatak.gov.in/sna/rajbhasha-rupambara.php accessed on 31 March 2019.

https://itunes.apple.com/in/album/the-raga-guide/1050729901 accessed on 5 May 2019.

https://www.amazon.com/Ravi-Shankar-Distinguished-Musician-Remastered/dp/B00OLA7AQC/ref=sr_1_1?fst=as%3Aoff&qid=1557124317&refinements=p_lbr_music_artists_browse-bin%3ARavi+Shankar&rnid=3458810011&s=dmusic&sr=1-1 accessed on 5 May 2019.

https://play.google.com/music/listen?gclid=CjwK CAjwk7rmBRAaEiwAhDGhxEG4G-pv9a1t_

hmostPQ1kFU2Zajh3bCQwLTkhA5jyOg5qx82vGT5xoCKbkQAvD_
BwE&gclsrc=aw.ds#/wst/artist/Ab6njtn6de7xmpyjgf37lcolcvq accessed on
5 May 2019.
https://open.spotify.com/user/thesoundsofspotify/
playlist/4JtowPifE700fO0oqyMFSD accessed on 5 May 2019; https://
gaana.com/album/yaman accessed on 5 May 2019.
https://www.jiosaavn.com/search/yaman accessed on 5 May 2019.
http://www.twaang.com/music-on-twaang.html accessed on 5 May 2019.
https://www.instamojo.com/payment-links/ accessed on 5 May 2019.
https://trueschool.in/courses/hindustani-music-lessons/# accessed on 5 May
2019.
http://globalmusicinstitute.in/three-year-graduate-diploma/ accessed on 5 May
2019.
https://www.shankarmahadevanacademy.com/learn-raga-alhaiya-bilaval-
khelori-hori-madhyalaya-teentaal/HVS801/ accessed on 5 May 2019.
https://www.youtube.com/channel/UCs6OTIFV53Z-EGT84lxTvqQ accessed
on 17 May 2019.
https://wikisource.org/wiki/Author:Neela_Bhagwat accessed on 2 May 2019.
https://underscorerecords.com/Catalog accessed on 2 May 2019.
https://swarasankula.org/index.php/media/bhatkhande-project/ accessed on
2 May 2019.
https://www.darbarplayer.com accessed on 5 May 2019.
http://www.hclconcerts.com/about/ accessed on 3 May 2019.
https://play.google.com/store/apps/details?id=com.hcl.music&hl=en_IN
accessed on 3 May 2019.

ALBUMS

Sanchay: Bandish Sangraha, Underscore Records Private Limited, New Delhi,
2007.

INTERVIEWS

Interview with Batuk Diwanji held in January 1993 and reproduced in Aneesh
Pradhan, *Hindustani Music in Colonial Bombay*, (Gurgaon: Three Essays
Collective, 2014).
Interview with Kaushalya and Dinker Manjeshwar held on 10 September 1993,
and reproduced in Aneesh Pradhan, *Hindustani Music in Colonial Bombay*,
(Gurgaon: Three Essays Collective, 2014).

Interview with Dinker Manjeshwar held on 30 March 2011, and reproduced in Aneesh Pradhan, *Hindustani Music in Colonial Bombay*, (Gurgaon: Three Essays Collective, 2014).

PERSONAL COMMUNICATION

Personal communication with Irfan Zuberi, Project Manager, NCAA, on 15 and 16 June, 2018, and on 9 November, 2018.

Personal communication on 26 September 2017 from curator Amarendra Nandu Dhaneshwar.

Personal communication from Sunilkant Gupta, flautist and director of music I/C, Films Division, government of India, on 21 August 2017.

Notes

Preface

1   Balwant Triumback Sahasrabuddhe, *Hindu Music and the Gayan Samaj* (Madras: The Madras Jubilee Gayan Samaj, 1887), pp. 82–83; Gopal Hari Deshmukh 'Lokhitwadi', 'Sangeetshastra' in *Lokhitwadikrit Nibandhsangraha: Gopal Hari Deshmukh* (Marathi), ed. Anant Kakba Priyolkar (Mumbai: Popular Prakashan, 1996), pp. 521, 524.

2   V.N. Bhatkhande, *A Short Historical Survey of the Music of Upper India* (Bombay: B.S. Sukthankar, 1934), p. 34.

3   Raja Sir Sourindro Mohun Tagore 'Universal History of Music: Compiled from Diverse Sources Together with Various Original Notes on Hindu Music' in *The Chowkhambha Sanskrit Studies*, Vol. XXXI, 2nd ed. (Varanasi: The Chowkhambha Sanskrit Series Office, 1963), pp. 87–88. For a biographical sketch of S.M. Tagore, see Surendra Mohan Tagore, *Public Opinion and Official Communications about the Bengal Music School and Its President* (Calcutta: Panchanun Mookherjee, 1876), pp. 225–234. Also see Allyn Miner, 'The Sitar: An Overview of Change', in 'The World of Music, le monde de la musique, die welt der musik India', *Journal of the International Institute for Comparative Music Studies and Documentation*, Vol. XXXII, No. 2 (1990), (Berlin), p. 44; Laxminarayan Garg, *Hamaare Sangeet Ratna,*

Pratham Bhaag, (Hindi) (Hathras: Sangit Karyalaya, 1957), pp. 67–71. For an analysis of patronage to music in Bengal and the work of S.M. Tagore, see Michael David Rosse, 'The Movement for the Revitalization of "Hindu" Music in Northern India, 1860–1930: The Role of Associations and Institutions' (PhD diss., University of Pennsylvania, Philadelphia, 1995), pp. 12–63; Adrian McNeil, 'The Dynamics of Social and Musical Status in Hindustani Music: Sarodiyas, Seniyas and the Margi-Desi Paradigm' (PhD diss., Department of Music, Monash University, Melbourne, 1992), pp. 115–125. For similar support provided in the Bombay Presidency, see Sahasrabuddhe, *Hindu Music*, p. 43.

4   Sahasrabuddhe, *Hindu Music*, pp. 66–73; B.R. Deodhar, *Gaayanaachaarya P. Vishnu Digambar* (Marathi), (Mumbai: Akhil Bharatiya Gandharva Mahavidyalaya Mandal, 1971), pp. 51, 62.

5   Pestanjee Firozeshah Kapadia, *Gayan Uttejak Mandali: Tenee Ponee Sadinee Tawaareekhno Ahewaal*, (Gujarati) (Mumbai: Mrs Freni M. Cama, 1946), pp. 36–37.

6   Deodhar, *Gaayanaachaarya P. Vishnu Digambar, op.cit.*, pp. 78–79.

7   Government of India Act, 1935, pp. 303–308. See also, Vrinda Uday Mishra, 'Decolonising the Raj: Bombay under Provincial Autonomy, 1937–1939' (PhD diss., Faculty of Arts, Monash University, Melbourne, 2003), p. 9.

8   A detailed account of cultural policy in India from the 1950s to recent times has been co-authored by Raghavendra Tenkayala, P. Radhika, Ashish Rajadhyaksha, and is available at http://www.worldcp.org/india.php?aid=1 accessed on 14 February 2019.

9   From Jawaharlal Nehru's speech at the inauguration of the Indian Council of Cultural Relations, New Delhi, 9 April 1950, cited in *The Essential Writings of Jawaharlal Nehru*, Volume I, eds. S. Gopal and Uma Iyengar (2003) (New Delhi: Oxford University Press 2003), p. 113.

10   https://www.mea.gov.in/Images/pdf1/S7.pdf accessed on 14 February 2019.

11   See History on the drop-down menu under About Us at http://www.indiaculture.nic.in/history accessed on 14 February 2019. Another source mentions the date for the creation of an independent ministry of tourism and culture as May 2004. See http://www.indiaculture.nic.in/sites/default/files/budget/Performance_Budget_Chapter_1.pdf accessed on 14 February 2019.

12   Kapila Vatsyayan, 'Cultural Development: A Profile' in *A Centenary History of the Indian National Congress*, Vol. Four, 1947–1964, ed. Iqbal Narain (New Delhi: All India Congress Committee (I) and Vikas Publishing House Private Limited, 1990), p. 315.

13   http://inc.in accessed on 14 February 2019; http://www.cpim.org accessed on 14 February 2019; http://www.samajwadiparty.in/index.php accessed

on 14 February 2019; http://rjd.co.in/index.html accessed on 14 February 2019; http://www.bspindia.org accessed on 14 February 2019; http://aiadmk.org.in/en/ accessed on 28 June 2016; http://dmk.in/home accessed on 28 June 2016; http://ncp.com.nu accessed on 14 February 2019; https://aamaadmiparty.org accessed on 19 March 2019; http://aitcofficial.org/the-party/ accessed on 19 March 2019.

14 http://www.bjp.org/en/core-issues/vision-of-modi accessed on June 28, 2016.

15 ibid.

16 http://shivsena.org/m/art-academy/ accessed on 28 June 2016.

17 http://pldkalaacademy.org/about.html accessed on 28 June 2016.

18 ibid.

19 ibid.

20 http://manase.org/# accessed on 28 June 2016.

21 For an analysis of the working of the Sangeet Natak Akademi and the National School of Drama with regard to theatre in the context of the larger framework of cultural policy of a new nation-state, see Anita Elizabeth Cherian, 'Fashioning a National Theatre: Institutions and Cultural Policy in Post-Independence India' (Unpublished doctoral dissertation, New York University, New York, 2005).

22 Daniel Neuman, *The Life of Music in North India: The Organisation of an Artistic Tradition* (New Delhi: Manohar Publications, 1980), pp. 202–229; Huib Schipper, 'Hindustani Music: Resilience and Flexibility in Recontextualizing and Ancient Tradition' in *Sustainable Futures for Music Cultures: An Ecological Perspective*, eds. Huib Schippers, Catherine Grant (New York: Oxford University Press, 2016), pp. 94–136.

Introduction

1 *Role of Media in Promotion of Music in India* (Mumbai: ITC-SRA Western Region, January 2012), p. 95.

2 https://mumbaimirror.indiatimes.com/opinion/columnists/sumana-ramanan/upholder-of-a-great-tradition/articleshow/67239004.cms accessed on March 5, 2019.

3 *Role of Media in Promotion of Music in India*, (Mumbai: ITC-SRA Western Region, January 2012), p. 96.

4 Most musicians refer to such collaborative ventures as fusion music concerts. Ashok Da. Ranade classifies them under a broad category that he calls 'confluence music'. See Ashok Da. Ranade, *Perspectives on Music: Ideas and Theories* (New Delhi: Promilla & Co. with Bibliophile South Asia, 2008), pp. 68–86. I have, however, chosen to use the term 'fusion music', as this has found popular acceptance.

5   Peter Lavezzoli, *Bhairavi: The Global Impact of Indian Music* (Noida: HarperCollins Publishers India, 2009), p. 392.

6   Ashok Roy, *Music Makers: Living Legends of Indian Classical Music* (New Delhi: Rupa & Co., 2004), p. 213.

7   http://indianexpress.com/article/lifestyle/art-and-culture/fusion-has-existed-in-india-for-a-thousand-years-tabla-maestro-zakir-hussain/ accessed on 14 February 2019.

8   Ashok Roy, *Music Makers*, p. 212.

9   ibid, p. 328.

10 ibid.

11 Kumar Prasad Mukherji, *The Lost World of Hindustani Music* (New Delhi: Penguin Books, 2006), p. 27.

12 Lavezzoli, *Bhairavi*, p. 381.

13 ibid, p. 385.

14 Roy, *Music Makers*, op. cit., pp 312-14.

15 Aneesh Pradhan, 'Perspectives on Performance Practice: Hindustani Music in Nineteenth and Twentieth Century Bombay (Mumbai)' in *South Asia: Journal of South Asian Studies*, Vol. XXVII, No. 3 (December 2004) (Carfax Publishing, Taylor and Francis Group). For a brief overview of the discourse concerning the question of authenticity with regard to folk music in various parts of the world, see Bonnie C. Wade, *Thinking Musically: Experiencing Music, Expressing Culture* (New York: Oxford University Press, 2004), pp. 140–145.

16 P. Vishnu Narayan Bhatkhande, *Hindustaanee Sangeet Paddhati: Kramik Pustak Maalikaa, Chauthi Pustak*, Hindi translation, ed. Prof. Harishchandra Shrivastav (Allahabad: Sangeet Sadan Prakashan, 2005), p. 42; See also, P. Vishnu Narayan Bhatkhande, *Hindustaanee Sangeet Paddhati: Kramik Pustak Maalikaa, Chhati Pustak*, Hindi translation, ed. Prof. Harishchandra Shrivastav (Allahabad: Sangeet Sadan Prakashan), pp. 30–31.

17 ibid., p. 16.

18 Vamanrao H. Deshpande, *Indian Musical Traditions: An Aesthetic Study of the Gharanas in Hindustani Music* (Bombay: Popular Prakashan, 1987), pp. 116–117.

19 ibid, pp. 117–118.

20 Romila Thapar, *Cultural Transaction and Early India: Tradition and Patronage* (New Delhi: Oxford University Press, 2001), pp. 7–8.

21 The efforts of sections from the Indian intelligentsia to establish Hindustani music as a symbol of national culture with an ancient Hindu-Sanskritic past, particularly in the context of the educated middle class in colonial Bombay, have been examined in Aneesh Pradhan, *Hindustani Music in Colonial Bombay* (Gurgaon: Three Essays Collective, 2014), pp. 1–2, 47–49, 71–72, 87–88.

22 http://www.ravishankar.org/reflections, accessed on 14 February 2019.

23 Ashok Ranade, 'Gandharvas and Musical Changes – Attempt at Cultural Perspectives' in *World of Gandharvas*, eds. Balawant Joshi, Dr Dilip Inamdar, Prof. Charudatta Bhagwat, Dr S.S. Gore (New Bombay: Sound Library Project of Akhil Bharatiya Gandharva Mahavidyalaya Mandal, 1993), p. 17.

1. Riding the Airwaves

1 http://prasarbharati.gov.in/default.aspx as on July 8, 2016. The name Akashvani was adopted in 1956 and is used synonymously with All India Radio. http://allindiaradio.gov.in/Profile/Growth%20and%20 Development/Pages/default.aspx accessed on 14 February 2019.

2 Rajiv Takru, 'Inaugural Address' in *Role of Media in Promotion of Music in India*, ITC-SRA, p. 9.

3 ibid, p. 11.

4 http://prasarbharati.gov.in/PBAct.php accessed on 25 March 2019.

5 http://indianexpress.com/article/india/india-others/prasar-ceo-hits-back-why-cant-ministry-send review-results-to-us/ accessed on 25 March 2019; http://bureaucracytoday.com/latestnews.aspx?id=2166 accessed on 14 February 2019; http://indiatoday.intoday.in/story/prasar-bharti-information-and-broadcasting-ministry/1/359913.html accessed on 14 February 2019.

6 http://www.business-standard.com/article/companies/prasar-bharati-can-sircar-turn-it-around-112102400078_1.html accessed on 14 February 2019.

7 http://jawharsircar.com/about_Career.html accessed on 14 February 2019.

8 http://blogs.timesofindia.indiatimes.com/toi-edit-page/why-india-cant-have-its-bbc/ accessed on 14 February 2019.

9 http://theindianawaaz.com/air-dds-content-quality-has-come-down-prasar-bharati-chief/ accessed on 14 February 2019; http://www.business-standard.com/article/news-ians/prasar-bharati-ceo-bats-for-youth-savvy-content-115090800919_1.html accessed on 14 February 2019.

10 https://thewire.in/229362/smriti-irani-latest-star-ministrys-serial-wars-prasar-bharati/ accessed on 14 February 2019. See also https://thewire.in/ government/angered-prasar-bharatis-defiance-smriti-irani-blocks-salary-funds-dd-air accessed on 6 March 2019.

11 http://indianexpress.com/article/opinion/columns/a-deceit-called-autonomy-prasar-bharati-act-5071837/ accessed on 16 April 2018.

12 http://prasarbharati.gov.in/Mission.php accessed on 8 July 2016.

13 http://prasarbharati.gov.in/PBAct.php#Fu accessed on 11 July 2016.

14 http://allindiaradio.gov.in/profile/milestones/pages/default.aspx. accessed on 6 March 2019. See also, U.L. Baruah, *This Is All India Radio—A*

Handbook of Radio Broadcasting in India (New Delhi: Publications Division, Ministry of Information and Broadcasting, Government of India, 1983), pp. 1, 8; Sumati Mutatkar, 'Music and the Radio (Looking Back and Beyond)' in the *Akashwani Sangeet Sammelan 1998 Brochure* (New Delhi: Prasar Bharati Broadcasting Corporation of India, Ministry of Information & Broadcasting, Government of India, 1998); Alasdair Pinkerton, 'Radio and the Raj: Broadcasting in British India (1920–1940)' in *Journal of the Royal Asiatic Society,* Series 3, 18, 2 (2008), (London), pp. 167–191, doi: 10.1017/ S1356186307008048.

15 Balkrishnabuwa Kapileshwari, *Shrutidarshan* (Marathi), (Pune: Continental Prakashan, 1963), p. 68.

16 B.R. Deodhar, *Thor Sangeetkaar* (Marathi), (Mumbai: Akhil Bharatiya Gandharva Mahavidyalaya Mandal, 1973), p. 68.

17 Daniel M. Neuman, *The Life of Music in North India: The Organisation of an Artistic Tradition* (New Delhi: Manohar Publications, 1980), p. 172.

18 Susheela Misra, *Music Profiles,* (n.p., 1955), pp. 49, 57.

19 Laxminarayan Garg, *Hamaare Sangeet Ratna,* p. 173.

20 Lionel Fielden, *Report on the Progress of Broadcasting in India: Up to the 31st March 1939,* (Delhi: Manager of Publications, 1940), p. 60.

21 B.R. Deodhar, 'School of Indian Music' in *Deodhar's School of Indian Music, Golden Jubilee Souvenir,* (Marathi), (Mumbai, 1975), n.pag.

22 Fielden, *Report on the Progress of Broadcasting,* p. 21. The term 'mirasi' refers to a caste of hereditary musicians that was low in the social order.

23 ibid.

24 G.C. Awasthy, *Broadcasting in India,* (Mumbai: Allied Publishers Private Limited, 1965), p. 38.

25 ibid.

26 Fielden, *Report on the Progress of Broadcasting,* p. 21.

27 ibid.

28 ibid, p. 20.

29 ibid, p. 134.

30 Deodhar, *Gaayanaachaarya P. Vishnu Digambar,* op. cit. p. 122.

31 Baruah, *This Is All India Radio,* op. cit, p. 8; Fielden, *Report on the Progress of Broadcasting,* op. cit., p. 25; Neuman, *The Life of Music,* op. cit., p. 184.

32 http://allindiaradio.gov.in/Profile/Growth%20and%20Development/ Pages/default.aspx accessed on 16 February 2019;. See also, Baruah, *This Is All India Radio,* p. 8.

33 Jawhar Sircar, 'Remembering Akashvani' at http://akashvanisamvaad. blogspot.com/2014/05/prasar-bharati-ceo-jawhar-sircars.html accessed on 5 July 2016.

34 'Music as Compulsory Subject in Schools: Dr. Keskar's Suggestion' in *The Times of India*, 6 November, 1957, p. 3. www.proquest.com accessed on 21 March 2017

35 ibid. For a discussion on Keskar's role in propagating art music on AIR, see David Lelyveld, 'Upon the Subdominant: Administering Music on All-India Radio' in *Consuming Modernity: Public Culture in a South Asian World*, ed. Carol A. Breckenridge (Minneapolis: University of Minnesota Press, 1995), pp. 55–60.

36 Baruah, *This Is All India Radio*, op. cit., p. 10. For an examination of Keskar's role in propagating art music on All India radio, see Lelyveld, 'Upon the Subdominant', op. cit., pp. 55–60.

37 Baruah, *This Is All India Radio*, ibid., pp. 9–10. Jawhar Sircar mentions that the first Akashvani Sangeet Sammelan was held over three days beginning 23 October 1954. See http://jawharsircar.com/assets/pdf/Akashvani_Sangeet_Sammelan_Jawhar_Sircar.pdf accessed on 14 February 2019.

38 http://jawharsircar.com/assets/pdf/Akashvani_Sangeet_Sammelan_Jawhar_Sircar.pdf accessed on 14 February 2019.

39 'AIR Audition Tests at Bombay: 400 Artistes on List' in *The Times of India*, 26 September 1952, p. 1; www.proquest.com accessed on 12 July 2015.

40 'Bombay Artistes Resent A.I.R. Audition System: Decision To Boycott Programmes' in *The Times of India*, 14 May 1953, pp. 1, 3; www.proquest.com accessed on 12 July 2015; 'Audition Tests' in *The Times of India*, 15 May 1953, p. 6; www.proquest.com accessed on 12 July 2017; 'Audition Test Issue: Offer to Hear Artistes' Views' in *The Times of India*, 16 May 1953, p. 11; www.proquest.com accessed on 12 July 2017; 'Struggle Against A.I.R. Will Continue' in *The Times of India*, 24 May 1953, p. 2, www.proquest.com accessed on 19 May 2016; 'Agitation Will Benefit All Artistes: Mandal Gives Assurance' in *The Times of India*, 28 May 1953, p. 3; www.proquest.com accessed on 12 July 2015; '"Campaign Of Vilification Must Stop"—Reply to Radio Artistes' in *The Times of India*, 3 June 1953, p. 3; www.proquest.com accessed on 19 May 2016; 'A.I.R.'s Tests: Mandal's Views Misunderstood' in *The Times of India*, 12 June 1953, p. 3; www.proquest.com accessed on 19 May 2016; 'Audition Test Controversy: A.I.R. Blamed' in *The Times of India*, 27 June 1953, p. 11; www.proquest.com accessed on 12 July 2015. Also, based on information procured during interview with Kaushalya and Dinker Manjeshwar held on 10 September 1993, and with Dinker Manjeshwar held on 30 March 2011. See also, Kapileshwari *Shrutidarshan*, pp. 219–221.

41 S.K. Chaubey, *Indian Music Today* (Allahabad: Kitab Mahal, 1945), p. 136.

42 ibid, p. 135.

43 ibid, pp. 135–136.

44 *The Times of India*, 24 February 1952, p. 2.

45 Ravindra Kumar, chief ed., *The Selected Works of Maulana Abul Kalam Azad: Vol. III—1947–48*, (New Delhi: Atlantic Publishers & Distributors, 1991), p. 28.

46 ibid, p. 29.

47 ibid, p. 53.

48 http://allindiaradio.gov.in/Profile/Mission/Pages/default.aspx   accessed on 14 February 2019.

49 http://allindiaradio.gov.in/Profile/Growth%20and%20Development/Pages/default.aspx accessed on 29 January 2017. The Prasar Bharati Annual Report for 2014–2015 mentions the total number of stations as 414 and the website in a section entitled 'Facts at a Glance' states that there are 419 stations. See http://prasarbharati.gov.in/Annual_ReportPDF/English_14-15.pdf, p. 17 accessed on 25 March 2019; http://allindiaradio.gov.in/Profile/Factss%20at%20Glance/Pages/default.aspx accessed on 14 February 2019.

50 http://allindiaradio.gov.in/Profile/NationalPrograms/Pages/default.aspx accessed on 29 January 2017.

51 http://allindiaradio.gov.in/Oppurtunities/Music/Pages/Music.aspx accessed on 14 February 2019.

52 Leeladhar Mandloi's address in 'Electronic Media: The Role of All India Radio' in *Role of Media in Promotion of Music in India*, ITC SRA, op. cit., pp. 68–69.

53 ibid, p. 70.

54 http://allindiaradio.gov.in/Profile/Growth%20and%20Development/Pages/default.aspx accessed on 14 February 2019.

55 Leeladhar Mandloi's address in *Role of Media in Promotion of Music in India*, ITC-SRA, op. cit., p. 70.

56 Chandawarkar, 'Mass Media and Music in *World of Gandharvas*, eds. Balawant Joshi, Dr Dilip Inamdar, Prof. Charudatta Bhagwat, Dr S.S. Gore (New Bombay: Sound Library Project of Akhil Bharatiya Gandharva Mahavidyalaya Mandal, 1993), p. 121.

57 Data compiled, analysed and communicated to the author by Abhimanyu Herlekar on 29 May 2016.

58 http://prasarbharati.gov.in/Annual_ReportPDF/2015-16-English.pdf, pp. 13, 28, 33, 49-50, accessed on 25 March 2019.

59 Data collected by Vighnesh Kamath, Dhaivat Mehta and Siddharth Padiyar, and compiled, analysed and communicated to the author by Abhimanyu Herlekar on 12 May 2017.

60 See 'Appendix 1: All India Radio Contract'. The All India Radio contract contains clauses in Hindi and English. I have provided the English version in the appendix.

61 http://allindiaradio.gov.in/Oppurtunities/Tenders/Documents/New%20 Music%20Gradation%20Policy%20of%20AIR-2014%20(Modified).pdf accessed on 16 February 2019.

62 *Dadar Matunga Cultural Centre Golden Jubilee Souvenir*, Mumbai, 2003.

63 For papers presented at this seminar, see *Journal of the Sangeet Natak Akademi-20*, New Delhi, April–June 1971.

64 https://www.facebook.com/ravindra.katoti.1/posts/10155707810278369 accessed on 14 February 2019;. http://www.deccanherald.com/ content/667361/harmonium-solo-air-four-decades.html accessed on 14 February 2019.

65 http://allindiaradio.gov.in/Profile/NationalArtists/Pages/default.aspx accessed on 14 February 2019.

66 This information is based on my personal experience and the informal discussions that I had with staff artistes.

67 Leeladhar Mandloi's address in *Role of Media in Promotion of Music in India*, ITC-SRA, op. cit., p. 68.

68 http://pbinfo.air.org.in/feedback/ReceptionReport.aspx accessed on 14 February 2019.

69 http://prasarbharati.gov.in/Annual_ReportPDF/English_14-15.pdf , p. 6, accessed on 8 July 2016.

70 http://allindiaradio.gov.in/Information/RTI/Pages/default.aspx accessed on 29 January 2017.

71 http://prasarbharati.gov.in/Annual_ReportPDF/English_14-15.pdf, pp. 69–70, accessed on 25 March 2019; http://prasarbharati.gov.in/ Annual_ReportPDF/2015-16-English.pdf, pp. 80–81, accessed on 29 January 2017.

72 Fielden, *Report on the Progress of Broadcasting*, op. cit., pp. 72–74.

73 Baruah, *This Is All India Radio*, op. cit., p. 1.

74 https://www.facebook.com/AkashvaniAIR/ accessed on 25 March 2019; https://twitter.com/AkashvaniAIR accessed on 25 March 2019.

75 Leeladhar Mandloi's address in *Role of Media in Promotion of Music in India*, ITC-SRA, p. 62.

76 ibid, p. 67. According to the Prasar Bharati Annual Report of 2014–2015 and of 2015–2016, the AIR Central Archives have, since April 2003, released eighty-five albums of archival recordings featuring Hindustani and Carnatic music under the banner *Akashvani Sangeet*;. http://prasarbharati.gov.in/ Annual_ReportPDF/English_14–15.pdf, p. 63, accessed on 25 March

2019; http://prasarbharati.gov.in/Annual_ReportPDF/2015-16-English.pdf, p. 63, accessed on 25 March 2019.

77 Leeladhar Mandloi's address in *Role of Media in Promotion of Music in India*, ITC-SRA, op. cit., p. 67.

78 http://prasarbharati.gov.in/Annual_ReportPDF/2015-16-English.pdf, p. 64, accessed on 25 March 2019.

79 http://prasarbharati.gov.in/Annual_ReportPDF/2015-16-English.pdf, p. 63, accessed on 25 March 2019.

80 http://doordarshan.gov.in/about-doordarshan accessed on 25 March 2019.

81 Examples of these can be viewed here: https://www.youtube.com/watch?v=hadACBHTcsM accessed on 14 February 2019; https://www.youtube.com/watch?v=_3nMytTVJ3s accessed on 14 February 2019; https://www.youtube.com/watch?v=wlkIGgCXqlE accessed on 14 February 2019.

82 Examples of these can be viewed here: https://www.youtube.com/watch?v=jViVTBioWWc accessed on 14 February 2019; https://www.youtube.com/watch?v=QZGrOfzSM9Q accessed on 14 February 2019.

83 Author's personal experience. Also see, Chandawarkar, 'Mass Media and Music', in *World of Gandharvas*, op. cit., p. 122.

84 Personal communication on 26 September 2017 from Amarendra Nandu Dhaneshwar who curated the series.

85 http://prasarbharati.gov.in/Annual_ReportPDF/English_14-15.pdf, p. 97, accessed on 25 March 2019.

86 ibid.

87 ibid.

88 Section 38 and 39 of the Indian Copyright Act, 1957. http://copyright.gov.in/documents/copyrightrules1957.pdf accessed on 14 February 2019.

89 https://www.facebook.com/shubha.mudgal/posts/10155910989665820 accessed on 14 February 2019; https://www.facebook.com/shubha.mudgal/posts/10156052024745820 accessed on 14 February 2019.

90 http://doordarshan.gov.in/program-highlights?field_sub_sites_tid_1=2325 accessed on 25 March 2019.

91 The author exchanged tweets with DD Bharati regarding this anomaly. https://twitter.com/aneesh/status/717750319531352065 accessed on 20 October 2017.

92 http://www.prasarbharatiarchives.co.in/doordarshan/music accessed on 14 February 2019.

93 http://www.mib.gov.in/# accessed on 14 February 2019.

94 http://filmsdivision.org/about-us.html accessed on 14 February 2019.

95 http://filmsdivision.org/fd-archieves.html accessed on 14 February 2019; http://filmsdivision.org/distribution.html accessed on 14 February 2019.

96 Personal communication from Sunilkant Gupta, flautist and director of music I/C, Films Division, Government of India, on 21 August 2017.

97 http://rstv.nic.in/about-us accessed on 14 February 2019.

98 https://www.youtube.com/results?search_query=shakhsiyat accessed on 14 February 2019.

2. From Facilitating Culture to Governing It

1 Cited from Devdutt, 'Culture Policy: Some Reflections' available at http://www.theatreforum.in/static/upload/docs/National_Cultural_Policy_Reflection.pdf accessed on 25 March 2019; *Approach Paper on the National Policy on Culture & Observation, Comments, Recommendations Thereon*, 1992, Government of India, available at http://www.worldcp.org/india.php?aid=421 accessed on 9 May 2017.

2 *Report of the Working Group on Art and Culture for XII Five-Year Plan (2012-2017)*, Ministry of Culture, Government of India, New Delhi, January 2012, p. i.

3 http://www.indiaculture.nic.in/mission-statement accessed on 14 February 2019.

4 http://www.indiaculture.nic.in/schemes accessed on 14 February 2019; http://www.indiaculture.nic.in/sites/default/files/Schemes/Minutes%20of%2023rd%20meeting.pdf accessed on 14 February, 2019. See also, Shubha Mudgal, 'Monetary Ambiguity' at https://www.livemint.com/Leisure/D4AWZl5oY4RrH2ztfyp5HJ/Monetary-ambiguity.html accessed on 14 February 2019.

5 http://www.indiaculture.nic.in/sites/default/files/CulturalMapping/MissionDocument.pdf, p. 10 accessed on 14 February 2019.

6 http://www.indiaculture.nic.in/sites/default/files/CulturalMapping/MissionDocument.pdf accessed on 14 February 2019.

7 http://www.sangeetnatak.gov.in/sna/introduction.php accessed on 14 February 2019.

8 ibid.

9 ibid.

10 ibid.

11 http://sangeetnatak.gov.in/sna/constitution.php accessed on 14 February 2019.

12 *Estimates-Committee—1960-61: Hundred and Thirty-ninth Report (Second-Lok-Sabha) Ministry of Scientific Research and Cultural Affairs, Cultural and International Activities* (New Delhi: Lok Sabha Secretariat, 1961), pp. 3–4.

13 *Report of HPC on the Akademis and other Institutions under the Ministry of Culture*, May 2014, pp. 27–33, 39–41.

14 http://www.sangeetnatak.gov.in/sna/introduction.php accessed on 14 February 2019.

15 http://www.sangeetnatak.gov.in/sna/publication.php accessed on 14 February 2019. See also, http://www.sangeetnatak.gov.in/sna/journal.php accessed on 14 February 2019; http://sangeetnatak.gov.in/sna/journal-sangna.php accesses on 31 March 2019; http://sangeetnatak.gov.in/sna/rajbhasha-rupambara.php accessed on 31 March 2019.

16 http://www.sangeetnatak.gov.in/sna/introduction.php accessed on 14 February 2019. See also, http://sangeetnatak.gov.in/sna/documentation.php as on 14 February 2019.

17 http://sangeetnatak.gov.in/sna/cds-dvds.php accessed on 14 February 2019.

18 http://www.sangeetnatak.gov.in/sna/introduction.php accessed 14 February 2019.

19 http://sangeetnatak.gov.in/sna/reports.php accessed on 14 February 2019.

20 *Report of HPC on the Akademis*, p. 111.

21 http://www.sangeetnatak.gov.in/sna/publication.php accessed on 14 February 2019.

22 ibid.

23 http://www.sangeetnatak.gov.in/sna/interpretation.php accessed on 14 February 2019.

24 ibid.

25 *Report of HPC on the Akademis*, p. 38.

26 ibid, p. 42.

27 http://ccrtindia.gov.in/aboutus.php accessed on 14 February 2019.

28 ibid.

29 ibid.

30 http://ccrtindia.gov.in/statistics.php accessed on 14 February 2019.

31 http://ezccindia.org/ezcc.html accessed on 14 February 2019.

32 http://www.nczccindia.in accessed on 14 February 2019; http://www.nczccindia.in/aboutus.html accessed on 14 February 2019.

33 http://www.rajeevsethi.com/projects/1986-Apna-Utsav-a.htm accessed on 14 February 2019.

34 http://www.nczccindia.in accessed on 14 February 2019.

35 Srimoyee Pandit, 'Mani Shankar Aiyar Committee on Zonal Cultural Centres formed to Revamp ZCCs submitted Report' http://www.jagranjosh.com/current-affairs/mani-shankar-aiyar-committee-on-zonal-cultural-centres-formed-to-revamp-zccs-submitted-report-1302869564-1 accessed on 14 February 2019; Poorva Rajaram, 'Why the Centre Should Not Hold' in *Tehelka Magazine*, Vol. 8, Issue 19, 14 May 2011 http://archive.

tehelka.com/story_main49.asp?filename=hub140511Why.asp accessed on 22 October 2017.

36 http://ignca.gov.in/about-ignca/organizational-structure/ accessed on 25 March 2019.

37 http://ignca.gov.in/divisions/kalanidhi/ http://ignca.bestbookbuddies. com and http://ignca.gov.in/divisionss/kalanidhi/cultural-archive/ sangita-music/ accessed on 24 May 2017.

38 http://ignca.gov.in/product-category/book/kalamulasastra-series/texts-on-music-dance/ accessed on 25 March 2019.

39 https://www.youtube.com/watch?v=sLJPlKPwnTs&t=675s accessed on 17 February 2019; http://ignca.gov.in/divisionss/kaldarsana/bhinn-shadj-innovative-classical-music-series/ accessed on 25 March 2019.

40 http://ignca.nic.in/PDF_data/vns_ic_Report_Siddhe_Devi_en.pdf accessed on 14 February 2019; http://ignca.gov.in/wp-content/uploads/2017/04/vnc_ic_Report_Sdevi_04_20174.pdf accessed on 14 February 2019; http://ignca.gov.in/wp-content/uploads/2017/04/vnc_ic_Report_Sdevi_04_20173.pdf accessed on 14 February 2019; http://ignca.gov.in/wp-content/uploads/2017/04/vnc_ic_Report_Sdevi_02_2017.pdf accessed on 14 February 2019; http://ignca.gov.in/wp-content/uploads/2017/04/vnc_ic_Report_Sdevi_04_20171.pdf accessed on 14 February 2019; http://ignca.gov.in/wp-content/uploads/2017/04/vnc_ic_Report_Sdevi_04_2017.pdf accessed on 14 February 2019.

41 http://ncaa.gov.in/repository/download/NCAA_Project_Progress_Report_(2014-17).pdf, p. 5, accessed on 14 February 2019.

42 http://ncaa.gov.in/repository/common/about accessed on 14 February 2019.

43 http://ncaa.gov.in/repository/download/NCAA_Project_Progress_Report_(2014-17).pdf, pp. 70–77, accessed on 14 February 2019.

44 http://ignca.nic.in/about.htm#BOARD and http://ignca.nic.in/about.htm#MEMBER accessed on 14 February 2019.

45 https://twitter.com/search?q=%40aneesh%20%40izuberi&src=typd

46 Personal communication with Irfan Zuberi, Project Manager, NCAA, on 15 and 16 June 2018, and on 9 November 2018.

47 http://ncf.nic.in/ncf_aboutus.htm accessed on 14 February 2019.

48 http://ncf.nic.in/Guidelines%20For%20Project%20Selection.pdf accessed on 14 February 2019. http://ncf.nic.in/ncf_annualreport.htm accessed on 14 February 2019.

49 http://ncf.nic.in/NCF%20Council.pdf accessed on 14 February 2019.

50 *Report of HPC on the Akademis and other Institutions under the Ministry of Culture,* May 2014, p. 3.

http://www.indiaculture.nic.in/sites/default/files/hpc_report/HPC%20
REPORT%202014.pdf accessed on 14 February 2019.
51 ibid, p. 11.
52 ibid.
53 ibid, p. 12.
54 ibid, p. 6.
55 *Report of the Working Group on Art and Culture for XII Five-Year Plan (2012-
2017)*, pp. 47–48.
56 ibid, pp. 14–16.
57 ibid, p. 19.

3. Civil Society and Corporate Patronage

1   Aneesh Pradhan, *Hindustani Music in Colonial Bombay*, pp. 45–71, 123–
135. This book has an overview of these organizations. Also see Kapadia,
Gayan Uttejak Mandali, p. 43; Ashok Da. Ranade, *Maharashtra: Art Music*,
Maharashtra Information Centre, Government of Maharashtra (New Delhi,
1989), pp. 66–67; Vamanrao Deshpande, *Between Two Tanpuras*, trans.
Ram Deshmukh and B.R. Dhekney from Marathi original *Aalaapini*, with
addition of piece on Bhimsen Joshi (Mumbai: Popular Prakashan, 1989), p.
154; http://suburbanmusiccircle.org/suburbancircle/about.html accessed
on 14 February 2019. Some of the information is also based on interviews
with music critic Batuk Diwanji held on 24 August 1992 and in January
1993.
2   For information regarding public patronage to Hindustani music in Kolkata
during the early twentieth century, see Anirban Bhattacharyya, 'From Salon
to Sammelan: Changes in the Contexts of Performances in Calcutta (1875–
1950)' (Unpublished MMus dissertation, School of Oriental and African
Studies, London, 2011.
3   Deodhar, *Gaayanaachaarya P. Vishnu Digambar*, pp. 19, 73–74; Michael S.
Kinnear, *Sangeet Ratna—The Jewel of Music: A Bio-Discography of Khan Sahib
Abdul Karim Khan* (Victoria, Australia: Michael Kinnear, 2003), pp. 41–42.
4   Interview with Kausalya and Dinker Manjeshwar held on 10 September
1993, reproduced in Aneesh Pradhan, *Hindustani Music in Colonial Bombay*,
pp. 257-273.
5   Ashok Da. Ranade, 'Gandharvas and Musical Changes', p. 17.
6   Sahasrabuddhe, *Hindu Music*, pp. 34, 49–50. Also see Deshpande, *Between
Two Tanpuras*, p. 158; Govindrao Tembe, *Maazhaa Sangeet Vyaasang*,
(Marathi), 2nd ed. (Mumbai: Maharashtra Rajya Sahitya Sanskriti Mandal,
1984), p. 24, and note prepared by S.V. Gokhale in Tembe, *Maazhaa Sangeet*.
7   http://suburbanmusiccircle.org/suburbancircle/about.html accessed on 14
February 2019.

8   ibid.

9   ibid.

10 Deshpande, *Indian Musical Traditions*, p. 126.

11 Smt. Gangubai Hangal interviewed by Dr S.S. Gore in *World of Gandharvas*, eds. Balawant Joshi et al., p. 42.

12 *The 80ᵗʰ Annual Report (2016-2017)* (Mumbai: The Suburban Music Circle, 2017), p. 2.

13 ibid, p. 4.

14 ibid, pp. 8–9.

15 Kapadia, *Gayan Uttejak Mandali*, p. 58.

16 Interview with Kausalya and Dinker Manjeshwar held on 10 September 1993, reproduced in Aneesh Pradhan, *Hindustani Music in Colonial Bombay*, pp. 257–273.

17 From the report of a panel discussion titled 'Changing in Organizational Aspects: Cultural Institutions/Organizations' held under the aegis of the Sangeet Research Academy in January 2010, Mumbai, contained in *Journal of the Indian Musicological Society*, Volume 41, 2011–2012 (Mumbai: Indian Musicological Society, 2012), pp. 197–198. For information about the Dadar Matunga Culture Centre, see http://dadarmatungaculturalcentre. org/preamble, http://dadarmatungaculturalcentre.org/facilities and https://weddingz.in/mumbai/dadar-matunga-cultural-centre-dadar-west/ accessed on 25 March 2019.

18 'Changing in Organizational Aspects', *Journal of the Indian Musicological Society*, ibid..

19 http://www.dnaindia.com/lifestyle/grandeur-he-blends-music-and-business- 1049333 accessed on 15 February 2019; Pandit Arvind Parikh and Ashok Damodar Ranade, 'Diversity and Media Explosion: A Dialogue of the Indian Scenario' in *Music Performance*, Volume 2, Issue 3 (United Kingdom: Harwood Academic Publishers, 2000), pp. 26–27. https:// books.google.co.in/books?id=ir2KQ8duankC&pg=PA26&lpg=PA26& dq=music+forum+arvind+parikh&source=bl&ots=VW_laOgb3n&sig= nJYU2T4tYlZ-p9tqgGHeKMdBaBM&hl=en&sa=X&ved=0ahUKEwi NrMvovZ3UAhXENo8KHVZQCao4ChDoAQgsMAI#v=onepage&q= music%20forum%20arvind%20parikh&f=false accessed on 15 February 2019.

20 http://underscorerecords.com/Resources accessed on 15 February 2019.

21 Joep Bor and Philippe Bruguierre, *Masters of Raga, Meister Des Raga, Les Maitres Du Raga* (Berlin: Haus der Kulturen der Welt, 1995), p. 20.

22 For the history of the Harivallabh Sangeet Sammelan, see http://www. harballabh.org/home.php accessed on 22 May 2016)

23 S.N. Ratanjankar, *Pandit Bhatkhande* (New Delhi: National Book Trust, India, 1967), pp. 45–46.

24 For details on conferences organized by Paluskar, see Deodhar, *Gaayanaachaarya P. Vishnu Digambar,* pp. 70-95, 114.

25 B.R. Deodhar, 'Sangeet-Sevak Shriman Damodardas Khanna, Calcutta' in *Sangeet Kala Vihar, Varsha 8, Ank 3* (Gandharva Mahavidyalaya Mandal, 1955), p. 30. Also see Deodhar, *Gaayanaachaarya P. Vishnu Digambar,* p. 59. Anirban Bhattacharyya, mentions the name as Bhupen Krishna Ghosh and the year of the first All Bengal Music Conference as 1934. See Anirban Bhattacharyya *From Salon to Sammelan,* p. 30.

26 Deshpande, *Between Two Tanpuras,* p. 154. See also G.H. Ranade, 'Sangeet ke Aadhunik Bheeshmaachaarya' in *Bhatkhande Smriti Granth,* (Hindi) (Khairagarh, MP: Indira Kala Sangeet Vishwavidyalaya, 1966), p. 328.

27 Bhatkhande, *Hindustaanee Sangeet Paddhati, Chhati Pustak,* op. cit. p. 30 Interestingly, contemporary incarnations of these listeners can be seen in present-day concerts as they message or speak on their mobiles during concerts with complete disregard for the music and the performers. Sadly, one also comes across musicians in the audience displaying such poor etiquette.

28 Deshpande, *Indian Musical Traditions,* op. cit., p. 119.

29 Chaubey, *Indian Music Today,* op. cit., pp. 120–122.

30 http://www.doverlanemusicconference.org accessed on 15 February 2019; http://xaviers.edu/main/index.php/indian-music-group-img accessed on 15 February 2019; https://www.thekendra.com/ssm-festival.php accessed on 15 February 2019.

31 http://sawaigandharvabhimsenmahotsav.com accessed on 15 February 2019; https://www.facebook.com/vishnudigambarjayanti/ accessed on 15 February 2019; http://www.allarakhafoundation.org/demo/a-homage-to-abbaji-on-his-barsi-3rd-feb-2018/ accessed on 15 February 2019.

32 Ashok Ranade, 'Gandharvas and Musical Changes', p. 18.

33 ibid, p. 17.

34 Mohan Nadkarni, 'Hindustani Music: Is It at the Cross-Roads?' in *World of Gandharvas,* eds. Balawant Joshi et al., p. 114.

35 Smt. Gangubai Hangal interviewed by Dr S.S. Gore in *World of Gandharvas,* eds. Balawant Joshi et al., p. 42.

36 Jyoti Easwaran, 'Pandit Shivkumar Sharma Is an Extraordinary Musician' in http://gulfnews.com/life-style/music/pandit-shivkumar-sharma-is-an-extraordinary-musician-1.716997 accessed on 15 February, 2019.

37 ibid.

38 For a detailed description of such performance contexts, see Aneesh Pradhan, *Hindustani Music in Colonial Bombay,* op. cit., pp. 29–46.

39 http://www.thehindubusinessline.com/todays-paper/tp-others/tp-variety/indian-music-group-continues-to-enchant-mumbai-students/article2166283.ece accessed on 15 February 2019; https://www.online.

citibank.co.in/portal/india-corporate-citizenship-report.pdf, p. 24, accessed on 15 February 2019.

40 http://www.itcsra.org/Origin-of-ITC-SRA as on May 30, 2017. See also, Sharbani Raut, "India: Surrogate Advertisements In India" at http://www.mondaq.com/india/x/606974/advertising+marketing+branding/CROSS+BORDER+INSOLVENCY+A+NEW+REGIME accessed on 15 March, 2019.

41 http://www.worldcat.org/title/saptarishi-a-constellation-of-stars/oclc/43977124 accessed on 15 February 2019.

42 http://ebook.mca.gov.in/Childwindow1.aspx?pageid=17923&type=CA&ChildTitle=Schedules&SearchText= accessed on 15 February 2019. See also *Handbook on Corporate Social Responsibility in India* (Gurgaon: PricewaterhouseCoopers Private Limited, 2013), p. 12, https://www.pwc.in/assets/pdfs/publications/2013/handbook-on-corporate-social-responsibility-in-india.pdf accessed on 15 February 2019.

43 For a discussion on venues built in the Western world, see Tim Blanning, *The Triumph of Music: Composers, Musicians and Their Audiences, 1700 to the Present* (London: Penguin Books, 2008), pp. 122–172.

44 http://www.ncpamumbai.com/about accessed on 5 June 2017; .

45 https://www.tajmahalteahouse.com/pages/taj-mahal-tea-house-sessions accessed on 19 March 2019.

46 Michael S. Kinnear, 'The First Indian Disc Record Manufacturers', in *The Record News: The Journal of the Society of Indian Record Collectors*, Vol. 5 (Mumbai: January 1992), pp. 25–43; Michael S. Kinnear, 'Reading Indian Record Labels: "RAMAGRAPH" – The History of the RAM-A-PHONE and RAMA-GRAPH disc records' in *The Record News: The Journal of the Society of Indian Record Collectors*, Vol. 20, (Mumbai: October 1995), pp. 25–44; http://www.saregama.com/static/about_us accessed on 15 February 2019.

47 These recordings have often been recompiled, repackaged and marketed under new names of albums. http://www.musictoday.in/inside.phtml?genere_id=1 accessed on 15 February 2019.

48 http://www.timesmusic.com/genre/indian-classical-9-1.html accessed on 15 February 2019.

49 https://www.discogs.com/artist/1600354-AshaRani-Mathur, accessed on 17 March 2019; https://www.linkedin.com/in/asharani-mathur-2615b610/?ppe=1 accessed on 25 March 2019; http://sursanjeevan.com/RPSur_PtKatti.html accessed on 15 February 2019.

50 https://www.indiatoday.in/swarutsav/about_us.jsp accessed on 15 February 2019;

51 Daya Kishan Thussu, 'Privatizing the Airwaves: the Impact of Globalization on Broadcasting in India' in *Media, Culture & Society*, Vol. 21 (London, Thousand Oaks and New Delhi: Sage Publications, 1999), p. 125.

52 Personal communication on 26 September 2017 from Amarendra Nandu Dhaneshwar who curated the first thirty episodes.

53 Some of the episodes from the *Sadhana* biopic series are available at https://www.youtube.com/results?search_query=sadhana+vrindavan+gurukul accessed on 15 February 2017.

54 Personal communication on 26 September 2017 from Amarendra Nandu Dhaneshwar who curated these programmes.

55 https://www.youtube.com/user/InsyncChannel accessed on 15 February 2019.

56 Some of the Art Talk shows can be accessed at https://www.youtube.com/watch?v=K-AleMLtWsE accessed on 15 February 2019, https://www.youtube.com/watch?v=vd2IPYeKZ1c accessed on 15 February 2019, https://www.youtube.com/watch?v=0AP8cmvuoUM accessed on 15 February 2019, https://www.youtube.com/watch?v=VddfTbjOIzU accessed on 15 February 2019.

57 Surajeet Das Gupta, 'What is WorldSpace radio all about?' at https://www.rediff.com/money/2005/aug/19radio.htm accessed on 19 March 2019; https://en.wikipedia.org/wiki/1worldspace accessed on 15 February 2019.

58 This information is based on the experiences shared by Geeta Sahai, who headed the Radio Gandharv initiative, in 'Electronic Media: Television' in *Role of Media in Promotion of Music in India*, ITC-SRA, op. cit., pp. 50–51.

59 Interview with Batuk Diwanji held in January 1993 and reproduced in Aneesh Pradhan, *Hindustani Music in Colonial Bombay*, pp. 236-249.

60 https://www.shiksha.com/hospitality-travel/event-management/colleges/colleges-india accessed on 15 February 2019.

61 For a description of artiste management primarily for Indian rock bands, see Ritnika Nayan, *Indie 101: The Ultimate Guide to the Independent Music Industry in India* (New Delhi: Music Gets Me High, 2017).

62 Donald S. Passman, *All You Need to Know about the Music Business*, UK ed. (London: Penguin Books, 2002), p. 13.

63 ibid, pp. 31–32.

64 ibid, pp. 32–42.

4. Personalized and Institutionalized Education

1 Adrian McNeil, 'Generational Friction: An Ethnographic Perspective on *Guru Seva* Within a Lineage of Tabla Players in Kolkata' in *MUSICultures*, *Vol. 44 No.1*, (Edmonton: Canadian Society for Traditional Music, 2017), pp.116-133.

2 For an overview on the adaptive strategies that evolved in the realm of pedagogy during this period, see Aneesh Pradhan, *Hindustani Music in Colonial Bombay*, pp. 137–156.

3   ibid, pp. 137–140.

4   For a brief analysis on the state of institutionalized music education in Hindustani music, past and present, see Aneesh Pradhan with additional inputs from Shubha Mudgal, 'Institutionalized Music Education in North India: Some Observations', in *Sangeet Natak*, Vol. XLIII, No. 2 (New Delhi: Sangeet Natak Akademi, 2009), pp. 23–34.

5   Deodhar, *Gaayanaachaarya P. Vishnu Digambar*, pp. 49–51.

6   ibid, p. 104.

7   http://abgmvm.org/about-us/ accessed on 15 February 2019.

8   ibid. For a list of courses and examinations conducted at the ABGMM's Vashi Centre, see http://abgmvm.org/courses-and-examination/ accessed on 15 February 2019.

9   *Annual Report, Balance Sheet and Income & Expenditure of A.B.G.M.V. Mandal and Sangeet Kala Vihar for the Year 2016-2017* (Mumbai: Akhil Bharatiya Gandharva Mahavidyalaya Mandal, 2019), p. 22.

10 http://abgmvm.org/music-teachers-conferences/ accessed on 15 February 2019; http://abgmvm.org/workshops-seminars/ accessed on 15 February 2019.

11 Vilayat Hussain Khan, *Sangeetagyon ke Sansmaran*, (Hindi) (New Delhi: Sangeet Natak Akademi, 1959), p. 15.

12 http://www.pracheenkalakendra.org/?page_id=91 accessed on 15 February, 2019;

13 http://www.sangitmahabharati.org accessed on 15 February, 2019; http://www.saptak.org/saptakDesk/saptakArchives accessed on 15 February 2019.

14 http://www.saptak.org/saptakDesk/saptakSchool accessed on 15 February 2019.

15 https://ajoychakrabarty.com/mobile/shrutinandan.php accessed on 15 February 2019.

16 http://ajivasan.com accessed on 15 February 2019;

17 http://www.extraprepare.com/mumbai/listing/kangaroo-kids_3838.html accessed on 15 February 2019; http://www.ajivasanhall.com accessed on 15 February 2019; http://timesofindia.indiatimes.com/city/mumbai/Private-school-wedding-halls-on-plots-given-to-artistes-in-Mumbai-despite-rules-saying-land-cant-be-sub-let-or-used-for-business/articleshow/50881934. cms accessed on 15 February 2019.

18 N.R. Marulkar, 'Aajche Shikshan-Satra Aani Tyaachi Saangataa' in *Sangeet Kala Vihar, Varsha 8, Ank 3*, ed. B.R. Deodhar (Miraj: Gandharva Mahavidyalaya Mandal, March 1955), p. 12.

19 Deodhar, *Gaayanaachaarya P. Vishnu Digambar*, p. 67.

20 ibid., pp. 70–75, 85–86, 92–93; B.R. Deodhar, 'School of Indian Music', (Marathi), *Deodhar's School of Indian Music, Golden Jubilee Souvenir* (Mumbai, 1975).

21 Surendra Mohan Tagore, *Public Opinion and Official Communications*, p. 230.

22 *Report of the Students' Literary and Scientific Society, and of the Vernacular Branch Societies, together with the Reports of the Girls' Schools for the Session of 1862-63* (Bombay, 1863), pp. 7–8. See also *Report of the Students' Literary and Scientific Society for the Session of 1871-72* (Bombay, 1874), pp. 5–6.

23 *Report of the Committee for Music Education, 1948-49*, Government of Bombay (Bombay: Education & Industries Department, 1949).

24 ibid, p. 10.

25 ibid.

26 ibid, p. 4.

27 ibid, pp. 3, 50–51.

28 'S.S.C. Chaa 1959 March Paasun Amlaat Yenaaraa Sangeetaachaa Navaa Kaaryakram', in *Sangeet Kala Vihar, Varsha 11, Ank 8*, ed. B.R. Deodhar (Miraj: Gandharva Mahavidyalaya Mandal, August 1958), p. 362.

29 *The Report of the University Education Commission (December 1948–August 1949)*, Volume I, First Reprint Edition (Delhi: Ministry of Education, Government of India 1962), http://www.educationforallinindia. com/1949%20Report%20of%20the%20University%20Education%20 Commission.pdf accessed on 15 February 2019. Also see *Report of the Education Commission (1964–66) Education and National Development*, First Edition (Delhi: Ministry of Education, Government of India, 1966), https://archive.org/details/ReportOfTheEducationCommission1964-66D.S.KothariReport accessed on 15 February 2019.

30 *National Curriculum Framework 2005* (New Delhi: National Council of Educational Research and Training, 2005), pp. 54–56,. http://www.ncert. nic.in/rightside/links/pdf/framework/english/nf2005.pdf accessed on 15 February 2019.

31 *Secondary School Curriculum 2017-18, Volume – I: Main Subjects for Classes IX & X* (New Delhi: Central Board of Secondary Education, 2017), pp. 113–126; *Senior School Curriculum 2017-18, Volume – III: Music and Dance for Class XI & XII* (New Delhi: Central Board of Secondary Education, 2017), pp. 15–24,. http://49.50.70.100/web_material/Curriculum17/ SrSecondary/Senior%20School%20Curriculum%202017-18%20 Volume%20-3.pdf accessed on 6 August 2017.

32 https://www.youtube.com/results?search_query=NCERT+music accessed on 15 February 2019.

33 'Appendix 2: Questionnaire for Schoolchildren'.

34 V.N. Bhatkhande, *A Short Historical Survey*, p. 50.

35 M.R. Jayakar, *The Story of My Life, Vol. II, 1922-1925* (Mumbai: Asia Publishing House, 1959), p. 568.

36 Margaret E. Cousins, *The Music of Orient and Occident: Essays Towards Mutual Understanding*, (Madras: B.G. Paul and Co., 1935), pp. 169–170.

37 Pankaj Chandra, *Building Universities that Matter: Where are Indian Institutions Going Wrong?*, Reprinted (Hyderabad: Orient Blackswan Private Limited, 2018), p. 7.

38 https://targetstudy.com/colleges/ba-hons-music-degree-colleges-in-kolkata.html accessed on 15 February 2019; http://mu.ac.in/portal/department-of-music/ accessed on 15 February 2019; http://www.unipune.ac.in/dept/fine_arts/centre_for_performing_arts/cpa_webfiles/academic.htm accessed on 15 February 2019; http://www.iksv.ac.in/about accessed on 15 February 2019; https://www.youtube.com/watch?v=hbFojsXZSGk&t=2s accessed on 15 February 2019.

39 http://www.msubaroda.ac.in/faculty.php?fac_id=12&action=home accessed on 15 February 2019.

40 ibid.

41 http://www.bhu.ac.in/performing_arts/ accessed on 15 February 2019.

42 http://www.bhu.ac.in/performing_arts/vocal_music/index.php accessed on 15 February 2019; http://www.bhu.ac.in/performing_arts/instrumental_music/index.php accessed on 15 February 2019.

43 http://www.bhu.ac.in/performing_arts/vocal_music/index.php accessed on 15 February 2019.

44 http://www.iksv.ac.in/about accessed on 15 February 2019; http://www.iksv.ac.in/affiliated-colleges accessed on 15 February 2019.

45 http://www.iksv.ac.in/vission-mission accessed on 15 February 2019.

46 http://bhatkhandemusic.edu.in/history/ accessed on 15 February 2019.

47 http://bhatkhandemusic.edu.in/message-from-vc/ accessed on 15 February 2019.

48 Aneesh Pradhan with additional inputs from Shubha Mudgal, 'Institutionalized Music Education in North India' pp. 23–34.

49 For a detailed analysis of the state of university education in India, see Pankaj Chandra, *Building Universities that Matter*.

50 See sleeve notes for the audio album *Sanchay: Bandish Sangraha*, Underscore Records Private Limited, New Delhi, 2007.

51 https://w.soundcloud.com/player/?url=https%3A//api.soundcloud.com/tracks/282848791&auto_play=true&hide_related=true&show_comments=false&show_user=true&show_reposts=false&visual=true&sharing=false&download=false&liking=false&%22 accessed on 15 February 2019; http://www.itcsra.org/Aims-and-Objectives accessed on 15 February 2019; http://www.itcsra.org/Facilities-and-Library accessed on 15 February 2019;

http://www.itcsra.org/Full-Term-Scholarship accessed on 15 February 2019; http://www.itcsra.org/ITC-SRA-Publication accessed on 15 February 2019.

52 http://www.gangubaihangalgurukul.gov.in/aboutus.htm accessed on 12 August 2017; http://www.gangubaihangalgurukul.gov.in/vision.htm accessed on 12 August 2017;

53 Vittal Shastri, 'Hubballi: Hangal family plans stir over Gurukul affairs' at https://www.deccanchronicle.com/nation/current-affairs/020316/hubballi-hangal-family-plans-stir-over-gurukul-affairs.html accessed on 21 March, 2019.

54 Deodhar, ed., *Sangeet Kala Vihar*, p. 36; Chaubey, *Indian Music Today*, op. cit., pp. 112–113; Deshpande, *Indian Musical Traditions*, op. cit., pp. 149–150.

5. Tangible Resources and Creating Awareness

1 For an overview of publications from the nineteenth and early twentieth centuries see Aneesh Pradhan, *Hindustani Music in Colonial Bombay*, op. cit., pp. 59–61, 80–83, 92–93, 154–158.

2 For an overview of English writing on Indian music, see Daniel M. Neuman, 'Indian Music and the English Language Fifty Years Later' in *Proceedings: International Seminar on 'Creating & Teaching Music Patterns'* (Kolkata: Department of Instrumental Music, Rabindra Bharati University, 2013), pp. 15–34.

3 http://ashokdaranade.org/wordpress/index.php/about-adr/publications/ accessed on 15 February 2019.

4 http://www.indiaifa.org/india-foundation-arts.html accessed on 15 February 2019; http://www.indiaifa.org/grants-and-projects.html?keys=hindustani+music&tid=All&tid_1=All&date=All accessed on 15 February 2019.

5 http://www.sangeetkaryalaya.in/page/about-us accessed on 15 February 2019.

6 Personal communication from Snehal Muzoomdar, President of the Indian Musicological Society, received on 14 August 2017.

7 https://www.indiastudies.org/ethnomusicology/ accessed on 15 February 2019; https://www.indiastudies.org/ethnomusicology/collections/ accessed on 15 February 2019.

8 https://eap.bl.uk/search/site/chandvankar accessed on 15 February 2019.

9 https://music.washington.edu/ethnomusicology-archives accessed on 15 February 2019; https://www.soas.ac.uk/courseunits/15PMUH025.html accessed on 15 February 2019.

10 https://www.facebook.com/pg/Dr.AshokDa.RanadeArchives/about/?ref=page_internal accessed on 15 February 2019.

11 I might add here that I have had personal experience in this regard and have on occasion voiced my opinion publicly. See http://www.aneeshpradhan.com/tender-archives-at-ncpa/ accessed on 15 February 2019.

12 Based on my experience.

13 Anthony Seeger, 'Intellectual Property and Audiovisual Archives and Collections' in *Folk Heritage Collections in Crisis* (Washington DC: Council on Library and Information Resources, May 2001), p. 43. Also available at http://www.clir.org/pubs/reports/pub96/rights.html) accessed on 15 February 2019.

14 ibid, pp. 43–44.

15 ibid, p. 44.

16 http://www.spicmacay.com/about accessed on 15 February 2019.

17 ibid.

18 ibid.

19 ibid.

20 ibid.

21 ibid.

22 *Chintan: Reflections on SPIC MACAY and Its Core Values* (Delhi: SPIC MACAY Communications, 2007). See http://www.arvindguptatoys.com/arvindgupta/spicmacay-eng.pdf accessed on 15 February 2019 and http://www.spicmacay.com/chintan accessed on 15 February 2019.

23 http://spicmacay.com/coordinators accessed on 15 February 2019.

24 http://spicmacay.com/basic-page/how-organise-spic-macay-events accessed on 15 February 2019.

25 http://www.spicmacay.com/about/activities accessed on 15 February 2019; http://www.spicmacay.com/coordinators accessed on 15 February 2019.

26 http://pib.nic.in/newsite/PrintRelease.aspx?relid=177210 accessed on 15 February 2019.

27 https://www.youtube.com/user/spicmacay/videos accessed on 15 February 2019.

28 http://spicmacay.com/naadbhed accessed on 15 February 2019.

29 ibid.

30 ibid.

31 ibid.

32 ibid.

33 *Chintan: Reflections on SPIC MACAY*, pp. 12, 18.

34 ibid, p. 18.

35 http://www.spicmacay.com/about/four-pillars-spic-macay assessed on 15 February 2019.

36 Based on personal experience.

37 *Chintan: Reflections on SPIC MACAY*, p. 10.

38 http://spicmacay.com/our-supporters accessed on 15 February 2019; http://www.spicmacay.com/about accessed on 15 February 2019.

6. New Formats for Dissemination

1 Major works in this area include Michael S. Kinnear, *A Discography of Hindustani and Carnatic Music* (Westport: Greenwood Press, 1985); Michael S. Kinnear, *The Gramophone Company's First Indian Recordings, 1899–1908* (Mumbai: Popular Prakashan, 1994); Michael S. Kinnear, *The 78 r.p.m. Record Labels of India*, 2nd ed. (Victoria: Bajakhana–Michael Kinnear, 2016); Peter Manuel, *Cassette Culture: Popular Music and Technology in North India* (Chicago: The University of Chicago Press, 1993). See also the volumes of *The Journal of the Society of Indian Record Collectors*, Mumbai.

2 Jacques Attali, 'Noise: The Political Economy of Music', English translation Brian Massumi in *Theory and History of Literature*, Volume 16, Tenth Printing (Minneapolis: University of Minnesota Press, 2009), pp. 105–106.

3 http://www.rediff.com/money/2007/sep/29spec.htm accessed on 15 February 2019.

4 http://www.livemint.com/Consumer/aaoA9lQQYq1PadcNJEpBEJ/Saregama-India8217s-largest-aggregator-of-digital-music.html accessed on 15 February 2019.

5 http://underscorerecords.com/Catalog accessed on 15 February 2019; https://www.facebook.com/MeeraMusic/ accessed on 15 February 2019; http://www.sonicoctaves.com/store/ accessed on 15 February 2019.

6 http://underscorerecords.com/catalog/listing/Merchandise/1 accessed on 15 February 2019; http://www.singingsleeves.com accessed on 15 February 2019.

7 http://underscorerecords.com/catalog/listing/Print/1 accessed on 15 February 2019.

8 This information is based on the author's experience as one of the directors of Underscore Records Pvt Ltd., an online production and distribution platform. See www.UnderscoreRecords.com accessed on 15 February 2019.

9 http://www.shubhamudgal.com/shop/ accessed on 15 February 2019.

10 https://www.youtube.com/watch?v=Mtk6ZN70ktU accessed on 29 March 2019.

11 https://www.sudeepaudio.com/profile/article/vocal accessed on 15 February 2019.
12 http://artclickindia.com/AboutUs.aspx accessed on 15 February 2019.
13 https://itunes.apple.com/in/app/itablapro-tabla-tanpura-player/ id337350026?mt=8 accessed on 13 September 2017; http://tampura. bzhtec.com/en/Introduction.html accessed on 15 February 2019.
14 https://www.radel.in accessed on 15 February 2019; http://www. soundlabs.in/dumas-chukame-1137.html accessed on 15 February 2019.
15 Based on discussions with tanpura makers.
16 https://musicmumbai.wordpress.com accessed on 15 February 2019; http://debatesangeet.blogspot.in accessed on 15 February 2019.
17 http://www.parrikar.org accessed on 15 February 2019; http://swaratala. blogspot.in accessed on 15 February 2019; https://www.swarganga.org accessed on 15 February 2019.
18 http://www.mohannadkarni.org accessed on 15 February 2019.
19 http://sangeetkosh.net accessed on 15 February 2019.
20 http://underscorerecords.com/Resources accessed on 15 February 2019; http://underscorerecords.com/Podcast accessed on 15 February 2019.

7. Hindustani Music Overseas

1 Joep Bor and Philippe Bruguierre, *Masters of Raga*, op. cit., p. 28.
2 ibid., p. 40. See also, Govindrao Tembe, *Maazhaa Sangeet Vyaasang*, p. 91.
3 Susheela Misra, *Great Masters of Hindustani Music* (New Delhi: Hem Publishers Pvt. Ltd., 1981), p. 121.
4 ibid, p. 106.
   For Inayat Khan's writings, see Hazrat Inayat Khan, *The Divine Symphony or Vadan*, Sufi Movement, 2nd ed. (Geneva, 1931); Hazrat Inayat Khan, *Notes form the Unstruck Music from: The Gayan* 4th revised ed. (Holland: N.V. Publishing Co., 1936); Hazrat Inayat Khan, *Nirtan or The Dance of the Soul*, 2nd ed. (Holland: N.V. Publishing Co., 1938). Also see, Joep Bor and Philippe Bruguierre, *Masters of Raga*, p. 40 and Gerry Farrell, *Indian Music and the West* (Oxford: Clarendon Press, 1997), pp. 144–155. For current work inspired by Inayat Khan, see http://www.sufimovement.org accessed on 15 February 2019.
5 Susheela Misra, *Great Masters*, op. cit., p. 66;. Farrell, *Indian Music*, op. cit., p. 165.
6 Joep Bor and Philippe Bruguierre, *Masters of Raga*, op. cit., p. 64.
7 Deodhar, *Thor Sangeetkaar*, op. cit., pp. 65–66.
8 Susheela Misra, *Great Masters*, op. cit., pp. 66, 106, 121, 142; Bimal Mukherjee, 'Jaipur Binkar/Sitar Gharana' in *Seminar on Sitar* (Sangeet Research Academy,

1990), p. 24; Laxminarayan Garg, *Hamaare Sangeet Ratna*, op. cit., p. 259; Vamanrao Deshpande, *Between Two Tanpuras*, op. cit., p. 147.

9   Laxminarayan Garg, *Hamaare Sangeet Ratna*, op. cit., p. 126.

10 https://scroll.in/magazine/881709/how-an-indian-man-and-his-english-wife-introduced-george-harrison-to-ravi-shankar-to-create-history accessed on 15 February 2019.

11 http://iccr.gov.in/content/constitution accessed on 15 February 2019;. http://iccr.gov.in accessed on 15 February 2019.

12 For funds allotted by the Ministry of External Affairs to ICCR for the years 2016 to 2019 see https://www.indiabudget.gov.in/ub2018-19/eb/sbe28.pdf accessed on accessed on 23 March 2019.

13 http://iccr.gov.in/content/outgoing-troupes accessed on 15 February 2019.

14 http://iccr.gov.in/content/list-centres accessed on 15 February 2019.

15 http://iccr.gov.in/content/empanelment-artists accessed on 22 February 2017.

16 http://iccr.gov.in/sites/default/files/empanelmentguidelines.pdf accessed on 15 February 2019.

17 http://iccr.gov.in/sites/default/files/RLIST2017.pdf accessed on 24 March 2019.

18 http://iccr.gov.in/content/dancemusic-institutions accessed on 15 February 2019.

19 http://iccr.gov.in/content/incoming-troupes accessed on 15 February 2019.

20 Based on personal experience.

21 Lavezzoli, *Bhairavi*, op. cit., p. 7.

22 ibid.

23 Farrell, *Indian Music*, p. 176.

24 Ravi Shankar, *My Music, My Life*, Sixth Reprint (New Delhi: Vikas Publishing House Pvt. Ltd., 1978), p. 96.

25 Lavezzoli, *Bhairavi*, op. cit., p. 12.

26 http://webtv.un.org/watch/ravi-shankar-and-yehudi-menuhin-human-rights-day-concert-10-december-1967/2033645153001 accessed on 15 February 2019.

27 https://www.britannica.com/biography/Ravi-Shankar accessed on 15 February 2019; https://aacm.org/ali-akbar-khan/ accessed on 25 March 2019.

28 Lavezzoli, *Bhairavi*, pp. 192–193.

29 http://www.khabar.com/magazine/features/every_concert_teaches_me_something_different accessed on 30 March 2019; http://www.georgeharrison.com/dark-horse-records-announces-ravi-shankar-

george-harrison-box-set-release/ accessed on 30 March 2019; https://en.wikipedia.org/wiki/Ravi_Shankar%27s_Festival_from_India accessed on 15 February 2019; https://en.wikipedia.org/wiki/Ravi_Shankar%27s_Music_Festival_from_India accessed on 15 February 2019.

30 Daniel M. Neuman, *Studying India's Musicians: Four Decades of Selected Articles* (New Delhi: Manohar Publishers & Distributors, 2015), p. 156.

31 ibid, pp. 160–162.

32 https://www.icmca.org/about/mission-vision/ accessed on 15 February 2019.

33 http://www.basantbahar.org/about/history accessed on 15 February 2019.

34 http://www.icmcdfw.org/about.aspx accessed on 15 February 2019.

35 https://www.musiccircle.org/our-founders accessed on 6 August 2018.

36 http://www.ragamala.ca/about-us/ accessed on 25 March 2019.

37 http://www.amc.org.uk/about_us.html accessed on 25 March 2019.

38 Jennifer C. Post ed., *Ethnomusicology: A Contemporary Reader* (New York: Routledge Taylor & Francis Group, 2006), p. 2.

39 For an overview of research undertaken and courses offered in Indian music at North American universities, see Neuman, *Studying India's Musicians*, pp. 164–172.

40 http://www.india-arts.pitt.edu/over.html accessed on 25 March 2019.

41 ibid.

42 Personal communication from Balwant N. Dixit on 30 September 2017.

43 https://music.calarts.edu/programs/north-indian-music accessed on 15 February 2019; https://music.calarts.edu/programs/world-percussion accessed on 15 February 2019; https://www.ethnomusic.ucla.edu/music-of-india-ensemble accessed on 15 February 2019.

44 https://www.codarts.nl/worldmusic/ accessed on 15 February 2019.

45 https://www.womex.com/virtual/codarts_research accessed on 26 September 2017.

46 See chapter titled 'Music Education' in this book.

47 Balwant N. Dixit, 'Globalization and Indian Classical Music: The North American Scene' at http://www.india-arts.pitt.edu/globalization.html accessed on 15 February 2019.

48 *Role of Media in Promotion of Music in India*, ITC-SRA, pp. 103–104.

49 http://www.pjim.org/Locations.html accessed on 15 February 2019.

50 https://www.discogs.com/label/95098-Chhanda-Dhara accessed on 15 February 2019; https://www.facebook.com/pg/neelamaudiovideo/about/?ref=page_internal accessed on 15 February 2019.

51 https://www.wyastone.co.uk/catalogsearch/result/?q=india accessed on 15 February 2019.

52 http://www.momentrecords.com/#section-about accessed on 15 February 2019.

53 https://www.discogs.com/label/155986-India-Archive-Music accessed on 15 February 2019; https://www.discogs.com/label/504229-Makar accessed on 15 February 2019.

54 https://www.youtube.com/watch?v=KksTVgmSQ1s accessed on 15 February 2019.

Conclusion

1 For a list of Padma awardees in the field of music, see http://dashboard-padmaawards.gov.in/?Field=Art accessed on 22 August 2017.

2 Lavezzoli, *Bhairavi*, op. cit., p. 395.

3 ibid, p. 394.

4 Romila Thapar, *Cultural Transaction*, op. cit., p. 26.

5 *Report of HPC on the Akademis*, op. cit., p. 12.

6 ibid, p. 14.

7 ibid, p. 13.

8 ibid.

9 ibid, p. 20.

10 Anup Satphale and Zainab Kantawala, 'GST relief for music and theatre performances' at https://timesofindia.indiatimes.com/city/pune/gst-relief-for-music-and-theatre-performances/articleshow/62652300.cms, accessed on 24 March 2019; https://cleartax.in/s/musical-instruments-gst-rate-hsn-code accessed on 24 March 2019.

11 'Schedule of GST Rates', p. 8, available at https://cbec-gst.gov.in/pdf/Schedule%20of%20GST%20rates%20for%20services.pdf accessed on 22 April 2019; Pritam Mahure, *GST in India*, 7th ed. (n.p., 2018), pp. 129–130, https://drive.google.com/file/d/13baoX7goPWRrqtr_JI2aA_asWE7ObRfD/view accessed on 16 February 2019.

12 Some of these issues were discussed in a conference on Intellectual Property Rights for musicians held by Underscore Records Pvt. Ltd. in 2009. See https://www.youtube.com/watch?v=QLFZj7IwNR0 and https://www.youtube.com/watch?v=iY2Z_giTMb0 accessed on 29 March 2019.

13 https://www.mid-day.com/articles/furore-over-sangeet-natak-akademi-awards/19557153 accessed on 16 February 2019.

14 See Appendix 3: Questionnaire for Young Professionals.

15 An attempt was made in 2007 to customize insurance policies for performers, but this has not met with widespread success thereafter due to the absence of a collective voice. See https://timesofindia.indiatimes.com/india/Now-

Big-B-can-insure-his-voice/articleshow/1560517.cms accessed on 29 March 2019.

16 https://itunes.apple.com/in/album/the-raga-guide/1050729901 accessed on 5 May 2019; https://www.amazon.com/Ravi-Shankar-Distinguished-Musician-Remastered/dp/B00OLA7AQC/ ref=sr_1_1?fst=as%3Aoff&qid=1557124317&refinements=p_lbr_ music_artists_browse-bin%3ARavi+Shankar&rnid=3458810011&s =dmusic&sr=1-1 accessed on 5 May 2019; https://play.google.com/ music/listen?gclid=CjwKCAjwk7rmBRAaEiwAhDGhxEG4G-pv9a1t_ hmostPQ1kFU2Zajh3bCQwLTkhA5jyOg5qx82vGT5xoCKbkQAvD_ BwE&gclsrc=aw.ds#/wst/artist/Ab6njtn6de7xmpyjgf37lcolcvq accessed on 5 May 2019.

17 https://open.spotify.com/user/thesoundsofspotify/ playlist/4JtowPifE700fO0oqyMFSD accessed on 5 May 2019; https:// gaana.com/album/yaman accessed on 5 May 2019; https://www.jiosaavn. com/search/yaman accessed on 5 May 2019.

18 http://www.twaang.com/music-on-twaang.html accessed on 5 May 2019.

19 https://www.instamojo.com/payment-links/ accessed on 5 May 2019.

20 *Swarna Samaroh: Festival of Music and Dance* (New Delhi: Sangeet Natak Akademi, 1997).

21 Examples of contrary views held by two journalists: https:// narenmusicnotes.wordpress.com/2013/09/05/need-to-promote-younger-hindustani-music-talent/, accessed on 16 February 2019, http://www. outlookindia.com/article/heir-gloom/232619, accessed on 16 February 2019.

22 For an overview of the processes involved in creating the Hindustani tradition, see Madhu Trivedi, *The Emergence of the Hindustani Tradition: Music, Dance and Drama in North India, 13th to 19th Centuries* (Gurgaon: Three Essays Collective, 2012).

23 http://cpcb.nic.in/noise-pollution/ accessed on 16 February 2019.

24 *Role of Media in Promotion of Music in India,* ITC-SRA, op. cit., p. 95.

25 Smt. Gangubai Hangal interviewed by Dr S.S. Gore in *World of Gandharvas,* eds. Balawant Joshi et al., op. cit., p. 42.

26 'Changing in Organizational Aspects', *Journal of the Indian Musicological Society,* op. cit., p. 199.

27 https://trueschool.in/courses/hindustani-music-lessons/# accessed on 5 May 2019; http://globalmusicinstitute.in/three-year-graduate-diploma/ accessed on 5 May 2019.

28 https://www.shankarmahadevanacademy.com/learn-raga-alhaiya-bilaval-khelori-hori-madhyalaya-teentaal/HVS801/ accessed on 5 May 2019.

29 For extracts from discussions held during a conclave on music education in schools, see https://www.youtube.com/watch?v=7QLtSXPz-Vg, https://www.youtube.com/watch?v=ZAckVRVStfA, https://www.youtube.com/watch?v=Jac2ENe93Sw, https://www.youtube.com/watch?v=puP8KUHKy2w accessed on 16 February 2019.

30 https://www.youtube.com/channel/UCs6OTIFV53Z-EGT84lxTvqQ accessed on 17 May 2019.

31 https://wikisource.org/wiki/Author:Neela_Bhagwat accessed on 2 May 2019; https://underscorerecords.com/Catalog accessed on 2 May 2019.

32 https://swarasankula.org/index.php/media/bhatkhande-project/ accessed on 2 May 2019.

33 https://www.darbarplayer.com accessed on 5 May 2019; http://www.hclconcerts.com/about/ accessed on 3 May 2019; https://play.google.com/store/apps/details?id=com.hcl.music&hl=en_IN accessed on 3 May 2019.

Index

Acknowledgements

This book would not have been possible without the generous guidance, help and encouragement that I have received during the course of this and even a few decades earlier. To begin with, I am indebted to my mentors, revered tabla maestro Nikhil Ghosh, who shared his immense knowledge and musical passion with me; eminent scholar-musician Ashok Da Ranade, whose prolific writings and advice have shaped my understanding of Indian music as an organic whole rather than a homogenous entity or a mix of disparate elements; and historian J.V. Naik, whose guidance was invaluable in defining my research methodology.

My wife Shubha Mudgal has been a partner in more ways than one. During the course of the numerous projects that we have undertaken together, I have had the opportunity to discuss with her various issues that are included in this book. She also very kindly read drafts of the text and shared her comments and suggestions. I cannot thank her enough for her immeasurable support and involvement.

Over the past few decades, my interaction with musicians, teachers, scholars, concert organizers, private collectors, archivists and members of the audience has enlightened me in multiple ways. The limited space available here does not allow me to thank each one separately, but I am grateful to all of them for having expressed their opinions on many matters concerning the Hindustani music ecosystem and for patiently tolerating my incessant questions. There were many with whom I have had discussions focusing on specific areas that have been included in this book. I have mentioned their names below in no specific order and I would like to express my gratitude to them:

Sudhir Nayak, Murad Ali, Seema and Pankaj Rajgarhia, Harshesh Mehta, B.S. Shashidar, S.D. Pillai, Niranjan Rajadhyaksha, Naresh Fernandes and Ragini Pasricha.

I am thankful to Adrian McNeil and Sudev Sheth for commenting on drafts of some chapters.

Vighnesh Kamath, Dhaivat Mehta and Siddharth Padiyar conducted a few surveys specifically for this book, under the able guidance of Abhimanyu Herlekar. They were kind enough to set aside their time for this purpose and I thank them for their help.

Many thanks to Raghav Pasricha for kindly shooting and providing my photograph for the back flap.

My parents, Kisan and Vasant Pradhan, have been a great source of inspiration right through my journey with music. I could not have embarked on this journey without their support and it is their constant encouragement that has brought me thus far. I am eternally grateful to them. My sisters Nishita Mhatre and Deepti Pradhan, and their families, have also wholeheartedly and unstintingly supported me on my journey. I thank them all.

My heartfelt gratitude to my literary agent Kanishka Gupta, my editor Amrita Mukerji and the rest of the team at HarperCollins India.